From birth to present day, I have experienced numerous tests of endurance, pain, grief and survival. There are many things we have not included in this book. Some of which would explain who I was when I met my ex and who I am now. We are all given choices in life. How our choices affect others is called 'The Butterfly Effect'. It can ripple out changes that are good or bad, dependant on individual decisions and actions. Tortures to my body, mind and soul were inflictions endured that were caused by men who were dominant in their force and control. God knows I am a survivor on a mission fighting for Justice and Freedom for all victims. No one should steal your identity, happiness and dreams. Break the silence, speak out and get out! Writing, poetry, art and photography are my release forms, vital to my very being. My work with Women's Aid is mainly raising awareness and funds for the ongoing silent disease that is domestic violence. If we all stand together with a united global voice, change will come!

YOU CAN'T RUN

THE TERRIFYING TRUE STORY
OF A YOUNG WOMAN TRAPPED
IN A VIOLENT RELATIONSHIP

MANDY THOMAS
with KATE MOORE

EBURY
PRESS

1 3 5 7 9 10 8 6 4 2

Ebury Press, an imprint of Ebury Publishing
20 Vauxhall Bridge Road
London SW1V 2SA

Ebury Press is part of the Penguin Random House group of companies whose
addresses can be found at global.penguinrandomhouse.com

Penguin
Random House
UK

First published by Ebury Press in 2015

www.eburypublishing.co.uk

A CIP catalogue record for this book is available from the British Library

ISBN 9781785030185

Printed and bound by CPI Group (UK) Ltd, Croydon, CR0 4YY

Penguin Random House is committed to a sustainable future
for our business, our readers and our planet. This book is made
from Forest Stewardship Council® certified paper.

For my Babies

Daniel, Jahméne, Corice, Isaac, Junior and Darren

'Freedom is what you do with what's been done to you'
Jean-Paul Sartre

'You must be the change you wish to see in this world'
Mahatma Gandhi

'I can do all things through Christ who strengthens me'
Philippians 4:13

*'Justice will not be served until those who are
unaffected are as outraged as those who are'*
Benjamin Franklin

Foreword

Mandy Thomas's book is probably one of the most important books you will ever read. This book could potentially save the lives of thousands of women who are prisoners in their own relationships.

I am in awe of Mandy's continued strength, determination and pure survival instinct. It cannot have been an easy decision for her to write this book and speak so openly and honestly about her ordeal. But while Mandy's story is horrific, it still gives us all hope; hope that we can speak out and stand up to those who try to control us. When life feels dark and hopeless you stumble across a story like this and realise in our darkest hours and deepest despairs there is still a point in fighting. It's hard not to feel angry when reading how many times people failed and let Mandy and her beloved children down. It could have been very easy for Mandy to retreat into herself and become angry and bitter. I'm a huge believer in turning a negative event into a positive situation – after all, it's not what happens to us that defines us, it's what we choose to do with it afterwards that truly matters. By sharing her story Mandy has chosen to turn years of vile abuse into a vehicle to help and empower other families.

Today Mandy shines bright, as a beacon of hope to other women. Anyone at any time can find themselves a victim of domestic violence. Someone tried to burn Mandy's bright light out countless times, but they failed. It's heart-breaking to read how many times she got knocked down but absolutely inspiring to read how many times she got back up – and won her fight and right to survival.

Katie Piper
July 2015

One man's choice:
Fear …

Fear rules
Our night and day
In every way.
We have no say.

The aftermath will be:
'She tried to tell you,
But you didn't see … '

Prologue

Lives change in an instant. With a look. With a smile. With a promise.

My life changed with a touch. A soft touch: a gentle tap on my shoulder. It was innocent, unthreatening, nothing to fear. Just a man with an everyday question for me.

This stranger, he asked me: 'Have you got the time?'

I looked at my watch, and I told him. But whatever the dial on my wrist said, whatever minutes and hours I mentioned, I answered him wrongly.

Because …

From that moment on, my time was running out.

PART ONE

FALLING
UNDER
A SPELL

*How sad
You feel to steal
My summer's tune
And turn it
Into winter's gloom.*

Chapter One

It was 1984 when my life changed forever. May 1984. Duran Duran were at the top of the charts – and I was on top of the world. I was eighteen years old, living with two girlfriends in a shared house; a house where all our mates used to come to chill out, to watch movies or simply hang with a coffee and a nice slice of conversation. That day – that fateful day – the girls and I had headed from our hometown of Rugby to the big city: to Birmingham and its famous Bullring Shopping Centre. I'd been there the week before for the very first time, shopping with my mum for her birthday, and when I'd raved to my housemates about how amazing the shops were, we planned a girls' day out, just the three of us.

I was a short, skinny teenager then: a bubbly girl with distinctive bright red hair – and an even more distinctive quiff fringe, which I used to flick out of my eyes when I was dancing to Simon Le Bon in the nightclubs; dancing till my feet ached. I loved to dance – and to paint and to draw and to write. Music was in my soul – I sang everywhere. I loved anything that expressed myself.

I'd discovered writing when I was nine years old, after my father had died suddenly of a heart attack at the age of just thirty-eight. The only way I could express my crushing grief was through words. My English teacher, Mrs Mickleborough, told me I was a born writer; she said I'd moved her to tears with a poem I'd written about my father when I was ten. After that, she entered me into competitions for my poetry – competitions I won. I have continued to write poetry throughout my life, and I've included some of my poems in this book because they help to express what I was feeling, even in the darkest times. I also excelled in art. I drew all the time, anything from Beatrix Potter books for an old lady I knew to cartoons and my own artworks. The colours seeped into my dreams, and I hoped to make a career of it one day. Just one of my dreams.

Life at home was hard after my dad passed away. I won't go into it here, but let's just say I moved out as soon as I could, not long after my sixteenth birthday in November 1981, into a little bedsit. I worked like a demon to support myself. Even at home after school, when I was fifteen/sixteen, I was a waitress at a local hotel. Then when I left school, I worked in a newsagents/grocers, went on to selling windows and worked for an American health company. I then started in a bar in a working men's club, collecting glasses and doing other odd jobs as I was sixteen. At seventeen, I helped a woman run exercise classes; a good job for me, as I'd done gymnastics as a child and got into formation street-dancing as a teenager. It was another way of letting out any pain I had inside. You can't feel down, not when your feet are pounding in time to your own heartbeat, and your limbs are wild and free. I may have been on my own, but I was surviving. I was doing OK. I was doing the odd painted portrait for people too, putting my beloved art skills to good use.

Fashion was another one of my loves – especially clothes in bright colours, like those I swirled in my paint palettes – so this day at the Bullring was a real treat. The girls and I had only been living together for a few months at that time, and we really felt like a team as we browsed through the outfits on display, giggling over some of the more outlandish gear and oohing over other items. I had a sweet, kind boyfriend back then, a six-foot-four basketball player who also body-popped, and my brain was ticking over thoughts of what I might wear on our next night out clubbing together. I was fretting about our friendship a bit; I kept telling him he was too nice for me, that he deserved someone who wasn't quite so fragile inside, but he wouldn't listen. He was so nice he couldn't even see the damage in my heart.

It was on our second loop round the shops when it happened. We'd been shopping for a few hours by then, exploring most of the stores in the Bullring, so we were all flagging. We decided to sit and have a rest and a cuppa. It was a hot day and we were done in.

There was a café on the ground floor in an open area not far from where we were, so we headed for that. I strode across the mall towards the escalator in my sensible grey court shoes, my heels scoring a soundtrack to a scene I will never ever forget.

I was about to step onto the escalator when I felt that gentle tap on my shoulder. I heard his voice for the very first time, from behind me. It was slow and polite. Smooth and velvety. Charming, you might call it. I could hear a smile in it, infusing the words he said.

'Have you got the time?'

I turned around. A man about my age stood before me, dressed in jeans and a red sweatshirt. He was around my height, five foot three, with a head full of curly hair and a beaming smile that displayed a fine set of white teeth. His eyes gleamed a light brown, like his skin. They seemed to drink me in as my gaze flickered over him. There was a breathless pause, and then he smiled again.

And in that moment, everything changed.

It was as if he'd cast a spell. To this day I say that. As though he'd magically waved a wand and made my whole world stop stock-still. It wasn't sexual chemistry, nor the romance of falling in love – it was a powerful, hypnotic incantation. An enchantment, if you will.

Or a curse.

Not realising his request was a classic pick-up line, I dragged my eyes away from his to check the numbers on my watch. I didn't normally wear a timepiece, but something had impelled me to slip it on that morning. I was dressed very conservatively for me, in a white blouse and a grey skirt, and perhaps I had thought it suited my outfit.

Thinking about it now, I must have looked like a schoolgirl that day. Innocent. Sweet. Corruptible.

We chatted all the way down the escalator. My friends and I went to get a drink from the café, just like we'd planned, and he followed. For some reason, it seemed OK. He was asking us questions in that charming voice of his, finding out where we were from and simple stuff like that. The feeling was really weird, like everything was glazed. Still under this haze of magic, I chatted away, quite happily. Before I knew it, my friends had wandered off, back to the shops, and it was just me and him sitting in the café talking. But it was a busy public place, right in the middle of the mall, and I thought, *I'll be all right*.

I don't remember what we talked about. I have no idea. Knowing me, it was a load of twaddle because I always ramble.

All I remember is the escalator and then me falling under a spell; and me thinking he was very charming, with his white teeth and his big smile. He mentioned that he went to the gym. I remember thinking that with the gym and those fine white teeth he must look after himself well. Something inside me – and perhaps it started that same afternoon – wanted him to look after me, too.

No one ever really had.

My friends came back, eventually, and we all got the train to Rugby, back to our shared house. There was a whole group of people who came with us because my housemates were social girls, just like me, and they'd made some new friends and invited them back. But amidst all the chatter, he and I sat talking, just the two of us alone. We chatted all the way back on the train like I'd known him all my life. And that's what made me think, *This person's the person*.

He stayed the night. Nothing happened, not in that way, but in some ways everything happened because my life as I knew it was never the same after that. The next day, I broke up with my boyfriend, with this soft teddy bear of a boy, and I broke his heart. Seeing the hurt in those bright, kind eyes of his, I did think to myself, *What on earth am I doing?* But the spell I was under was a strong one, and it said: *Just do it anyway*.

The man from the mall soon came back. It might have been the next day or a few days afterwards, I can't remember now, but he pretty much moved himself in, to my delight, and we continued our long, deep conversations. I told him everything about myself: the good, the bad, the painful … the shameful. Every last detail of everything about my life and my history; all my hopes; all my fears. I'd never met anyone before who made me feel like I could let go and show my true self, but he did.

He told me his name – Dusty – but the rest of his world was closed off. I didn't realise that at the time. It was only afterwards, long afterwards, that I realised I'd told him everything, but he'd told me nothing. I'd ask him questions and he would change the subject or give me a brief, nothing kind of answer. He'd say he didn't want to talk about it. He'd say he was way more interested in what *I* thought and what *I* dreamed, and why didn't I tell him another little secret? I was overwhelmed by his interest, thinking, *This person really cares about me.* (How wrong I was. How *stupid* I was.)

But it was breezy, in the beginning. He made me laugh. I actually looked on him as my knight in shining armour who was going to whisk me away to a bright new future. He bought me chocolates and flowers; I'd never had that before. It made me feel special and wanted. And it was even more special because he knew everything about me – all my hurts and sorrows that had maimed me deep inside – and yet he still wanted me.

(Later, I found out that my damage had attracted him, right from the start, from that day in the mall. Watching the hurt little 'schoolgirl' cross the mall, he'd bet his friend he could 'get' me. Oh, he won that bet. Big time.)

Before too long, he came to meet my gran, the most special person in my life. He was polite and charming, just as he had been on the day I met him: pleasant and nice. I met his parents, too, though it wasn't an arranged visit. It turned out that they'd wondered where he was, as he was always stopping at mine and he hadn't told them where he was going to. He had, however, scrawled my address on a mirror in his bedroom back in Birmingham, and eventually his folks came to check he was OK at this mystery location, as it had been so long since they'd heard from him. I found all that a bit odd, but when I asked him about it, he said, 'It's none of your business.'

What *was* his business, however, was me. Oh, I was his primary concern. And his interest was always so caring, of course. I felt almost touched by it, this man looking out for me. I'd mention some party I was planning to go to, or a new nightclub I wanted to check out, and he'd say, with seemingly genuine concern, 'What do you want to go there for?' In time, he might suggest that one of my pals, from my very wide circle of friends, perhaps wasn't looking out for my best interests, or he might say lightly that he didn't know what I saw in them. Naturally, we'd end up not really seeing that person anymore. He might turn up at the house unexpectedly, and I'd get in 'late' because I didn't know he was coming, and he'd say, 'Where have you been?', like I was in the wrong. Then I'd tell him where I'd been and he'd get so angry. *That's a bit weird*, I thought, but I didn't see it as any kind of warning sign. I was blind and deaf to everything but him.

In the end, I found it was easier to stay in, not to go out, to avoid my friends, not to speak to anyone he didn't like. It seemed to make him happy, they seemed mild requests, and I trusted him. So I thought, *Well, I want to be with him and I want to make him happy, so I best just do as I'm told, for the overall good*. I thought he was doing all of it with good intentions, after all, so there didn't seem to be any harm in wanting to please him.

My housemates tried to talk to me about him. Only a couple of weeks into our relationship, they pulled me aside.

'Mandy,' one of them said, struggling to find the words, 'we're not sure about him. There's something about him we don't like.'

Fool that I was, I thought, *They're just jealous*.

They didn't have boyfriends at the time, and I thought they didn't want me to have one, either. I didn't see what they saw.

Maybe I didn't want to.

As I stopped going out, my friends got more upset. We had been a team – three girls out on the town – but I wasn't part of the team anymore. Nonetheless, they didn't say anything to me again. What more could they say? They'd already told me they didn't like him and I'd just carried on seeing him. I was a lost cause.

One night, a few months into our relationship, I was 'late' home again. My housemate and I had nipped to the shops but the shop we'd planned to go to was shut, so we had to go to one further away, and then a friend offered us a lift back in his car, but he had to make a detour first before he took us home … Anyway, long story short, when I walked back into our crowded house, which was jammed as usual with our gang of pals hanging out, Dusty wasn't best pleased.

To say the least.

He led me up to my room and started asking me questions. *Where had I been? What had I been doing? Why did it take me so long?* And that velvety voice of his began to rise in volume until he was screaming at me. I was trying to explain, to stutter out about the shop and the lift and everything, but he just didn't want to know.

His questions got more and more heated.

I couldn't get a word in edgeways.

And then, with no warning, his hand shot out and he slapped me across the face.

That shut me up.

I stopped talking and lifted my hand to my cheek. It wasn't a really hard slap. But it was the first time he had hit me, and that made my skin sting more than the actual power of his strike.

I didn't say anything at all at first. I was too shocked to speak. But then I found my voice. I started shouting back at him, shouting that he'd slapped me, and he roared at me that he was leaving and he wasn't coming back. He took off into the night and I wandered slowly down the stairs, back into the warm mass of friends in the living room below.

I told my housemate what had happened. She hugged me. She said again that she thought he was a bad egg. And I spent the evening in the company of my friends, my head buzzing with confused feelings, even after the red mark of his flattened palm had faded from my skin.

He returned the next day, bearing chocolates and brightly coloured roses. He smiled sheepishly at me, and he said one word.

'Sorry.'

I stared at him, at all his bright white teeth curved into a toothy grin, trying his best to make me smile, and I felt the tug of that mysterious spell again. Something in my mind was telling me to make it work. He was the one.

I was young, and I was foolish, and I was blind and deaf and dumb.

That was the only 'sorry' he ever said.

Chapter Two

'This is the one!'

I spun round in excitement and looked at Dusty, a beaming smile spreading across my face. We were flat-hunting together, and we had found our new home.

It was a top-floor flat in the attic part of a building on Woodstock Road in Moseley, Birmingham. I wandered from room to room, which didn't take long as it was only small; a one-bed apartment that was just big enough for two. It had a good-sized living room, separate kitchen, bathroom and bedroom. Being on the top floor, we had a great view, too.

I started planning in my head what would go where and which items we still needed to buy. I linked my arm in Dusty's as I chattered animatedly about how we might decorate our home. With a head full of ideas and colours, I drifted into a happy place. He, however, had a vision for cork tiles and said he would put them up in the flat to keep the heat in. It was a bitterly cold and snowy January; the January of 1985. I'd known him for eight months. He hadn't hit me once since that first time, and I'd almost forgotten the incident.

I couldn't wait for us to move in together.

I can't recall now which one of us had suggested the move in the first place, but we were both excited as Dusty signed the mortgage deeds and we relocated to our new home. It felt like we were growing up together, and I felt like I was leaving my past behind, once and for all. Birmingham as a city held so many opportunities, too. I needed to find a job quickly, as I'd just missed out on a post as a cartoon-strip illustrator and was currently unemployed. There were loads more jobs in my new town than there were in Rugby; the possibilities seemed endless.

We unpacked together, although Dusty didn't have much to bring to our new home: a bag of clothes and a few other bits. I had got a fridge, bed, TV, wardrobe, saucepans and crockery. This was his first move away from home; it was my third. His parents gave us a sofa, we scraped together to get a cooker and a washing machine came much later. For the first year, I had to put all the washing in the bath to scrub and wring it out by hand, and then go down six flights of stairs to hang it out on a line in the shared garden below. It was a mammoth task each time.

Dusty was a technical whizz and got himself an Amstrad computer. He also had a Vectrex games console, which we would end up playing on for hours. That very first afternoon, though, I concentrated on unpacking my boxes and bags. As I lifted different garments to hang them in the wardrobe, Dusty came over with a smirk on his face. He pulled the clothes from my hands.

'I don't like that,' he said, slightly cross. 'You're not wearing that.'

The offending items were thrown in the bin. I shrugged – whatever made him happy, it was no skin off my nose – and unpacked another box instead. This time, it was full of old photographs (another art form I adored): snapshots of my friends and family, old boyfriends, a wide array of friendly faces and animals.

He went through them one by one, screwing up his nose in faint displeasure.

'You're not having that,' he said at each image. 'You're not having that, you're not having that.'

The pictures were torn and thrown in the bin.

I unpacked my most precious things next: things my father had given me before he died, when I was just a child. My favourite was a china ornament he had presented to me after a work trip – I think it was to Scotland – of a little girl with fluffy red hair, who looked a little like me.

She too was smashed and thrown away.

I protested at that, but Dusty took my hands and looked me deeply in the eye.

'You've got to throw your past away, Mandy,' he told me frankly. 'This is us now.'

I was not to have anything that had connections with my past.

I did what he said. I thought he was doing it because he cared and he wanted me for him alone. *This is a fresh start*, I told myself, *so start fresh*.

He bought me new clothes to replace the items he had chucked. Sometimes we went to the shops together; other times he'd bring me back an outfit and say, 'Here you are, that's for you.' The clothes weren't to my taste, but they made him happy. Though I had once loved to pick out my own outfits, to select the shapes and shades that suited me the best and expressed how I was feeling inside, it was a hobby and a passion that I slowly let slide. In the past, I had even designed and made my own clothes, with help from my granny, and one of my dreams was to become a famous fashion designer, but it was something that slipped through my fingers into the trash, just like my dolly with the bright red hair.

I had many dreams and ambitions that faded with time.

I didn't go out anymore at night, once we moved. I'd changed cities, after all, and no longer had any nearby friends to go out with. And anyway, after eight months of Dusty subtly suggesting that this person or the other wasn't to his liking, I'd fallen out of touch with lots of people. When I moved away from Rugby, there weren't too many friends left to say goodbye to.

There was still my granny, but Dusty said I shouldn't see her anymore; what did I need her for when I had him? I worried at his words; my granny was my rock, and she'd kept me alive and sane throughout my difficult childhood. She was far too precious for me never to see her again, but in those first few weeks in the flat I had other priorities than a visit back home, so I didn't push it. My first mission was to find a job.

I went to interview after interview, trudging through the freezing winter snow with a woolly hat pressed down firmly over my long red hair. I remember feeling sick with nerves every time – properly ill. But, even after my interviews were over, the sickness didn't stop. When I heard I'd got a job – as a full-time daytime barmaid at the Crown, a central, upmarket bar situated right next to the canal – I still felt really unwell. My whole body felt different, peculiar. I decided to go to the doctor.

I can still remember walking to the call box down the road to get the results of the tests the doctor gave me. A bag of nerves, I dialled the numbers shaking with anticipation, dropped the coins in the slot and waited for a voice.

I can still remember clearly what the nurse on the phone said: 'You're pregnant.'

I cried, I smiled, I laughed – I was above and beyond feeling blessed. I think I must have skipped or flown back to the flat. I was so happy. It was genuinely one of the happiest moments of my life. I wanted to tell the world – dance, sing. *How perfect to have my own little family*, I thought, *a precious little soul I can love and give everything to*. I couldn't wait for Dusty to get home from work.

I kept going over and over in my mind how I would tell him, picturing his excited reaction, those white teeth beaming at me as I told him he was going to be a dad. 'We're a family now,' I would say. I was fit to burst by the time he walked in the door, but I let him settle first; he was sometimes grumpy when he first came home and unconsciously I was starting to judge his moods and adapt my behaviour accordingly. Only once he seemed ready to talk did I share the news, my happiness popping out of every word like lemonade bubbles in a full-brimmed glass.

But his reaction wasn't quite how I'd imagined it. He didn't smile. He didn't say anything. Nothing apart from a quiet 'oh', and then it was as though a big wall had come up between us. I wondered, *Why aren't you happy? Why aren't you happy like* I'm *happy?* A dull flatness entered the conversation, sucking out the joy. The room just lurched, the floor falling away from me. His reaction threw me into a headspace of: *Oh my God, he's not taking this how I thought he was going to take it.*

I knew only one thing. There was no way on God's earth I was *not* having the baby. The thought drummed in my head, neatly in time with my new child's heartbeat: *I'm having this baby, he will come round, it's the shock.*

*

After that, Dusty started staying out more. 'I'm doing overtime at work,' he'd say, or 'They're sending me on a course.' I barely saw him. I tried to be understanding about his reaction; after all, we were both young, only nineteen years old, and I knew blokes were a bit more immature than women. *Maybe he's not ready yet*, I thought. *Maybe that's it.*

He seemed to come round to the idea, in time. We told his parents, and he appeared happy: 'She's pregnant,' he said, with that smile I so admired. 'She's having our baby.' We got a machine so he could listen to the heartbeat through my swelling belly, and he played music so the baby could hear the melodies in the womb. I loved all that. I was so excited about the new life growing inside me, and I loved being pregnant. I bought books and videos and learned everything I could. I was determined that my child would have a happy life; an idyllic childhood; a doting, caring, loving mum.

We were out shopping one day when he decided to get me a ring. It was a dark red, garnet-stoned engagement ring. He didn't ask me a question to go with it, though. He simply said, 'We're engaged,' to his parents, who sent a card to congratulate us. There were no celebrations; no party; no cake or flowers.

To this day, I don't really know what that was all about. Maybe he did it to make his mum happy. And I guess it made me happy too, for a short while, thinking he wanted to marry me at some point, which made me feel needed. But it was hardly the romantic proposal I might have dreamed of. I still don't know, even now, if it was his parents' suggestion that we get engaged. It was odd because it felt like he didn't want to. Like it wasn't special.

Dusty was starting to unnerve me, now. Though he put on a happy, charming face in public, he seemed to have another one at home.

On the rare occasions he was in the flat, he made his presence felt. He would interrogate me when I got home from work, with what I thought were stupid questions.

'Which way did you walk back today?' he'd say, and wait for my answer with a stern expression on his face. At first I would laugh and think, *What's he asking me that for?*

That laugh became a problem. I already had a nervous habit of laughing or smiling when I felt under pressure, and when he used to grill me about my walk home, with all the intensity of a murder cop, I couldn't help the mirth that used to bubble up inside. If he shouted at me, I would giggle: a very real, nervous disposition. I'd try to reply to his questions, and I'd let a little laugh out with my response. I couldn't control it.

He hated that, absolutely hated it.

'Stop laughing,' he'd say. 'Stop laughing or I'll slap that smile right off your face.'

At that, I'd bite my lip and strive to keep the nervous giggles locked inside.

My face used to annoy him, too. Evidently, I unwittingly pulled faces that he didn't like. We'd just be chatting, and he'd suddenly go, 'You're pulling that stupid face again.' And I'd think, *God, what am I doing? What face* am *I pulling?*

Anything could set him off, pacing back and forth with annoyance across our small flat. I had a habit of biting my nails when I was feeling nervous, too, and that would drive him nuts – his simmering frustration would spiral into him batting my hands away from my face. That didn't help because the more upset I got, the more I bit my nails.

The pregnancy made me hotter than usual as the months progressed. I used to change my clothes throughout the day, putting on layers and taking them off, trying to get comfortable.

'Why have you changed?' he'd ask me, looking me up and down, not missing a thing. 'You weren't wearing that earlier.'

It seemed really weird to me, but I'd answer him anyway, and indulge his questions. I'd never understood men and I didn't have a clue what he was thinking. It was baffling, the things he would ask me over and over.

I knew that he didn't like me working, though. That was crystal clear. He'd pick fights with me about it when I got home, grilling me about who I'd spoken to, what had happened, where did I go, why was I home a few minutes later than usual – on and on and on. *Why? What? When? How? Who?* He wanted to know everything. He wanted to *control* everything. I wasn't doing anything wrong, but being constantly interrogated was turning me into a nervous wreck.

I already didn't socialise because I knew he didn't like it, and I had no friends. Now, though, he made it obvious that he didn't like me even speaking to *anyone* else. I had to stay in; I wasn't to tell anybody anything. I became this recluse, trying to 'behave'. I couldn't do anything I wanted, not even draw. He controlled my world.

His mum taught me how to knit and that became my new passion: knitting beautiful, unique, brightly coloured clothes for our unborn baby. That was the only hobby I was allowed – but he hated me knitting if he was there; the *click-click* of my needles would make him furious. So I spent all my spare time doing the washing and the cleaning, trying to keep our home nice and clean and tidy. I was striving to be this perfect 'wife' and mother-to-be, so that it would work …

But it just wasn't working.

It didn't matter what I did, I just seemed to irritate him. He was in his own world. Every now and then he would show affection, which would make me think there was hope. But, generally, he was just angry. He was always angry at someone, it seemed – be it a friend, someone at work, his parents, me … It was as though he didn't like people.

There were some people he liked, though – liked too much. It wasn't long before rumours started circulating from his friends and associates, who would pop into the pub where I worked, that he wasn't working late but was with other women. People told me they'd seen him here and there; anywhere but where he'd told me he'd been. I decided to confront him about it – and that was when it all went wrong.

How dare I ask! Who was *I* to ask! I didn't have the *right* to question him in any which way or form, he said. I had crossed a line by bringing it up.

It fuelled the bubbling temper in him. It brought it up to boiling point. And he started getting violent again. Not just threatening, not anymore – he'd actually do it. He smacked me to put me in my place. He slapped me because I was a free spirit with what he called 'attitude'. He hit me because he said I needed controlling. He strangled me because I wasn't doing as I was told. I'd be trying to stand my ground and he'd get so, so angry.

But, like before, his outbursts were sudden and short, like a summer storm. And while they were worse, in degrees, than that simple slap in Rugby, they were still rare, only every couple of months. And so I tried to cover up the marks he left, when he held me up against the wall by my throat with one strong hand; when he hit me in the face till my cheek bruised; when he punched me in the chest, or the arm, or the leg. I'd put on my make-up and wrap a scarf around my neck, and I'd go into work like nothing was wrong. I thought I'd got away with hiding everything.

My colleagues at the Crown were concerned, nonetheless. They knew what was going on – not only from the bruises, but because he'd turn up sometimes when I was working, raging angry, and cause a scene. I had to explain it somehow, so in the end I just told the truth. I said what he'd done. I stroked my growing belly to reassure myself as much as my unborn child, and then I said: 'You can't do anything about it because it will only make it worse.'

I'd already learned that much.

I didn't really know what else I could do. I was pregnant, having *his* baby, and I had nowhere else to go. Having stopped speaking to so many people over the past year, I couldn't very well phone up my old friends and ask for help. There was no way I could go back home. Everything felt out of my control, but I knew I'd put myself in this mess. It was up to me to get myself out of it. I reasoned to myself: *It's only every now and again that his temper flares up and he hurts me. Maybe it'll be different when the baby arrives. Maybe when the baby is born he'll mellow.*

Midway through my pregnancy, Dusty invited a work friend of his to stay over at our place while he house-hunted. I met his wife, Shania, later, and instantly liked her. She was a Londoner, loud and beautiful. She had a little boy around a year old. He was the most gorgeous, dark-skinned little lad, with bright green eyes and a mop of curly hair, like his mum. The two of us quickly bonded by chatting about children and girly stuff. I hadn't been allowed friends for so long that she was a warm welcome in my world. I guess she was allowed as she was the wife of Dusty's colleague.

But, to Dusty's displeasure, we became good friends, close friends. In time, she told me her husband hit her, too. We became more than friends then; we were allies. I was so proud of her when she managed to get away from him and went back to London; I missed her, but at least she was safe. She came back a couple of times to try to save her marriage, but it didn't work.

When I was eight months' pregnant, her fella was having a party while she was 'away', to which Dusty and I were both invited. I was banned from attending; Dusty planned on going alone.

On the evening of the party, though, Dusty's mum came round and said I should go. She got me to put on a lovely green dress that hugged my big bump, and encouraged me to have a good night, to get out of the flat and enjoy myself … to surprise Dusty. She said I looked positively blooming and beautiful; she even dropped me off at the party. I was nervous and a bit anxious, but I walked up to the door and rang the bell.

As soon as someone let me in, I knew I shouldn't have gone. Shania's husband came over to say hello and I was shocked at the décor I saw behind him; he'd painted over the pretty wallpaper Shania had picked out with thick streaks of black paint. Everywhere was black. I found it very disturbing and felt extremely uncomfortable. I wandered through the throngs of partygoers looking for Dusty, trying to squeeze past the jumbled bodies with difficulty, just wanting to go home. No one looked me in the eye. I clearly wasn't meant to be there.

What happened next happened so quickly, in a haze. I found myself at the bottom of the staircase and saw a couple canoodling on it. I started to stutter out an apology for interrupting them – when my jaw dropped. It was Dusty on the stairs, entwined with a stranger. I couldn't breathe. *What is he doing?* Though I'd heard the whispered rumours, there's a big difference when you see it with your own eyes. That was the father of my child. That was supposedly my fiancé. That was my man, for better or for worse.

Watching him on the stairs that night, I felt something new fracture in my heart. I felt so hurt, so lost. I felt betrayed.

As soon as he saw it was me, he leaped up and started screaming at me. 'Why have *you* come?'

He'd banned me, after all – I wasn't supposed to be there. I was going against his word, and he was clearly in shock about that, more than anything.

I couldn't reply. I felt like my world was falling apart around me.

He went on the attack. 'What are you doing here? You're pregnant. You should be at home.'

I just thought, *I'm having your baby – what are you doing?*

He said it wasn't what I thought it was, but it was obvious what was going on.

His barrage of words continued: 'You shouldn't be here. I told you not to come. You get home right now, you *slag*.'

'Slag' wasn't a new insult. In fact, it had become a favourite word of his, to use for me, to put me down. I'd almost got used to the sting of its sibilant sound, but it was humiliating having him call me it in front of other people. A jagged thought snagged in my head: *You're always calling* me *a slag – but this is what you're doing while I'm pregnant with your child …*

I just wanted to get out of there, run away. Somehow, I did. I don't remember how I got home that night, but I do remember thinking, *This isn't right. There is something very, very wrong in this relationship.*

Other people would have thought that a lot sooner, I know. But I'd been blinkered. I'd been under his spell. I'd been trying so hard to make things work – for me, for my unborn child, for us – but everything was fracturing around me, falling apart into useless fragments of shattered, hopeless dreams. I felt like my very future was crumbling in my hands.

I felt like the spell was broken.

Not long after the night of the party, after I'd stopped work at the Crown and was counting down the days before my labour began, I spotted Dusty outside Burger King one evening, getting onto a bus with a girl. They were holding hands – until he spotted me; then he tried to make out she was just a workmate. I was with Shania that evening – we were just out shopping, picking up a few last things for the baby before it arrived – and she boldly shouted at him. She saw right through his lies. He'd been caught in the act and was clearly shaken, but he soon twisted it onto me, asking why I was out so late when I was pregnant. It was only 7 p.m., but it was 'late' according to his 'rules'. Normally, I would have been reliably at home, where I was meant to be, but we had missed our bus.

He was shocked, then angry with me. The whole story then became about me … how *I* was in the wrong.

I wasn't allowed to see Shania again after that, not after she'd spoken out against him in public.

The next day, and the day after that, and the day after that, I had only one concern.

What would happen when the baby came?

Chapter Three

When it comes to giving birth, there is no other feeling like it. It's miraculous. It's overwhelming. On Sunday, 10 November 1985, I welcomed my son into the world.

For nine months, he'd been growing inside me, part of me. It turns out that, even after your baby is born, they're still part of you, still connected to you, even once the umbilical cord is cut. You can feel their hurt and their happiness, their joy and their fear. You have that bond from the minute you know you're pregnant and it never, ever weakens.

My new-born son looked up at me from where he lay in my arms in the hospital bed. He was beautiful: big brown eyes, dark wisps of hair, skin the colour of honey. I remember counting all his fingers and toes, just to check he was all there. And he was. He was perfect, all five pounds eight ounces of him. He smelled so sweet and his skin was so soft. How precious he was: so tiny and delicate. He was a very alert baby, with bright eyes that seemed to latch onto mine immediately, and my love for him was instantaneous and huge. I'd never felt anything like it. My uncle gave me an enormous ET cuddly toy for him – about 40 centimetres tall – and my baby looked so tiny next to it. Of course, as he grew, slowly he started catching up with the creature, and I used to chart his development in photos by seating the baby and ET together. It was amazing how fast he grew.

I called him Booboo for a month, while we thought of a name. Dusty and I decided on it together: Daniel. I liked it; it was a fighting name, a survivor's name. The kind of name he would need in this world he'd been born into.

Dusty was a proud dad. He set up Daniel's cot at the end of our bed, squeezing it into our tiny bedroom. He enjoyed the post-birth drinks with his mates, with their masculine back-slapping congratulations on the arrival of his first-born son. And I think he enjoyed, too, the fact that I now had a reason to be at home 24/7. Because his rules and interrogations continued, without a break. If anything, the iron fist in which he now held my world stiffened and squeezed my horizons even narrower than before the birth.

Those rules didn't apply to him, of course. He was frequently out – where, I didn't know. When he said he was on a course, was that true? Or was he with another woman? His parents asked me about it once, soon after Dan was born; perhaps they'd seen their son with someone else, I don't know what prompted it. They came round and spoke to him, but it just blew up in my face and left things worse than before – as any intervention always did. Dusty stuck his face in mine and told me firmly, hissing his words into my ear: 'You're mine, you're not going anywhere. And you're not taking Daniel anywhere. You stay here, you stay put.'

Exhausted from the stress of being a new mum, lonely and scared, I desperately needed guidance and help, but I had nobody I could really talk to who was on my side – nobody except my granny.

My granny was like an angel on earth. I've never met anybody like her, before or since. She had the most beautiful soul, bound up in a tiny body. She was only four foot three. The two of us had been in a car accident when I was six – I'd been sitting on her lap when the crash happened and we both flew out of the car – and she came out worse, having broken bones. She already had curvature of the spine so the accident made things worse. But every inch of her was caring and loving. She had thin grey hair and wise eyes that showed me the depth of her soul. She was my rock. Dusty knew exactly what she meant to me from the long conversations we'd had when we first met, so he had banned me from seeing her, as punishment.

He also instructed me to stay in the flat and not go out. I'd left my job at the Crown to have Daniel, so – as he saw it – there was no longer any reason for me ever to leave the confines of what had become my prison. I knew only too well what the consequences would be if I disobeyed. But, miserable and frightened as I was, I decided a visit to my granny was worth the risk. And after all, I wasn't actually doing anything *wrong*, I reasoned. I only wanted to see my gran. Beyond anything else, I wanted to show her great-grandson to her. I was so proud of my little boy. The hours I spent cuddling Daniel as a baby were the absolute happiest moments of my life up to then. I could lose myself in the sheer wonder of his perfect beauty; lose time as I wallowed in my overwhelming, unconditional love for him.

When Daniel was just over a month old, Dusty took off on one of his extended absences. I thought he would be gone for a while so I took my chance. I secretly lifted the handset of our landline phone and called my granny – another risk, as Dusty tracked the calls coming in and out. She was surprised to hear from me, but relieved: she'd been worried about me, she said, as she hadn't been able to track me down over the past few months; it had been like I'd vanished off the face of the earth.

We arranged to meet that day at her house in Rugby. I bundled Dan up in a little pouch that I strapped to my chest, and snuck out of the flat. I looked around nervously as I pulled the door to and set off down the six flights of stairs, worried that someone might spot me and report back. Dusty was so charming with the neighbours that he always had them eating out of the palm of his hand.

No one stopped me. My son and I boarded the train to Rugby and I felt the most glorious sense of freedom, seeing the countryside flash by outside the windows. My granny lived in a little warden flat on the ground floor. I remember walking up the path, and the enormous hug she gave me when she opened the door. She cried when she held Daniel. I took pictures ... I don't know what I was thinking, taking pictures. I wasn't supposed to go there and I took pictures ...

My granny and I talked and talked and talked that day. And everything came tumbling out. I was crying as I told her what Dusty had done to me, what he was really like, and she wrapped her arms around me like a soft blanket and held me as I cried. Each tear seemed to make her hurt; I'd not said anything before because there was nothing she could do about it, but now I was desperate.

I sat next to her with hot tears streaming down my cheeks. 'I've got myself into a mess,' I confessed, and I felt the weight of it lift, just a little, for the simple act of telling. It gave me courage. I took a deep breath and told the absolute truth, even to myself: 'I need to get away from him.'

My granny, as she always seemed able to do, immediately saw a way to help me. 'You can come and stay here,' she told me, her kindness sugar-coating every word.

I longed to accept her offer, to never go back to Dusty and the one-bed flat, but I could only imagine his reaction if he found out where I was – and what he might do to the woman who was helping me. 'I don't think it's as easy as that,' I said, reluctantly, thinking of his sneering face and his vicious temper. 'I've got to sort this out … but I don't know what to do.'

She urged me to get away from him. She told me he was no good. We talked it over all day, as the winter shadows lengthened on the floor and Granny clicked on table lamps to light our desperate conversation.

But, in the end, I felt I didn't have a choice. I couldn't leave, not like this. I bundled Daniel back into his pouch and I retraced my steps to Woodstock Road. It was dark outside now, and I couldn't see the countryside as the train rushed me back to Birmingham. I could see only my reflection: a pale-faced, indistinct young woman who was blurry at the edges.

It was half-eleven at night by the time I trudged up the six flights of stairs and turned my key in the lock.

I had expected to find the flat empty and dark. Usually when he went away, he stayed away – for days at a time, for weeks.

Not this time.

When I walked in, he was there. He flew at me, shouting, 'I told you to stay in the flat! Where have you been? *Where* have you been? I told you not to go *anywhere*.'

I held my head up high and tried to draw strength from everything my granny had said throughout our long afternoon together. *I've done nothing wrong*, I told myself, even as Dusty's eyes blazed at me, his expression full of dark displeasure that I'd broken his precious rules.

'I went to see my granny,' I told him, with a little of my old defiance.

'I told you not to go there. Why are you going there? You're going there *against my will*.'

He went on and on and on, screaming at me, up in my face, his tongue sharp with insults and my crimes. He went on and on so much that, in the end, my defiance broke down and I apologised meekly for doing wrong. That's what he always managed to do. His interrogations made me feel so on edge and his clever manipulations took me in circles until I didn't know up from down, right from wrong, good from bad. He would repeat himself over and over and over until I agreed with what he'd said, even if he was spouting nonsense. He twisted my mind like that. He twisted words.

'The grass is green,' I might say, for instance. 'It's blue,' he'd riposte. I'd keep saying it was green, and he'd be saying it was blue, and he'd be shouting it, so many times, getting so angry, that in the end I'd say it was blue just to please him, just to shut him up. But, later, he'd say, 'The grass is green.' 'It's blue,' I'd respond, having learned my lesson. But I'd be wrong: the grass was green, *obviously*. And that's what he'd do with everything – where I said I'd been; who I said I'd spoken to; when I said I was sorry, even if I wasn't in the wrong. I never won. Whatever I said, whatever I did, it was always wrong.

I don't remember if he hit me that night. The problem now was that he didn't need to. I stayed in line anyway, my fear keeping me prisoner in an invisible cage.

That night, after I'd fed Dan and laid him to sleep in the crib at the foot of our bed, I lay down next to Dusty, mere inches from the man I now feared so much, and listened to him breathing beside me. I tried to sleep, but I couldn't. A living nightmare kept me awake. For that's when I realised, *He's never gonna let me go. He actually wants me* here. *He can go off, go out, do whatever, but he is always gonna want me here, holding our baby, on my own.*

And I simply thought, *What have I done?*

I was so tired all the time, with no reprieve, no help from anyone. My lovely Daniel kept me awake, of course, as all new babies do their mums, but worse by far was Dusty. He'd keep me awake with his interrogations. There was no time for sleep. I was exhausted by the baby and wanted nothing more than to catch forty winks when I could, but Dusty would prod me till my head jerked up, my eyes wide and startled. My fear of him, too, kept unconsciousness at bay. I felt like I hadn't slept for weeks, months; like I was going crazy. I had no help from him. He had his own life he was getting on with; I was just a hindrance to his plans.

I think I coped quite well, considering I was a young mum with no help or even conversation from another adult. Daniel consumed me: he was my world. I spent every day loving him, holding him, singing to him. He had my undivided attention. His first smiles and his uncontrollable laughter at my silly faces are embedded in my memory, and always will be.

One night, I was standing in our small kitchen, boiling milk on the stove. It had been a long, draining day. My right hand was resting gently on the handle of the pan, as my body swayed slightly back and forth, rocked by the migraine that came with lack of sleep. I stared into the pan, at the bubbling liquid, and I thought, *I'm shattered.*

That's the last thing I remember before I blacked out.

When I came round, it was to wild, burning pain. The boiling milk had scalded me; I'd knocked it from the cooker and it had gone all over my hand, down my arm, across my chest and onto my face as I collapsed to the floor. I awoke to Dusty's arms around me, throwing me into a freezing cold bath. We later found out that was the worst thing he could have done; I could have had a heart attack from the shock.

But we only found out later because – despite the alarming, brightly coloured burns searing my disfigured skin – he refused to let me go to hospital. 'You silly cow,' was all he said to me, by way of consolation. He blamed me for the accident. It annoyed him.

It was only the day after, when the burns bubbled up into frightening, ugly yellow blisters, that he permitted me to go to hospital. The doctors there told me I had third-degree burns. My skin had started to heal wrong, so they had to peel it off with tweezers, then let it set again. They had to do that three times over the following weeks and months, and it was agony. My hand went black at one point, and I feared I was going to lose the use of it altogether. I had to do painful exercises to keep the skin stretching correctly. Over a long period of time it eventually healed to snow-white tissue, like a glove.

Of course, I got no sympathy at home. It became even harder work to look after Daniel at that time, as my hand and arm were swathed in bandages I couldn't get wet and, until it healed, I couldn't use my right arm at all. Yet Dusty refused to help, delighting in observing my struggles when he was there. If anything, my clumsiness – and just me in general – seemed to make Dusty ever angrier, hour by hour. Out walking one day, with Daniel in his pram, my so-called fiancé picked a fight with me. He said something, then I said something back, and the next minute – to my shock – he just whacked me really hard in front of a load of people; clobbered me around the head. I was stunned: it was the first time he'd hit me in public and let that charming mask of his slip, even for a second.

'What was that for?' I asked, as though I might receive a sensible reply. I was still trying to work out the rules – if I obeyed them, I might not get hurt.

But the more I tried to ask him – 'What are you doing that for?' – the more he went mental.

A crowd gathered … not to help; to watch. In the end, Dusty grabbed Daniel's pushchair in a rage and stormed off. I had to run after them, to keep my baby safe. Not one person said anything to me, they just stopped and stared. They didn't want to get involved.

But if I thought he was bad in public, he was about to take things to an even darker place at home.

Our baby slept at the foot of our bed, as I've said. So when Dusty heaved himself on top of me one night, and held me down as he thrust his way, unwanted, inside me, I didn't cry out or scream or make a noise, even though I was screaming inside. I said no to him, I said I didn't want it, but why would he ever listen to what a 'slag' like me would say? He told me I was asking for it. He said I deserved it. He complained that I was dry.

He got some baby oil for the next time.

Chapter Four

'You're a slag. You're not worth anything.'

Dusty was on top of me, pounding hard inside me, his hand fixed around my throat to hold me still. He was enjoying this rape – he'd torn my clothes off and strangled me first, and now he was battering me inside, while he whispered poison into my ears.

'You deserve to be raped.'

I lay silently and took it. Daniel was sleeping at the foot of our bed, and I didn't want to wake him. I had to be really, really quiet, even though it really, really hurt.

'You can't run away from me. There's nowhere you can go that I wouldn't find you.'

I wanted to run – oh, how I wanted to. I wanted to escape so badly.

'If you run, I'll take Daniel. I'll take him away from you. You're a bad mum anyway, you slag. I'll find a better mum for him than you. You're not worth anything.'

Daniel was my world. I was so scared he was going to take my baby. My body tensed, and he reacted to my fear. He loved seeing the terror in my eyes, knowing he had that power over me. It fed him, as oxygen to a flame …

The rapes and the beatings were regular now. This wasn't a pathetic summer storm I was living through; it was a relentless, catastrophic tornado, which sucked up all familiar landmarks and left me stranded, far from home, without a clue of how I'd got there, but with the grim knowledge that the storm was here to stay.

The morning after that rape, my mind felt shot through, blasted into a swirl of crazed thoughts that I couldn't process. They burred through my brain: *I need to stop this. I have to stop this. What can stop this? A lock. A lock could stop this. I need to get a lock to put on my door. If I change the locks, I could lock him out.*

Still not thinking clearly, I fed and washed and dressed Daniel, tucked him into his pushchair and headed out to the shops. I wandered round a DIY store, the voices in my head all confused, chiming with my migraine and my sleep-starved head. I was in a right state, mentally and physically, and my hand trembled as I paused in the lock aisle and placed one mindlessly in the hood of the pushchair, before moving on, still trying to think. *What would he do if he found out? Perhaps I shouldn't get a lock after all. What should I do? I don't want to lose Daniel, I can't lose Daniel, he is my life, my world …*

I walked round and round the store, the thoughts swirling round and round my head. I walked out the shop.

A man's hand on my arm broke into my reverie. He was a heavy-set man with a forbidding expression on his face. 'Come with me,' he said, sternly.

I followed him back into the store and into a side room, not understanding.

'You've been stealing,' he told me, with disgust. 'The police have been called.'

'What?' I said, completely confused. And then I remembered – the lock! I'd forgotten that I'd put it in the hood of the pushchair. I tried to explain, but he wouldn't listen.

The police came, and arrested me, and locked me in a cell, prior to my interview. I balanced Daniel on my knee and I just sobbed and sobbed. I felt so guilty – for breaking the law; for having Dan with me; for being a bad mother, just as Dusty had said. I was hyper aware, too, of the time all this was taking. I wasn't supposed to leave the flat. What if I wasn't home by the time Dusty returned? What would he do then?

Worse still – what if he found out about this? He would beat me, for sure, for being stupid, for getting caught, for mixing his son up in all of this. He could never, ever know. He would kill me and take Daniel, I thought. I started panicking. I started begging them to let me out.

'I'll plead guilty!' I cried out, imploring the unseen officers on the other side of the metal door to set me free. Anything to get out of this cell. I wasn't scared of the legal consequences, of having a criminal record.

I was far more scared of him.

The police took me into an interview room. I was still sore and broken from the night before. When they asked me questions, I tried to explain – why I'd done it and why I was in such a state. I relived what Dusty had said as he raped me the night before; I relived the whole experience, spewing it out to the police, vomiting up an inner pain I'd held in for so long. I couldn't stop crying, choking on the hateful words as I spat them out. *He beats me. He rapes me. He hurts me. I'm too scared to leave. I'm so frightened of what he'll do. Please help me. I don't want to lose my baby. I don't know what to do.* I wrote it all down in a tear-stained statement for them.

And then the time came for them to release me.

'All right, then,' the police officer said, 'so we've charged you with theft, and we're letting you go.'

'Are you going to arrest him?' I asked, hopefully. 'I told you everything he did.'

But they said they couldn't do anything about all of that. There was no thought, no compassion from them – just a conviction for me. I can't remember now what their excuse was, as to why they wouldn't do anything, but let's just say that, back then, official attitudes to domestic violence were hands-off, to say the least. *Talk to each other, work it out*, that was their answer. Everything I'd told the policewoman fizzled away, like I'd never said anything. It had been so, so difficult, talking about being violated in that way, revealing what he'd done, but they simply didn't care.

They simply sent me back to the flat.

That was the first time I realised: *They're not going to help me.*

It made me think: *Why not?*

I could think of only one reason: maybe they thought I deserved it, too. Maybe they thought I was a bad person, a thief, that I didn't deserve their help.

Dusty found out about the incident, in time. Of course he did. Nothing stayed secret. I got a beating, and he mused out loud on the fact that I'd been caught stealing a lock. 'Why would you be shoplifting a lock?' he said sarcastically, his lips fixed in a grim line. 'What do you want a lock for? To lock me out? That won't stop me, you stupid cow. *You* can't stop me. You can't run, you can't hide … ' He sang the last bit to me, taunting me. He raised his forefinger to his lips, licked it and held it to the air. *Score to me*, he was saying. *I win again.*

I had nowhere to run to, no one to talk to and no one to help me.

Except ... there was one person, I realised. I could help myself.

And that whole incident changed me. Because, after it, I became not a victim, but a survivor. It woke my senses up, like fresh coffee on a winter's day.

From then on, I realised I had to be alert and in control of my own mind, all the time – even after being beaten and raped; even after no sleep. I'd been stupid, but I wouldn't be that way anymore. I would learn to be strategic. Because I had to survive this. I had to be there for Daniel.

I held my baby close to me and I hugged him till I thought my heart would break. 'We will get through this,' I promised him, pressing my lips to his dark-haired head. He smiled up at me and reached out a baby hand to mine. I took it and kissed his tiny fist.

I made a promise to myself. *We will get through this together.*

Chapter Five

'Look, Mummy, look!'

Daniel toddled up the hill ahead of me, pointing out some new marvel he wanted to show me, his little legs clad in summer shorts and his face alight with joy. We were on a camping holiday in Woolacombe, Devon, and my twenty-month-old was in his element. Recently, I had discovered that he had hearing problems, but his so-called 'disability' only brought us closer together as we spent even more time one-on-one, with him cleverly lip-reading every word I said.

'I'll be there in a second!' I called out to him, as I laboured up the hill behind him. I was four months' pregnant and I was feeling incredibly uncomfortable. I bit my lip, to channel the pain, and carried on. I didn't want to cause any trouble. Besides, swallowing down pain was second nature to me now.

It was the summer of 1987. Dusty, his parents, Daniel and I had all come away together for this trip. It was a time when things were OK-ish between me and Dusty; there were stretches when things were OK. I had tried not to fall pregnant again, given the situation at home, but my contraception had failed and, once pregnant, there was no way I could not have any child of mine. I loved children and I adored being a mother. The fact was, I wanted this baby, even though it was his; even though it had been conceived from rape. *It will be nice for Daniel*, I thought, *to have a sibling*. He was

42

a quiet little boy, serious and alert, always carrying his favourite toy: a Danger Mouse I had knitted him myself. Perhaps having a brother or sister would bring him out of himself a bit more.

We were still living in our small one-bed flat in Woodstock Road; Daniel was still sleeping in his cot at the end of our bed. Much of the time, it was just the two of us there, as Dusty would still do his disappearing acts, heading only God knows where. I could never ask him where he'd been or what he'd been doing – not unless I wanted a severe beating for even thinking I had the right to question him.

Occasionally, I'd gather snatches of information about his world without us, though. The police raided the flat, warrant in hand, to search for something they thought was there; they didn't find it, but they trashed the place anyway. Trouble seemed to follow Dusty everywhere. My first encounter with one of his enemies happened when he and I were out in Birmingham one day. A huge black guy with a scar down his face came up to me and punched me hard in the top of my head. 'That's for you,' he said to Dusty, before walking off.

'What was that about?' I asked Dusty, my hand rubbing the growing lump on my skull. 'That really hurt!'

He seemed anxious and just said, 'Keep walking, keep walking.' He never explained why.

Other men threatened me too, in time, physically – or the flat might get broken into, the door off its hinges and everything gone. If I ever saw them myself, I would say, 'If you've got a problem with him, go to him. Don't do anything to me. He doesn't care about me.' But they never believed me. They thought he was going to be affected by it.

I don't pretend to know what he was mixed up in; better off not knowing, I guess. When he was home, he would spend hours on his precious computers, honing his skills. He was a clever man. I would suggest to him that he could get a job in a bank or in computers, but he preferred to operate outside of that.

As for my work, to which I could have returned now Dan was older, he didn't allow me to get a job; but I had no help with childcare, anyway. So I had no money, and no chance of building my own life away from him. I just had to stay in, day after day, as he had decreed.

On very, very rare occasions, he would permit me a quick visit to my granny, just for ten minutes, so I'd shown my face, but I had no other adult conversation, and he would always be with us throughout the visit, listening to every word we said.

From time to time, I tried to raise the subject of me leaving. He beat me if I ever did. And from time to time, I would write to old friends or family members for help, but that always caused more trouble – people would then show up at the flat to see how I was, Dusty would act wonderfully to them … and they'd be fooled and leave, never to return. He'd beat me afterwards, of course, because he knew I'd contacted them and speaking out was against the rules.

Once, I would have asked him why. Why was he doing this? What had I done wrong? I would have said sorry for my 'misdemeanours'. I would have tried to reason with him. But I didn't now, not anymore. After a couple of years, you work it out: it's not you, it's them. There was nothing I could do because it was his own brain making it up, inventing reasons to give me pain.

The pain I was in at the moment, though, was not of his making – or at least it was, but only indirectly. I paused on the hill and rubbed my baby bump. It was very firm, sticking out slightly to the right, and it was much, much more painful than I ever remembered my pregnancy being with Daniel.

The following day, it got worse. Much worse. It was the most intense pain I'd ever felt. I dragged myself to the public loos on the campsite and locked myself in a cubicle. My body went into shock, sweating out bucketloads of water till it was dripping everywhere. I couldn't breathe, let alone cry out for help. My God, the pain was unreal. It felt like hours before I could move, even slightly. People were coming and going around me in the loos, and after a long time a lady asked me through the cubicle door if I was OK. I mumbled through the pain where our tent was located, panting out each word as I struggled to breathe. After she went off, I managed to get myself out of the cubicle and propped myself up by a sink, staring bleakly into the mirror. I was grey-skinned; my clothes soaked through with sweat.

Dusty's mum then appeared, worried and panicked. She took one look at me and said I needed to go to hospital; she called an ambulance. When the paramedic arrived, he touched my bump just once and then said urgently, 'We've got to go right now.'

Sirens blazing, we wormed our way at top speed through bendy lanes and busy roads in the ambulance. By then, though, I felt as though the pain had decreased, so I kept saying I was OK. I felt silly; I didn't need all this fuss. Nonetheless, the paramedic kept looking at me with concern, regularly taking my blood pressure, checking I was alert. His concern worried me. 'Stay with us,' he was saying at the end.

Dusty came with me while his parents watched Dan, following the ambulance in his car. He was by my side as the paramedics got me out of the ambulance onto a stretcher bed and rushed me down the corridors of Barnstaple Hospital, fifty miles away from the campsite. I remember gripping his hand, scared stiff. I was whisked into a ward, where a surgeon pressed my tummy. Like the paramedic before him, he had urgency written all across his face.

'Theatre – *now!*' he shouted.

They flew me through the corridors as I hung onto Dusty's hand. We were going at such a speed that Dusty got whacked in the face by all the plastic doors we went through; I remember that.

I don't remember much more. When we reached the theatre, I suddenly felt really tired – and then I blacked out.

What happened next was the strangest experience: floating lighter than light, having no pain, feeling calm and happy. Complete serenity. I was flying towards a white light at a great speed. It was beyond anything I had ever felt. I started going through chapters of my life from birth. I saw my dad – I was a little girl again – it was like a film reel of my life. It was *happy*: I was enjoying the experience. There was no hurt, no pain.

But then, suddenly, I felt myself being pulled backwards into darkness, fast. I didn't want to go back; I fought to go towards the light. But I couldn't fight hard enough; I heard the words: 'It's not your time yet … '

When I woke up, I was in a recovery room, wired up to all manner of machines and drips. The surgeon came to speak to me. I had been in theatre for many hours, he said. I had lost nearly eight pints of blood.

I'd been dead for six minutes before they brought me back.

He said I was lucky to be alive.

I'd had an ectopic pregnancy, he told me then. The baby had been growing at the end of my right fallopian tube and had burst into my stomach. If I hadn't got to the hospital when I did, I wouldn't have made it. The surgeon said in wonder, 'How did you cope with the pain? It should never have gone on this long.'

But I was an old hand at coping with pain.

I was confused, dazed. I wanted to go back to that place of no pain; of peace and tranquillity. For the pain was back now – tenfold. I felt like I had been run over by a truck: I was bruised, sore, everything hurt.

I had never heard of an ectopic pregnancy before, and I was inconsolable that I had lost my child. I struggled to deal with that loss. I went through so many emotions as I lay there in hospital. *Lucky to be alive?* I thought. *But my baby didn't make it.*

Pints of strangers' blood were infused into mine. I had a drip in my right hand, which was bleeding and sore; they'd struggled to get a vein so I looked like a pin cushion, all over: they'd tried my neck, hands, arms and ankles. All my blood had rushed to my stomach during the haemorrhage.

The doctors told me I had to stay in for ten days at least, but our holiday was over in three and Dusty said we had to get back to Birmingham. I had to sign myself out early; and then, as if we hadn't been through enough, we had a car crash on the motorway going home. I'd been lying flat on the back seat, not strapped in, so I went flying into the front seats. My stomach was on fire; the black wire stitches across my belly burned with hot pain as a few tore open.

Once we made it home, Dusty carried me crossly up the stairs to our flat, not even thinking of taking me to A&E, as I bled from my stomach. He hated me bleeding. I often bled after he raped me, and he was disgusted by the scarlet ooze of human fluid.

He was angry with me as he marched me up the stairs. He blamed me for everything.

'You slag,' he muttered at me, as he threw me down onto the bed. 'Only slags have ectopic pregnancies. This is why this has happened to you. Cos you're a whore.'

In the end he phoned my doctor to sort me out, and then took off. He left me to cope with Daniel on my own, despite the huge scar across my abdomen and my internal injuries. He left me to cope with my bleeding surgical wound – and my bleeding, broken heart. I questioned why I had been saved, why I was alive after all of this, especially as Dusty told me over and over that I was not worthy. Yet an inner faith and strength got me through the hardest of tests.

I would need them both in the years to come. Because I knew worse was on its way. I knew, even as I heard the door slam shut behind my so-called partner, that he would be back.

Chapter Six

In time, I learned that my friend Shania in London was getting married again. She phoned me up and asked: could I be her bridesmaid, and could I stay over with her to go dress hunting?

I never thought Dusty would let me, but to my surprise he was all for it. 'Why don't you get away?' he said. 'Just for a couple of days. Just you and Daniel.'

He didn't need to tell me twice.

I made plans for our trip to the capital, still in shock at his reaction. I wasn't allowed to go anywhere or have any friends – especially not Shania, as he didn't like her fiery, strong character – but now he had given his permission. I became excited. It would be the break Dan and I both needed; Shania had a little boy a year or so older than Daniel so they could play together. Dan was almost three now, he'd be starting school before too long and I was keen for him to play with other children. He was still very reserved, although not with me. He and I were a team. Together, we would spend hours playing with his toys, with ET and Danger Mouse, Dan's laughter rippling through our flat like raspberry sauce through vanilla ice cream, sweetening my days. He especially loved pretending to be a flying superhero – Superman, say, or Spider-Man. He'd climb up onto the back of the sofa when I wasn't watching, spread his arms out wide and then jump off. The amount of times I used to have to dive across the floor to catch him in my arms ... But he used to love that feeling: flying without wings.

As we arrived in London, I heard the sound of Erasure's 'A Little Respect', which was storming up the charts that autumn of 1988, coming from the concourse shops. It lifted my spirits – already high from the freedom of the unexpected trip – even further. *Maybe that's what's happening*, I thought hopefully, *maybe Dusty is finally showing a little respect.*

Daniel and I had a wonderful few days. It was like being set free. I went shopping with my friend, just as we'd planned. We must have tried on every wedding dress and bridesmaid dress in London! We talked for hours, just about fluffy, girly stuff, nothing heavy. It felt good to just be young and spend time with my friend, with no complications. I was only twenty-two, and that weekend, for the first time in ages, I acted my age. We went to the beach, breathed in the fresh air, revelled in the open space and freedom; a crisp, sunny day the backdrop to our fun and games. We laughed so much it reminded me I hadn't done that in a long while. We got back to her place in London that night exhausted and put the children to bed. I was ready for an early night myself; I had a headache coming on, strong and fast. It had been a lovely day ... but it wasn't to end well.

For Dusty suddenly appeared, bounding towards me, fuming with rage. As my friend and I stood motionless in shock he grabbed my hair, ripping it from my scalp, and dragged me out into the corridor of her apartment block. He was lifting me, throwing me from wall to wall, and then he dug his fingers into my long red hair and started banging my head against the wall, over and over. *Bang. Bang. Bang.* My headache was now full-blown skull-ache.

50

Curtains were twitching, Shania was screaming at him – but he didn't stop. *Bang. Bang. Bang.*

A neighbour down the corridor stuck her head out her door, and then quickly pulled it back in again. *Bang. Bang. Bang.* She must have phoned the police because the next thing I knew they were there, pulling him off me, while he fought them like a cat on steroids. It took about eight officers to hold him back, but they managed it, and bundled him into a police van outside.

'We've arrested him,' they told me – and I thought, *At last!* 'You come on down to court tomorrow morning,' they continued, 'to press charges, and we'll hold him until then.'

My ears still ringing from the beating, Shania took me back into her flat and dressed my injuries.

'Thank God he got locked up,' she said. I could only nod.

I was still in shock. I'd long given up trying to understand why he hurt me, but this was insane – he knew I was here, he'd given permission for me to go … what possible justification had his warped brain given him this time?

The next morning, we got up, got dressed for court and prepared the kids as well. I walked down the street with a newfound strength in every step. *They've locked him up*, I told myself, allowing a smile to creep across my face. *He's not going to get away with it this time. I'll press charges and he'll be put away, and Daniel and I will be free. Finally free.* I looked down at my son, walking happily next to me, with little idea of what was going on. I felt like his future was blossoming before me.

But then, in a screech of brakes, my daydream shattered. Before I could compute what was going on, Dusty's car drew up alongside us, he leapt out and he forced me, by my hair, into the back of the car. He grabbed Daniel and threw him in after me. My friend was screaming her head off at the side of the road, but no one came running. It was broad daylight, and he snatched us off the street and drove us at full tilt back to Birmingham. The police had let him out without telling me. *Talk to each other, work it out*, I could hear them saying in my head, between each pounding beat of my heart. All my stuff was back in my friend's apartment, but Dusty wasn't going back for anything or anyone. He drove thin-lipped, fast, in silence, all the way home. I sat shaking in the back, trying to paste on a smile for Dan, trying to pretend, as I always did, that I was happy and everything was OK.

I remember getting back to the flat, my heart as heavy as my feet as I climbed the six flights of stairs. Walking into our bedroom, I did a double take. Dan's cot wasn't there. My stuff wasn't there. The room had been changed around; several things were missing. The three of us were crowded into the small room, and I turned to Dusty in confusion.

'Where's the cot?' I asked.

I should have known better than to question him. He raised his fist and punched me hard. I kept saying, 'Not in front of Daniel,' so he backed off.

I found the cot out the back, all dirty, with all my stuff out on the back stairs. I tidied it up, cleaned and sorted it, and brought it back in without a word. I put Dan to bed and he rested his tired, confused little body down to sleep.

The air was icy. Dusty had a plan; I could feel it.

Before I knew it, he was coming at me with a pair of scissors somehow in his hand, which he was using to cut off my clothes, the silver blades swishing and slicing as his eyes went slanted and he trapped me in the corner of the bedroom. He raped me viciously, sticking the edge of the scissors in my throat. He revelled as he beat the living crap out of me, while our son slept on. His grimace, his anger, his hatred spewed from every pore of his being. I had to be silent and take it the whole time. I didn't want Daniel to wake and see this.

The next day, our downstairs neighbour pulled me to one side. Dusty had had someone in the flat, she told me, while I was away. She could hear everything that had gone on because the apartment had paper-thin walls. She'd heard him bring a woman back, she said. She'd heard them having sex in our bed. And it wasn't the first time.

I realised, then, that it was his own guilt he was taking out on me all the time. I understood, too, why he'd wanted me out of the way; why he'd urged me to go to London.

A few weeks later, an envelope arrived for me in the post. It was a court summons and a fine – for not showing up at court the day after his attack in London. I phoned the police up and I said, 'Look, you let him out; you weren't supposed to let him out. Why did you let him out?'

And they said they were sorry, it was a slip-up with something, and he got let out.

But they didn't try to put him back inside. They had no intention of helping me. I still had the summons and the fine, though, which didn't make sense at all. All it did was empower Dusty and decrease my faith in the justice system.

He would constantly lick his finger and hold it in the air. *I win again.*

I couldn't possibly compete when even the police were on his side.

'You can't run, you can't hide, you can't stop me' became words that rang constantly in my ears.

And then there came a day, not long after the London trip, when Dusty sat me down and said he wanted to talk. I was apprehensive – this was a man who liked to talk with his fists. But, for once, he was reasonable. It was a side of him I rarely saw anymore. It was like he was organising a meeting or something.

And what he had to say blew my mind.

'I'm leaving.'

Is this real? I thought.

'I'm leaving for good. I'm going to get a place of my own in Birmingham.'

Oh my God, oh my God, oh my God … I'm going to be free of his tortures. Finally. Finally!

It was all so amicable, it was unreal. He moved out, and Daniel and I went round to visit once, to see his new place.

There was a bottle of baby oil on the floor next to the bed, which unnerved me. Had he put it there to show me on purpose? Was it there for me?

Or did he have another woman; perhaps the woman he'd taken to our flat? Was that why he was leaving now, after all these years?

And I thought, *If he has someone else, he will leave me alone. I'll be free of him forever.*

I couldn't have been happier.

I got my own place, too, a home just for me and Dan. It wasn't in the best of areas, but it was untouched by his dad's bullying and violence. I could make it a happy home. Dusty sold the flat in Woodstock Road and he became, just like that, my ex.

This man had once cast a spell on me, one sunny afternoon in a shopping centre. Now, with one conversation, he cast that magic spell again and this time set me free.

And you know what happens next, at the end of fairytale stories?

They all lived happily ever after.

Right?

Wrong.

PART TWO

TRAPPED IN HELL

A blackened night
No point to fight
Inflicted pain
Over and again
Each blow and thrust
Turn mind to dust

Numbed by perpetual fear
Holding on to life's breath dear
Thinking of the day ahead
How I must hold my head …
Praying not to be left for dead.

Chapter One

Daniel and I moved into our new home in the spring of 1989. As I wasn't working, we were reliant on the council helping us out, and they housed us in a three-bed maisonette ground-floor flat in Nechells, a really rough area of Birmingham. It was properly run-down, the dregs of the city, and it wasn't what I would have chosen if I'd had a choice, but I had no money of my own so it was the only place we could go. Our flat was opposite high-rise tower blocks, but we were lucky: we lived in a red-brick building with only three apartments in it, and we had a garden.

Most importantly, it was just me and Dan. No Dusty. So it may have been grotty but, to me, it was paradise.

All the rooms were huge. It took me a while to get carpets in, but the walls were painted a soft cream colour from the start. There were no cork tiles. There was so much space in that flat – it was like a physical representation of our new-found freedom. Daniel had a bedroom of his own, with a *Count Duckula* bedspread, on which Danger Mouse and ET sat, looking almost as surprised as we were to be free. I got Dan into a local nursery, and he blossomed before my eyes, like a flower opening its petals to the sun. He'd always been a quiet boy before – you had to be, in my ex's presence; it was all part and parcel of obeying the rules – but now he became quite bubbly and chatty. He made friends – as did I, after a while. To begin with, I kept myself to myself, the years of speaking to no one keeping my tongue in check, but gradually, as other mums started saying hello to me at the nursery, I would respond and smile, and rediscover what it was to laugh with a mate.

Daniel being at nursery meant I could start looking for a job. I landed a position as the manager of a greetings-card shop, which I enjoyed, doing the cashing up and having real responsibility. It felt weird to be trusted after having my entire life controlled by Dusty for so long. But, like Daniel, I felt I could fly now, my wings stretching fully into fresh air.

I felt so much relief that Dusty was going to leave us alone now. I didn't believe it at first, but as the weeks and then months went by, I thought, *Yay! This is it. He's left. I can really do this. We're really free.*

I still saw him from time to time – we had a son together, after all, and every now and again he would turn up to see Daniel. I would tiptoe around him, back on my old tenterhooks at his dominating presence in my home, but he would always leave: that was the important thing. He would leave us on our own.

At Nechells, Daniel finally had an operation on his ears, during which the doctors fitted him with grommets. It sorted out his hearing immediately. I remember him coming out of theatre as I muttered some soothing words to him: he turned to me with a wondering smile on his face and said, 'I can hear you, Mummy!' And I just burst out crying – happy tears for my little, hearing Superman.

After a while, I left the card shop and started work at Techno Cameras, where I began selling cameras and equipment, and was later promoted to doing the developing and printing of images as well. I loved it. Photography had always been a passion of mine, and the team there were amazing. It was so much fun, I didn't even class it as work. I won an award for being top salesperson of the year; I was always honest with my customers, my enthusiasm for the different cameras coming through with genuine excitement, and I had one client who used to fly all the way from America just to buy his gear from us because he appreciated the service so much. Inspired by my job, I started taking my own pictures again, portraits of my beautiful boy, and I started painting again too, the colours a kaleidoscope for my emotions: heliotrope for happiness, sunshine yellow for joy.

And then … Dusty moved himself back in. I don't mean he suddenly turned up on the doorstep with a suitcase of clothes and unpacked, he just … *returned*. There was a knock on the door and I answered it and he was there, with a look on his face: 'I've come back.' He walked in and took over, and immediately started ordering me around. He's not the sort of person you can tell to, 'Go away', he's not that kind of man. I knew I just had to put up with him when he turned up.

I don't know why he 'came back' like that. I don't know if he fell out with the woman I thought he might be with or what the circumstances were: all I knew was that he was back, and more frightening than ever. The only good thing was that he didn't live with us full-time; instead, he'd stay for a day or two, or sometimes weeks, and then take off again.

I never knew when he would turn up or when he would leave. That was part of his game: nobody controlled him. He would come and go as he pleased. He didn't have a key, at first, but he acquired himself a key. If I tried to change the locks he'd circular-saw the whole thing off and put his own lock in. I couldn't stop him.

And, now he was back, he made the place his own. He cooked in my kitchen. He ate at my table. He slept in my bed.

I fought that. I fought hard. I would say strongly, with all the might I could muster, '*No*! I *don't* want you here. I *don't* want you doing this.'

But fighting just got me hurt more.

He'd climb on top of me and pin my arms down with his knees. And then he'd curl his hands into rigid fists and punch me till I was drunk, punch-drunk. He'd thump me until I shut up. He'd kick me. He'd hit me. He'd choke me.

'I come and take what I want,' he'd say. 'You're *mine*. You belong to me.' And then he'd rape me.

If I had any fight left, I would try to ask him, '*Why* do you do this? Why have you come back? You hate me – why, why, *why* are you doing this?'

But I would get beaten for bringing it up, so I learned to shut up and to take it. I stopped asking; I stopped talking. We didn't have conversations because conversations got me beaten. I just tried to stay quiet and do the housework, or lie still and let him do what he wanted. The way he saw it, I was his 'property', so he could do these things to me. He would pick me up like a plaything, and drop me when he was bored. He'd just stay until he'd done what he wanted, and then he'd leave again. And at least he did go away. Because that's when I'd have time to repair, and try to recover from what he'd done.

But his return caused difficulties on every front. The social security stopped my money because they said he was living at

61

mine. In desperation I went to their offices and tried to explain to the woman behind the counter what he was like, the whole story of us. She just said, 'Well, unless you tell him to leave and get him to go, then you're not getting any more money.' They wouldn't listen. Even when I begged them – saying, 'I can't sort him out. Please, can't you send somebody to sort him out? I don't want to see him. I don't want him living with me' – they ignored me. Just as with the police before them, my pleas fell on deaf ears.

As the months passed, I fell pregnant – again, and again. But the babies didn't survive. I had several miscarriages, and every time he blamed me. 'Only slags have miscarriages,' he would say, viciously. 'You don't deserve to be a mother.'

One afternoon at Techno, when I was twelve weeks' pregnant, I was out the back, doing stock-taking. I loved all my colleagues, who were great fun, and that day I was working with a young lad who was a real giggler. He was one of those stupidly funny people who just made you laugh. We were working away, with me chuckling merrily at the jokes he was cracking, little knowing that my ex had come into the shop and was out the front.

Dusty recognised my laugh. He hated me laughing. He jumped over the counter and came out the back to grab me. In front of this helpless young lad, he pinned me up against the wall and strangled me; I fought him desperately, but I couldn't loosen his hold around my neck. And then, in a flash, just when I thought I was going to pass out, he dropped me and ran out the shop.

My colleagues were gobsmacked; I hadn't told them what went on at home. My boss called me in and he was fuming at my ex. 'We need to sort this out,' he said, 'we need to get the police involved.'

I gave a wry smile. 'The police have been involved,' I said. 'They don't do anything. They don't lock him up; they can't stop him.'

Later, during my shift, I doubled over with pain, and my boss rushed me to the hospital. That day, I suffered another miscarriage: my third in less than two years.

This one was worse than all the others – because the doctors had some bad news for me afterwards; worse news even than that I had lost this baby. Because now, the doctors told me, I would never carry another child ever again. My insides were so messed up, so badly scarred with what they called 'keloid scarring' – which is where your scars don't stop growing, so they invade healthy skin and become bigger than before, and they rip and bleed and scar again – that I was now infertile.

To say I was devastated would be a massive understatement.

Being a mother was my world. It was my reason for living. I loved Daniel with all my heart and I had wanted to give him siblings. More than that, I had so much love to give and I had wanted to have more children, many more, to shower them with affection, to see them grow, to support and love them. Now, the doctors were saying none of that was possible. I would never again carry a baby in my womb, or breastfeed it, or hold it in my arms, or tuck it into bed at night. Yet another dream of mine was ripped to shreds – just like my newest paintings were in Dusty's hands. I felt heartbroken. I felt as though I was being punished for something.

I remember phoning my granny, who was very weak by now with life's woes and age, and sobbing down the phone to her: 'I can't have any more children.'

Her response perplexed me.

'You will,' she said calmly. 'You will one day.'

The way she said it was like it was going to happen.

I went to visit her not long after. She'd had to move in with my mum and stepdad after a heart attack. I hadn't gone back to that house since I'd left at the age of sixteen, but I wanted to see her so much I went. I took her a massive bouquet of brightly coloured flowers to cheer her up. But I knew, when I looked into her eyes, that she'd given up. I knew I wouldn't see her again. In May 1990, she died. I didn't think I could live without her, and I spiralled into depression.

Shortly after she died, I had a laser operation on my scars. The keloid scars were tearing and bleeding every time I bent down to clear up after Daniel or put away a saucepan in the cupboard, and the doctors hoped the laser op would stop me haemorrhaging and lessen my pain. I had the op and, not long after, Dusty came by on one of his 'visits'.

And, not long after that, I found out I was pregnant. The operation had reduced my scarring and I guess it had freed things up enough inside me so that I could conceive again. I was so beyond happy, I can't put it into words. I was shocked, overwhelmed and, most of all, delighted. Best of all, when I told Dusty, he took off and was gone throughout my pregnancy, which left me to plan for my future child in blissful peace. He told me I was a slag before he left, and intimated that the baby wasn't his. Yet his angry words fell painlessly on my happy ears. All I cared about was that he was gone.

Because I was working, I had money coming in, and I spent every penny on my unborn baby and Daniel. I knitted so many clothes for them, designing jumpers with Daniel's name on, and making little hats and sweaters. I remember splashing out on a mint-green-and-white silk blanket for the pram. It was a fair bit of money, but I budgeted and managed to make it work. I was happy. I hadn't been able to choose things for Daniel's babyhood – we got given things and made do – but I had choice now. I chose the cot, and the pushchair and the bumper. I was in control. I was doing this. I was going to be the best mother I could possibly be.

The baby arrived on 26 February 1991. He was four weeks late, and he was a massive eight pounds ten ounces, which was hard-going, especially as I'd been a size eight before I fell pregnant. He was very pale-skinned, with blue veins, and he was battered and bruised because they'd had to use forceps to pull him out. Daniel had been a tanned-looking baby and very tiny, like a little dot, but this one was different: he was white-skinned and solid.

That was something Dusty noted, when he saw him – noted to his displeasure. Daniel had resembled his father, but this baby didn't. To my mind, there was hate from Dusty for his second son, right from the start. He even said bluntly to me: 'He's not mine.'

But I adored everything about him. To me he was a miracle birth.

We decided to call him Jahméne.

Chapter Two

From the very beginning, Daniel loved being a big brother. I was very conscious when the new baby arrived that I should include him in everything, so he didn't feel left out or that this new person was taking over his mum. Daniel and I were very, very close; I'd basically brought him up by myself, he'd had my undiluted attention for the first five years of his life, and, with his deafness, we'd been even closer than most mothers and sons. I'd always had this thing about getting down to his level to communicate with him, so he could communicate openly back to me and not feel that I was different, a scary adult. I talked to him a lot about his new brother and what his arrival meant for our little family. He took to his new role like a duck to water. It was as though he almost felt responsible for Jahméne, and he'd look out for him and show him things – including his special superhero trick of jumping off the sofa (no matter how many times I told him not to). He liked his big-brother role, and my boys soon bonded.

Jahméne was a special baby. I'd been so sad that my granny hadn't lived to see her prediction come true, to see that I had given birth to another child, but as Jahméne grew older, I felt somehow that the spirit of her lived on inside my son. He'd been born almost nine months to the day since she passed away. And as he developed his character, and his looks and smiles, my heart would sometimes catch in my throat to see my granny's smile or spirit in his expression. He had her character of kindness and heart. He was very loud and open and caring and giving. He was a beam of sunshine, a bundle of joy in every sense of the word.

His father couldn't bear him.

I thought I'd worked Dusty out, by now. I thought I knew what he was capable of, and knew what was coming when he turned up for his visits. But, in the wake of Jahméne's birth, he became really nasty, and spiteful, and calculating.

He changed the rules of the game.

Now, when he raped me, he wouldn't just 'take what was his'. He would try different things to cause me more pain. If I got used to a certain pain, a certain way of it being done, he'd change it to make it worse for me; in a different position or pressing me against something hard so I'd have pain from both sides. Before, if I'd been on my period or bleeding from his attacks, it would put him off and I'd have some respite. Now, the blood only egged him on.

He was very violent when he'd thrust his way inside me, asserting all the masculine control he could, forcing me to submit. Even though I didn't fight him anymore, it was like he wanted me to. He'd rape me in a frenzy, grabbing anything within reach to beat me with. A kitchen utensil, a ruler, a tool. Slap, punch, push me down, kick. It got so bad I'd start trying to analyse what was in the room, trying to predict what he might use. But that was a dangerous game, because if my eyes landed on something he'd hadn't yet thought of, it could plant ideas in his head, like he could read my mind. He'd rip my clothes off and leave me standing there, naked and vulnerable, with all my parts exposed, while he weighed up what he wanted to do. He'd hit me as he forced his way inside, punching me in time with his thrusts. He'd punch me over and over. Blood would be spurting from my mouth, my eyes, my ears, yet he still carried on, raping me with gusto and energy, like he was super-fuelled to cause the utmost pain. If ever I showed that I was in agony, it fuelled him further. He used to get a thrill out of it: his face would have a grimace of pleasure and power. It made him feel bigger and better. And he would laugh and enjoy and revel in my pain. I tried to switch off, to become a robot, to not feel anything, because if he saw me react to something, he'd bank it and use it again. But switching off was almost impossible, at the start …

He'd rape me in my bed in these vicious attacks and he'd actually say to me, 'Be quiet, don't wake up the kids.'

As if I would. I kept everything locked inside, biting my cheeks as he raped me. I tried to be real quiet. I can probably count on one hand the amount of times I screamed out loud. For every shriek, there were a million times when I didn't make a sound. He would use my long red hair to push and pull me about – to force me to look at him or, if he didn't want to see my face, to push me down into the pillow, not caring whether I suffocated. And as he roughly yanked my head and drove himself deeper inside me, I would bite down hard on my cheeks to keep myself silent. I would bite down even as I tasted blood.

He had his own methods of shutting me up, too. He took to strangling me as he raped me. It felt like my eyeballs were going to pop out of my face from the pressure. My natural reaction was to try to pull his hands from around my throat, but that would start a massive fight because he saw it as me rebelling. I had to learn to lie still, and he was going to teach me that lesson, once and for all.

The strangling was a big part of his new rules. He didn't want me to die, though, because then the game would be over. So he would take me to the brink and bring me back again. All the time, this game of severity: up to the point of imminent death … and then stop. Years afterwards, I studied it, as he had clearly done too. When someone strangles you, there's a certain place where they can apply pressure so it won't kill you – it will stop you breathing, but if they let go after so many seconds you will stay alive. And that's what he'd do. I could feel him searching for that sweet spot, adjusting his vice-like grip. He'd get the wrong place and he'd mutter above me, 'No, it's not there … *there* it is.' And then he'd squeeze.

Many times, I thought he'd gone too far. When someone steals the air from your brain, you can't think straight and you feel yourself ebbing. Fear would strike right at my heart then, cutting through the panic, and I'd think in a rush of fright, *He's actually going to do it!* Through my dread, I'd remember my promise to Daniel, and I'd chant in my head: *You're not gonna kill me, you're not gonna kill me, I'm gonna stay alive, I'm gonna get through this, you're not gonna do this to me, you're* not …

I don't know how I got through it, but I did. I don't know where my strength came from – maybe an inner, suppressed faith – but I was determined to survive. My mind kept me alive. My mind kept me focused.

Afterwards, after all the craziness and immense pain, after he'd got his own way, he'd just roll over and go to sleep. I would lie next to him in the darkness, barely able to catch my breath, in extreme pain, with my blood pooling around me on the mattress. My heart would be going through the roof.

But I couldn't get up and clean myself – because I didn't want to risk waking him up. Only once I heard him settle into a deep, deep sleep would I ease myself out of bed as gently as I could, and limp slowly to the bathroom to patch myself up.

I went to the doctor and got myself put on the Pill. I was breastfeeding Jahméne so I knew it was unlikely I'd get pregnant, but I didn't want to take any chances, not when Dusty was being like this.

When Jahméne was only four months old, I started throwing up in the mornings. I knew what it was, instantly.

I was pregnant again.

Chapter Three

'Morning Mandy, how are you feeling today?'

I manoeuvred with difficulty to the chair beside the health official's desk, carrying Jahméne in my arms, just above my growing bump. I was four months gone and felt bigger than ever. Daniel was at school, and I'd taken the opportunity to visit the baby clinic.

'Not too bad, thanks.' I smiled at Karen. She'd been my midwife at the local clinic throughout my pregnancy with Jahméne, and we knew each other well by now.

'And how's this beautiful boy?' She took Jahméne from my arms to weigh him, cooing at him while he waved his little hands at her in delight and tried to clutch at strands of her long blonde hair, his ever-friendly face smiling up at her. Even if I said so myself, my children were adorable, and Karen loved my boys to bits.

By now, she knew all about the beatings at home. At first, I'd lied about the marks she saw on my face or neck during my appointments. I didn't want anyone to know how I'd got them because I didn't want any officials storming in at home: I knew full well they wouldn't put my ex away, they'd just make things ten times worse for me by revealing that I'd spoken out. But, over the months, I'd grown to trust Karen and opened up. I saw her regularly now, and she'd always ask if I was OK and we'd chat. She'd check over the red welts on my throat where he'd strangled me or examine my black eye, and if it was something more serious I'd go to the doctor for it. They logged it all, but they couldn't stop it. They just recorded what had happened.

The way the system worked in those days, the doctors didn't have any power. Social services didn't really have any power. And the police, as I'd already found out to my cost, weren't enforcing their power to make him stop. So I just had to get on with it.

I wasn't the only mother Karen saw at the clinic who was beaten. She used to tell me I was doing really well, and take pointers off me to help other women who were going through a similar thing. For me, it was all about keeping my mind strong. He could beat me black and blue, but he couldn't touch my mind, not if I didn't let him. I would do knitting or I would read books. I had to do things for me, to keep my mind straight, so I could remind myself: *You're not the one at fault; you're not the one who's causing all this; this isn't about you, it's* him. I knew I had to keep my mind in the right place for my children.

Speaking of which, it was time for my latest scan. Karen helped me up onto the clinic's bed and slathered my belly in a clear cool gel. I winced at its temperature and we giggled together. I felt free enough to have a giggle that day. Because, ever since I'd told Dusty I was pregnant again, he'd vanished from my life. 'Why have you done that?' he'd said crossly when I told him. 'You shouldn't be having my children.' And then he'd taken off and I hadn't seen him since. Good riddance was all I could say.

Karen ran the scanner across my stomach and I watched excitedly as a grainy black-and-white image filled the screen. I loved being pregnant. The feeling of it; the anticipation. I could write a book just on the emotions of having a child in your stomach, growing in your womb. I was happy I was pregnant again: I adored children, and I knew Dan and Jahméne and I were doing just fine without Dusty. This new little one would be a much-loved member of our gang.

'Do you want to know the sex?' Karen asked me, a smile playing on her lips.

'Yes, please,' I said, holding my breath in expectation.

'It's a girl.'

My first daughter. I went a bit mad, then. I must have bought every baby dress I saw – not ridiculously expensive things, because I'd had to leave Techno Cameras when Jahméne was born so I was living on benefits, but I went to Mark One and I waited for the sales. I got her so many outfits that, when she was born, I had to change her two or three times a day just to make sure she wore them all.

My little girl arrived on 7 January 1992. I called her Corice. She came three weeks early and was such an easy birth – she practically flew out. I felt fantastic afterwards: I got up from the hospital bed, went and had a shower and was home within the hour.

My daughter was adorable. She was like a little doll, not a blemish on her. She had the biggest eyes, and the darkest purest skin of all my babies. Unlike the boys, she was born completely bald, but in time she grew a mop of thick curly hair that I loved to plait and comb. She was a hit with her brothers from day one. Jahméne in particular attached himself to her and they were inseparable ever after. They were so close, and so close in age, that people used to think they were twins. They were just buddies. They did everything together.

I barely saw Dusty when Corice was small. He'd just come to visit for a couple of horrible nights and then go, never saying when he would be back – but making it clear that he would be, at some point, whenever I least expected it. He issued threats to keep me in line, telling me never to run, telling me that he would kill me if I ever took the children away from him. He would always be checking up on me to see if I was breaking the rules. Because, just as he had done in Woodstock Road, he liked to control my world, even when he wasn't living in it.

He had made friends with the neighbours, turning on that velvety voice he'd once used to tempt me, twisting his way into their sympathy. He could switch from monster to matinee idol in an instant; he was a master of disguise to fool the world, and people fell for it. And, once they were in his sway, they became, often unwittingly, part of his network of spies. He would make friends with everybody in the neighbourhood, so that he could ask them seemingly innocent questions, each one laced with a smile that didn't reach his eyes: 'Did Mandy go out? Who was she with? What time did she get home?' Like a spider at the heart of his lair, he'd ensnare information within the web he'd built so well. He knew everything. If I even started to make friends with someone, he would find out, and then he would make friends with them too and become the dominant player in the relationship, so they 'reported' to him what I said. I worked that out very quickly.

He was so paranoid, I wasn't allowed to talk to anybody. He would check the phone numbers I had rung, asking who they were for and even phoning them himself to check if I was telling the truth. He would time me on the school run to make sure I wasn't dawdling on the way home. As in Woodstock Road, I wasn't allowed out, other than to take Daniel to school. If I did go out for any other reason and he found out, I would get a beating.

Sometimes, I'd risk it: I'd go to a childcare centre and sit there for a few hours, or I'd take the kids to visit one of my old friends from Dan's nursery. I was careful not to tell people what was going on. I just needed to get out of the house and have a friend, even if I didn't tell them anything, to take me out of the bubble of fear in which I lived. It's so hard when you're on your own; if you don't have another soul to speak to it sucks you down into a pit. To keep strong, I had to escape every now and again, even just for an hour or two. That, I thought, was worth the risk.

On occasion, if I was feeling brave and he seemed relaxed, I would dare to ask him: 'Why can't I have a friend? Why do I have to stay in when you go out all the time?'

But he'd shout at me: 'What I do is none of your effing business. Stay out of it! It's nothing to do with you.' And that would be the end of it.

I battled on. I might not have been allowed out, I thought, but I was an artist. I could create my own magical world for me and my kids right inside the house, spun from love and colour and music and heart, and that's exactly what I did. I cracked on with my kids and we got on with *life*. There were such long stretches where we had normal, wonderful, loving, happy times. I remember in particular putting on music to do the housework and just singing at the top of my voice. I used to blast the house out with Whitney Houston. I used to play happy music and I used to play it *loud*. Even from a tiny age, Jahméne would try to copy the singers on the stereo, and he and I would warble along to Whitney, hitting all her high notes. All the kids would join in, and we'd dance and sing around the flat, me crooning to Corice in her bouncer as we all let it out, just let it out. She would giggle at me; she was a bubbly, happy little girl.

One of the best bits was reading stories to my babies as I put them to bed, as well as drawing pictures together and playing with toys. If ever I sat back and questioned my life, all I had to do was look at the children and I'd think: *This is such a goodness that has come out of a badness that it's meant to be.* My kids had turned out so good. They truly were a blessing.

I wanted my children to learn to love with as big a heart as I had. We got a huge fish tank for the living room that took up one whole wall, and I filled it with vibrantly coloured fish, sharks, neons and so on who became part of our family. Dan learned how to feed and care for them, as did the others in time, and we all enjoyed seeing these wondrous creatures swimming peacefully across the enormous tank, floating as serenely as fluffy white clouds in a summer sky. They brightened up our world.

In the August of 1992, a new song came on the stereo: 'Sweat (A La La La La Long)' by Inner Circle. But this wasn't one of our favourites. No way. It was one of Dusty's.

He took that melody and he twisted it, as he did everything. He used to rape me to it that long hot summer, crooning the words to me with a sick smile on his face. He loved to sing threats to me: 'You can't run, you can't hide …' UB40 was another favourite of his: 'One in Ten'. I didn't know what he meant by those words. I guess they were meant to make me feel like nothing; like I was just another statistic: another woman wounded by an angry, violent man.

Come the autumn, after that heated summer song, I was pregnant once again.

Chapter Four

'All right, sweetheart?' I tousled Jahméne's thick dark hair. He had beautiful hair, all curled into ebony ringlets, prettier even than Corice's growing wisps. She was asleep in her room, while Dan was off somewhere else, probably reading quietly, which he spent a lot of his time doing. He was a smart kid, quiet and studious even at the age of seven.

Two-year-old Jahméne was playing quietly on the floor in the living room, while I busied myself at the stove. It was good he was playing quietly because Dusty had returned on one of his infrequent visits. I was eight-months pregnant, and as with all my other pregnancies before this one, my ex had mostly been absent throughout. But, that afternoon, he was back.

I didn't see what happened next. I just heard Dusty talk to his second-born son. He called him Mark.

I didn't think. I just asked him, automatically, the question tripping off my tongue: 'Who's Mark?'

In a flash, my ex was beside me. *How dare I ask him questions...* I think he was angry at himself, too, for slipping up, for saying the wrong name. He grabbed me hard by the throat and held me up against the wall, till I was gasping for breath. He lifted my feet off the ground; my eyes bulged in my head and I actually thought they were going to explode. Somehow, he got a knife in his hand, suddenly, grabbed from the counter or some other spot, and he slashed viciously at my clothes. *Swish. Swish.* My shirt sliced open and fell to the ground.

And then …

'Daddy, no!'

A fierce little voice. A little figure coming between us, pushing his knife-wielding father away from me with two-year-old arms.

'Jahméne, get out of the way!' I yelled, more frightened for him than I'd ever been for myself. 'Move!'

His father's eyes dropped onto him. Dusty picked him up and moved him out the way, roughly, firmly, his big hands shifting the little boy with ease. 'Stay out of it!' he growled.

'Don't you touch him,' I said, my hands rubbing the red welts on my neck, standing up for my boy, just as he had done for me. 'Don't you *dare* touch my kids.'

He let me go to him, thank God. Jahméne was crying his eyes out. I think Dusty was shocked, more than anything: shocked at Jahméne's audacity and courage; that he would dare to push his father out the way. Jahméne had that rebelious side in him, just as I used to have, back in the day. He was more like me than I'd ever realised. It went beyond his chin, which was just like mine, right into his spirit. His natural reaction, when his dad attacked, was to come between us.

But that instinct, commendable as it was, could get him killed. That was something I knew only too well.

I ushered him away from his father's hateful gaze. My boy was crying so hard.

'Why was Daddy doing that to you, Mummy?' he asked me through his tears. Though he knew our world became quieter and stricter when his dad was around, he'd never ever seen him hit me before. We kept all that behind closed doors to protect the children.

I dodged the question. Even I didn't know why Daddy did it; I couldn't possibly answer him when I didn't know myself. Instead, I said, 'I know you want to stop him. I know you want to get in the middle. I'm very proud of you for that.

'But you mustn't do it, sweetheart. It will get you hurt. You need to stay out of the way if anything like that ever happens again.'

'But …' he interrupted.

'Shh,' I said. 'I'm a big person, Jahméne. I can handle myself.'

Jahméne looked seriously at me, and then nodded. He was only two, but like his brother Daniel, he was a smart kid. Smart in so many ways. Both he and Daniel learned, from a very young age, that it would cause trouble if they spoke up, even when they wanted to. They learned it was dangerous and so they didn't do it. If they hadn't learned that lesson, it could have got us all killed.

I made sure that, as well as staying safe, they understood the wrongs and rights of anything they saw at home, though. I knew that if I didn't explain, they weren't going to know any different; they wouldn't know that this wasn't a normal way to behave. If ever they saw something – which was rare, but it did sometimes happen – I would sit with them and explain clearly that I hadn't done anything for it to occur. Their dad would be yelling insults at me – 'This is because you're a slag! You deserve this, for sleeping around! This is your fault!' – and I had to say: 'No. None of that is true. Your dad is just in a bad mood and this is what he does.' I would try to train them into a certain way of behaving to make sure they stayed safe. I did all I could, even more importantly, to try to make sure that they didn't grow up just like him.

My son Isaac was born a few weeks later, on 21 July 1993. It had been a shock to me to find out I was pregnant again – I'd been breastfeeding Corice and I was on the mini-Pill – but I wanted him just as badly as all my other kids once I learned he was on his way. I was overjoyed to have another little soul to love, even though I knew it would be tough. But I was getting a handle on my ex by now, I thought. Yes, the rapes were horrific, but – strange as it may sound – I could cope because they were only every now and again, and because he would leave again afterwards, for weeks or even months, I had plenty of time to recover. The bulk of my life was spent loving my children, and that was something so joyful it eclipsed the darkness.

Dusty wasn't there for the birth. It was another easy one, and I remember going home afterwards and hanging out the washing because it was a sunny day.

I remember clearly what Isaac looked like when he was born. Like Jahméne, he was very pale-skinned.

He had the brightest blue eyes.

He had wisps of blond curled hair.

Dusty took one look at him and said, 'That's not mine.' And he just went off his trolley. I was beaten black and blue and accused of sleeping around. It was awful. He was so, so angry. Nothing I said made the blindest bit of difference. He thought my disobedience was staring him in the face, and he had to teach me a lesson. He went away and came back and I got beaten again, and again. Every time he came back he kept saying that Isaac wasn't his. He got so mad that he turned up to my flat one day with a bucket of red paint and scrawled 'SLAG' in crimson capitals all over the walls of my living room. I had a photo montage in there of the kids, six or seven photographs I'd taken of them growing up, as well as shots of my granny, and he just went in and spoiled it all. 'GRANNY OF WHORE' he painted next to my gran's face. He painted all over the living room: 'slag', 'whore', 'he isn't my child'. He painted all over the children's pictures: 'SLAG, SLAG, SLAG'.

I was so humiliated by it. I tried to wipe it off, but he grabbed the sponges out of my hands and forced me to leave it. 'It's gotta stay there,' he insisted. 'You do not wipe it off.'

The kids asked me about it, of course. 'Just ignore those words,' I said brightly, hoping they couldn't understand them. 'He's just put those words up. We've just got to ignore them.'

I told myself I could get through it. I had done it before, I'd do it again. And, that autumn, I found even more inspiration to find courage from within. Dusty and I had a rare night out together, and we went to see *What's Love Got to Do with It* at the cinema, the Tina Turner biopic about her life with her abusive partner, Ike Turner. Ironically, Dusty got angry at the film – angry at the way Ike behaved towards Tina. He couldn't see that his own actions exactly mirrored the domestic abuse onscreen, even as he took me home and raped me afterwards.

But I could see the parallels, and the message I took from the film was …

Tina got out.

I came home empowered. It gave me so much energy, mentally. I thought, *If she can do it, I can do it. I can leave this evil man.*

No matter what my ex had once told me, I thought to myself: *I* can *run* …

Chapter Five

'Jingle bells, jingle bells, jingle all the way … '

The children's voices lilted with mine as we sang along to the radio at home, Corice and Jahméne duetting together on the high notes, as they often did. They were still glued to one another, and both of them loved to sing. I had Isaac in a sling as I dusted and cleaned, readying the house for Christmas. The kids' schools and nurseries were about to break up for the holidays, and I was so looking forward to giving my children a Christmas they would never forget, filled with treats and presents and laughter. Daniel was eight, Jahméne was nearly three, Corice was almost two and Isaac was coming up to six months old. Dusty was so little in our lives at the time, it was just a joy.

I had spent weeks preparing, saving up money to buy the kids their longed-for gifts, and wrapping the presents in swathes of beautiful festive paper. I didn't even let the trouble that still came to my door because of my ex bother me. As had happened in Woodstock Road, the police raided my home – looking for him or items he might have hidden; I never knew exactly why. Though I said, 'He doesn't live here,' they replied that they'd been given my address to search and then battled their way through the house. They didn't search nicely, either. They broke stuff and tipped things over, yanked up the floorboards and ripped up the carpet. I told them, in all sincerity, 'If he'd left something here,

I'd tell you, believe me. If you can lock him up it does me a favour,' but they carried on without bearing me any mind. And then they triumphantly seized on a briefcase of his, which was hidden behind a box. I'd never seen it before and I peered at it with curiosity, wondering what was inside. The police smashed it open, and I soon found out.

There was a birthday card in it. 'Happy Birthday Daddy', it read, with a child's sketch of a father and son. It was signed: Mark. The name Dusty had called Jahméne just a few months before. Like a jigsaw puzzle piece, it formed a picture for me of where my ex might go when he wasn't with us. Perhaps he was with Mark ... and Doreen, the name I saw inside an engagement card that was also in the case. I wasn't about to ask Dusty about them, whoever they were. The time for asking him questions about his personal life had long gone.

Hopefully, I thought, *he will be with Doreen and Mark over Christmas*. I expected him to turn up at some point, bearing gifts for the kids as he sometimes did, his arms overflowing with overcompensation. As if a Barbie doll or a new train track could make up for his behaviour the rest of the time. But I was pretty confident he wouldn't stay for long; he never did, these days. And that would leave me free to be with the kids, to delight in their shining faces and their 'Mummy Mummy Mummy!' excited cries.

Two weeks before Christmas, as I'd expected, Dusty walked through the door. He never said hello to me when he came back; he was never nice. He just walked in and took over, and that's exactly what he did that December. The kids were off school by then, so I was trying to entertain them. But he didn't like me spending time with my children. When he was around, he'd stop it, and that's what he did. He ordered them to go to their bedrooms or he'd order me to the kitchen, and tell the children I had to do chores and couldn't play with them. Then he'd sit himself down on the couch and pull Corice onto his lap. She was a daddy's girl, easy to love with a ready smile, and he spoiled her. Or he might sit down next to Daniel and talk quietly with him; I never knew what he was saying to my son.

I tried to keep the peace. I knew something would set him off, so I tried my very best to do none of the things that had been a trigger in the past. I peeled the potatoes properly. I cooked the dinner right. I wore the clothes he had picked out for me. I tried to keep my face neutral and expressionless. I slowed my breathing down so he wouldn't hear it and complain. I analysed everything, looking at the whole picture, 360 degrees. It was what I had learned to do, like an animal, to try to stop him from kicking off.

But it never, ever worked.

Once the kids were asleep, he ordered me to the bedroom. We both went in and then he started hitting me; then he raped me; then he fell asleep. The usual vicious, horribly familiar pattern. I took it, and thought of Tina Turner, and I told myself, *You can get through this. He'll be gone in a day or two. Just hold on. You will survive.*

But that December … he didn't leave. He stayed, day after day after day. He told me he was stopping for Christmas, which was still weeks away. He was determined to stay and be part of it. It felt like he was trying to destroy everything I'd planned for the children. But, worse than that, it felt like he was trying to destroy me.

My repair time was usually when he was gone. I needed that time, to cope, to survive. I was really struggling because he wasn't going anywhere. His abuse, now, was every day. It was constant.

He would belittle me in front of the kids. He would just poke me, here, there, with his finger, or a ruler, prodding me, trying to get a reaction. He would disparage me in conversations, and make snide comments, and push me as I walked past him, trying to trip me up. He would ramble on in front of the kids about what a bad mum I was. It was like he was trying to drill me into submission.

Worst of all, though, were the violent rapes. He took it to another level, and it was all out of my control. I could tell he was planning what he was going to do each night, for every night he'd put me through a different routine, each one worse than the evening before. I never knew what was coming next; I couldn't second-guess him anymore. And I thought, *I've just got to get through this alive because I don't know where this is going. I don't know what his plan is.*

He'd go to sleep afterwards and I'd think, *I've got to stay awake because if he wakes up and I'm asleep … what's he going to do then?*

I started thinking of all manner of scenarios. I feared for every minute, not knowing what might make him flip.

Every day in the run-up to that Christmas was a battle to get through. I was so stressed I couldn't eat, my stomach balled up with bruising and the tension of living with my ex; I was so scared I couldn't sleep even for a second. Yet each morning I would drag myself out of bed, and force myself to pretend to the children that everything was OK. I was in severe internal pain, but I had to keep going: lifting up the babies and changing nappies and doing all the normal things mums do when they've got four kids. Some days I would have to take myself off to the bathroom for a minute and just stand there and tell myself: *Breathe. Just let yourself breathe. You've got to keep it together.*

Then I would paste on my smile, unlock the door and head back out into my prison. But, inside, I felt like I was breaking. He was wearing me down, inch by inch.

I tried my best to enjoy the holidays for the kids because it was their Christmas and I wanted it to be happy for them. I didn't want anything bad to mess it up; I was trying so hard not to let that happen.

Christmas Eve came round, and I helped the children hang up their stockings, and read them a festive story. Then I tucked them into bed, pausing for a minute in the doorway of each of their rooms, to watch them dream, of candy canes and flying reindeer, with an innocence that made my heart break.

Dusty was waiting for me as I shut their doors. He was waiting for me to come into the bedroom. He'd planned a special surprise for me that Christmas, and I think he deliberately chose Christmas Eve to give it to me.

Because every year, ever after, I would think of him on Christmas night and remember.

That evening, as the kids slept in the rooms next door, he threw me down on the bed, at a weird angle. I was naked. And straight away – without missing a beat, because he'd planned this – he held me steady, and he buggered me.

I screamed.

I couldn't help it.

I was in shock: I didn't see it coming. He was vicious, and he delighted in his new game. It was beyond degrading. He took all my dignity and threw it out the window.

Afterwards, he told me, 'Nobody else is going to want you now. No decent man is going to touch you, not after I've done that.'

86

He hated me himself, but he didn't want anyone else to have me. I was *his*.

Christmas morning dawned, inevitable as death. I was badly injured; far more than the other kinds of rape had ever done to me. I limped as the children darted around me, their faces alight with Christmas spirit. I couldn't take pleasure in any of it; I was in far too much pain.

Dusty set up a video camera in the corner of our lounge. He wanted to film the children unwrapping their presents, like we were an ordinary family. Yet there was a weird atmosphere pervading everything. The kids weren't stupid. They tried just to be kids and open their presents, but they were only pretending everything was OK as well. You could feel that heavy mood, weighing down the day, and they knew something was going on, even if they didn't know exactly what. I think they had bouts where they would forget and start giggling, but then they would remember, and their laughter would take on a hollow, empty tone, like they were faking it for Daddy's camera. Everything was false, a stage set, with everybody acting. And all the time, in the corner, the camera whirred.

As I crossed its shot, going to help one of the kids with something, Dusty raised his palm and slapped me on the behind.

To anyone else, it might have looked like a cheeky husband's move, manhandling his wife with a mischievous spank on the arse.

But for me, it was agony, after what he'd done the night before. He did that deliberately. I winced visibly, sucking in my breath, but the kids were all splayed out on the carpet in front of me, and I had to swallow down my pain in silence.

I hated him in that moment more than I'd ever hated him before.

And still he didn't go. Boxing Day came and went, with its new tortures. He kept up his campaign of hate, provoking me during the day, abusing me at night. He'd opened a Pandora's box now, and he just went psycho. Raping me, buggering me, using implements. He tore me apart. He forced me to do things I am ashamed of now. New Year's Eve came and went, fireworks lighting up his face as he took perverse joy in hurting me harder, deeper, further than he ever had before.

I'm going to break, I thought. *I cannot bear this. I cannot take this. After all these years, he's going to win.*

On 5 January 1994, Daniel had to go back to school. Dusty had gone somewhere that morning – I didn't know where because, like always, he didn't say anything to me, he just left, though I knew he'd be back later – so it was down to me to take my son to school and the other children to nursery. I dressed the kids in their winter coats in a daze, and together we walked the short distance to Daniel's school. I was in such a state, I didn't even take my wallet with me. I had four pence in my pocket, Isaac in a sling on my chest, and Corice and Jahméne hanging onto each hand. Daniel walked slowly beside me, as I tried to limp my way through the pain without him noticing.

I dropped him off at school. I couldn't stop thinking about the fact that I would have to go back to the house. *Dusty will be waiting*, I thought. *He'll be timing me. I don't have long.*

But I didn't want to go home.

And then I realised: *I* can't *go home.*

If I did, I might never get out of there alive.

I looked at my children: baby Isaac and my two toddlers; I thought of Daniel safely at school. I thought of everything babies and children need, just to get through the day. Nappies. Clothes. Food.

I can't go back to get anything, I thought, *because he might already be there.*

I patted my pockets. No wallet. No money. Not even enough change to call someone for help. *I've not done this right*, I thought. *I haven't thought this through.*

I wandered slowly to the shops across the road from the school, the little ones trailing in my wake. There was a woman there, behind the counter, and she looked at me as I entered her shop. I felt sick and dizzy and confused, and my head was pounding.

I stared helplessly around the store, knowing I could afford nothing in there, knowing what I wanted couldn't be lifted down from a shelf and scanned, the barcode reading: FREEDOM. I wandered out again, and traipsed with the little ones down to their nursery. It was a place I knew well because I helped out there from time to time and had drawn some murals of Disney characters on the walls. The staff were always saying what a credit the kids were to me: how well-behaved, how smartly dressed, how clean and happy. They were thoughtful children, caring towards the others in the crèche, even at that young age: a complete contrast to their father's viciousness at home.

When we walked in, Jahméne and Corice ran straight into their groups, excited to be back with their friends after the Christmas break. And as they parted from me, it was like a dam was breached. I just broke down, crying uncontrollably. I sat down on a chair in a corridor of the crèche, clutching Isaac to me, and I sobbed and sobbed and sobbed. I had been imprisoned in Dusty's torture for weeks, raped and buggered and strangled, and being outside, with the sounds of normality crashing around me as the kiddies giggled and played and their teachers welcomed them back, was too much to bear. Fresh air and people: they tipped me over the edge.

I felt my head spin in fast circles, confused, sick and hurting. I felt guilt, shame, embarrassment and failure. I had no words. I just kept sobbing.

One of the teachers, someone I knew well who had become a friend of sorts over time, came over and sat down next to me. I could see concern and confusion in her eyes. I had kept so much hidden for so many years. I wore my mask well; no one had a clue. It was easier for me that way – a chance to be 'normal'.

Now she said, 'What's wrong?'

How on earth could I tell her?

Yet I focused on her, my heart beating hard in my chest, my skull throbbing. I could have said, 'Nothing, I'm fine,' even though it wasn't true. I could have ducked my head, and scurried back home, as I had so often before; rushing to get home before my time ran out.

'What's happened?' she asked again. Her voice was thick with kindness and compassion.

And I raised my eyes to hers. I opened my mouth to speak. And, before I could stop myself, before I could take it back, the truth came tumbling out.

PART THREE

DESPERATE FOR REFUGE

The mind is plagued
By troubles deep
And head lays heavy
No time to sleep
Days filled with chaos
The future unsure
The question is:
How much more
Must I endure?

Chapter One

The truth came spluttering out of me in sharp-edged, ugly words. They poured from my mouth between heaving sobs, and I didn't even think how the teacher listening would take it; how crude it all was. I relived the incidents, and every word I said made me retch with shame.

To the teacher's credit, she listened and she didn't judge. She looked shocked, but she put her arm around me. That felt strange: to be touched in a way that was caring and gentle; to experience a gesture intended to help, not harm.

She went off to get the head of the nursery, who said, in a firm but kind voice, that she needed to ring the police.

I told her there was no point: that the police wouldn't help. *Been there, done it before, it just makes things worse.*

But the head looked me in the eye. 'What are you going to do if I don't ring?' she asked me. 'Have you anywhere to go? Family? Friends?'

I sobbed again at that, knowing there was no one to help me … no one but me. And I think that steeled my resolve. Because there seemed no other way *but* to phone the police. I wasn't going back to the house so Dusty could carry on as before.

Before I knew it, two police officers arrived, a man and a woman. I was rambling, shaking, my head was spinning. The female officer interviewed me sensitively, but the man drilled me with questions, real fast: we need to know this, we need to know that. 'Where is your ex now? What is his name? What has he done?'

I couldn't think straight to answer them; my migraine was sucking away my sentences. It felt unreal to be doing this. I just wanted them to put my ex away and keep us safe. That was all I asked. I felt terrified – terrified of talking, terrified of going home, terrified of running away. *What is the right thing to do?*

I had to think of the children. We had nowhere to go, no money, nothing. We had to ask the police for help. But I also knew that Dusty had threatened me with death if I ever took the children away from him. Every line he had ever said about that was burned into my brain. His words ran through my mind now, like shards of glass, cutting me with every bitter word he had ever said. I knew full well he was more than capable of carrying out the threats.

But if I did nothing, the way he was acting now, he would probably kill me anyway.

I felt a futile sense of déjà vu as I sat across from the police officers and, in halting words, still unsure if I was doing the right thing, I told them what he'd done to me. *Here we go again*, I thought. My experience with the police to date made me think that my ex was just going to get off, but I kept on talking anyway. It was different, this time. I kept on saying to them, 'We've been down this route before, but you have to help me. Please. It's not the same as before. He's on another level now, and this is a worse level than before. If he takes it up another level …' I paused then, in sheer fear of what could possibly be worse than what he'd already done to me, unable to imagine. Sickened, I shook off my dread to press home my point. 'If he takes it up another level, that's *really* dangerous. I need to tell you now; I need to do this now because it could be really, really serious if he's not stopped.'

They assured me they would find him and arrest him as there was a warrant already out for his arrest, for another crime they believed he had committed, which I didn't know anything about. 'While we're doing that,' they said, 'let's get you back to your flat so you can grab your stuff, and then we'll get you to a refuge.'

They accompanied me back to my home. My ex was still out there, somewhere, so I was terrified, my eyes flickering every which way, desperately trying to look everywhere at once, so I could see him coming if he suddenly rounded the corner of the red-brick building. *My God*, I thought, *if he comes back now we're all dead. If he comes back now and he sees this and then he runs off, he's gonna organise something, and something really bad is gonna happen …*

'Right,' the police told me. 'Let's make this quick. In and out. You've got a minute to grab what you need.'

I ran inside. My skull was still banging, my body was battered and bruised. I felt sick being back inside the flat, with all its memories; and sicker still at the thought that he might be there at any second. I ran from room to room, trying to think, but my pounding heart wouldn't let me. I reached out and grabbed things, stuffed them in a bag. I got the nappies. I took clothes for the five of us, a handful of mismatched outfits that were the first things I laid my hands on. I didn't think clearly about what I should have been picking up. I didn't grab the right stuff. All I could think was that my ex could be back at any second. I kept saying it to the police: 'If he catches us doing this, he's gonna kill you, and then he's gonna kill me. He's gonna kill all of us.' They were trying to calm me down, but it didn't work. My fear was too real for their empty reassurances to touch it.

We all piled into the police van and went to Daniel's school to collect him. He was startled at first, and then became angry and upset when he realised we were running away. He joined his siblings in the back of the police van, and it revved off with the five of us inside, taking us far away from Birmingham.

'Have you got him?' I kept asking the officer who was with us. 'Have you locked him up yet?'

'Don't worry about your ex,' they said. 'We've just got to get you to a safe place.'

They took us to a women's refuge forty miles away, in Worcester. The first thing I did was visit a solicitor and change all our names by deed poll, legally, so my ex couldn't track us. I was determined to do everything right this time, to do everything the officials told me so that we'd stay safe. 'You can't run,' Dusty had told me. 'You can't hide.' *Yes*, I thought, as I signed the legal documents, *I bloody well can*.

The refuge was a dive. It was dirty, and small, and strange. There was no privacy. The five of us were given a room together, smaller even than my bedroom had been at Woodstock Road, with a couple of beds in it that we had to share. There was barely space for the kids to get changed into their pyjamas.

Daniel was livid. 'I hate you!' he shouted at me. 'Why have you brought us here? It's *horrible*.'

I tried to explain to him why, and he knew why, but he was only eight, and he was understandably upset at being snatched away from the life he knew.

'It's only for a little while,' I promised him. 'Just while we get our heads together and sort ourselves out.'

But he didn't want to listen. Because, as well as forgetting to pick up money and food when I'd made my mad grab for our things, I'd forgotten something even more critical: the children's toys.

'I wanted to get my toys!' Daniel howled at me. He was inconsolable.

In all honesty, I was angry too. Angry that I'd had to bring my kids here to get away from their father. *We* were the victims. Why did *we* have to leave our home? Dusty was the one who should be punished, not us.

I felt guilty, as well. Guilty for taking the children away from their home, especially to such a disgusting place. Guilty for forgetting their toys. Guilty for running when I hadn't thought it through. Most of all, guilty for possibly making things even worse for us all, because I still didn't feel safe. The police had told me they'd got my ex and were keeping him in, but I didn't trust them. I had no money. I had no job. I had no home.

I had no idea what we were going to do next.

I didn't sleep that night in Worcester. My head was banging in time with the noises from all the other disturbed families who were crammed into the refuge's tiny, unclean, desperate rooms; in time with my heart, which was racing nineteen to the dozen. I just wanted to have space to think, to figure out what had happened and what I had to do next, but my body wouldn't let me relax. It was still in fight-or-flight mode, on edge at what the next move would be in my ex's sick game.

The following morning, we found out.

There was a fierce *rat-a-tat-tat!* on our door, and before I could even get up to answer it, the door flew open and the woman who ran the refuge came rushing into our room. My kids and I all looked up at her, startled. She was clearly panicking.

'He's tracked you!' she cried. 'The police have let him out and he's coming. He's on his way, right now. You need to get out *now*. Get your stuff together, you need to go.'

Fear shot through all of us, but even as I shoved our handful of clothes back into my bag, I was angry too. Of all the ways to tell us … Couldn't she have pulled me to one side, so the kids didn't have to hear it? I could feel, through that invisible umbilical cord, that each of my kids was terrified. And as for the police … Well, thanks to them, there was no time for that, not right now.

'How the heck did he find us?' I asked her, as she helped me carry the kids down the stairs and into a waiting car. 'This is all supposed to be private. We're supposed to be safe here! How on earth is this possible when I've done it the legal way, the way you've all told me to?'

'We can't talk about that now,' she said. She slammed the car door and it pulled away at speed. We didn't know where we were going. We didn't get a choice.

It turned out, later, that it was changing our names that had allowed him to track us down. He always used to tell me he would find me if I ran. 'There's always a link,' that's what he'd say, his dark eyes gleaming. And even though I was only doing what the officials had told me to, I'd bloody well given the link to him this time. Because I'd gone to the solicitors and changed our names legally, there was a record of it – a record he'd found with just a few clicks of his computer mouse. I'd done it to make us untraceable but I'd led him straight to us. Stupid.

I tried to calm the kids down as the miles rolled past outside, but inside I was panicking. *I'm not safe anywhere*, I thought. *I've not done this right. He's gonna find us and he's gonna be even more angry than before because I took off. I thought these people were supposed to help us, but all this is only gonna make things worse.*

I couldn't get Dusty's voice out of my head, his threats running through it constantly like tickertape. He used to say he would kill me if I ran.

Soon, I would find out if he really meant it.

Minutes turned into hours on our journey. The kids, exhausted, fell asleep in the car. I couldn't sleep. I felt like I would never sleep again. I stared blindly out the window, wondering what on earth I was going to do.

After a couple of hours, we passed a sign.

'Welcome to Bath', it said.

We had arrived at refuge number two.

Chapter Two

We got the top-floor room. It was tiny, only about three metres square, even though this refuge was bigger than the last, in a bigger building with more rooms. A couple of beds were crammed into this minuscule space we'd been allocated, and we squeezed in with our five bodies and all our stuff. Isaac was crying. Everywhere in that refuge, kids seemed to be crying. There were loads of families there.

We didn't speak to them. That first night, we all huddled together in the room and we didn't communicate with anyone else in the building. We fully expected, at any moment, my ex to come tearing through the walls, huffing and puffing like the big bad wolf we knew him to be. This could be our last night on this earth. We just wanted to spend it together.

Again, I didn't sleep. I watched my children instead. Watched them like a hawk, drinking in their every movement, measuring their breaths and the steady rise and fall of their chests. I was amazed they could sleep, but children are resilient.

A full day passed. There was no desperate banging on the door. There were no clean clothes, either.

I gathered the kids together. Isaac in a sling on my chest, Corice and Jahméne balanced on each hip, a rucksack of washing on my back, and Daniel following me, dragging his grumpy eight-year-old feet. I couldn't – wouldn't – leave the kids anywhere, so we all had to go everywhere together. Like a five-headed monster, we traipsed down eight flights of stairs to the laundry room in the basement. It would have been a slog for anyone, but I was still battered and bruised from the final attacks, still trying to come to terms with the degradation he'd inflicted on me, mentally and physically. Up and down those stairs I went, carrying the kids and the washing, till my knees were shot too.

I was scared of the other people in the refuge. I didn't know anything about them. It took me a couple of days before I gained the courage to speak to anyone, but in the end I did start talking to some of the other ladies. A lot of them had kids, so my kids started talking to their kids, too.

Each woman had her own story of horror. One had her ear bitten off. Another had her arm melted to the elbow in a deep-fat fryer. They all said the same thing: it wasn't a one-off incident. It would be the twentieth incident; the two-hundredth. But their attackers would walk free if they were ever arrested for their crimes (which in itself was a rarity). The perpetrators of the violence got away with it, over and over. They'd get locked up, they'd get let out, they'd find the women and they'd hurt them again. And these weren't petty injuries, they were serious things – but they'd get away with it, all the same. The women would try their hardest to run away from them, but the men would track them down and force them back. The refuge was full of people like that.

There was one girl in particular I got chatting to. Her bloke had taken a hammer to her, all over her body, and her bones were shattered all up her legs. Listening to her story, knowing my own, I wanted so much for this to be what it *should* be: a final escape. No going back.

Then and there, I decided: this time, I was going to do everything right. He *wasn't* going to find me.

I was determined to cover my tracks.

I made a list: things we had to do to stay safe. I changed our names again – *not* by deed poll. We chose new ones; I plucked 'Iona Bennett' out of the phone book and that became my new identity. The kids all got new names, too: a new first name, and a different surname; each one different, so he couldn't look for a family of five. We all got new dates of birth as well.

I racked my brains. What else? My hair! My distinctive, long red hair. It was down to my knees, my pride and joy. I hacked it off with scissors and stared at myself in the mirror. It still wasn't enough. I called my new friend over, and she got some hair dye for me. I didn't want to go outside in case he was watching, and waiting; in case he'd already tracked us down.

'Are you sure about this?' she asked me, as we stood side by side in the poky bathroom, the dye bottle on the sink between us. 'You're not thinking clearly. You've got lovely hair, Mandy – think it through.'

I shook my head, not missing a beat. 'My hair sticks out like a sore thumb. Anyone can spot me a mile off. I could wear a hat or whatever, but do you really think that will stop him?

'This is the way it has to be.'

Together, we transformed my appearance. She rubbed the cheap dye into my short hair and we waited for the allotted time. But something went wrong. My ear went green, and my hair was such an odd shade I don't even know how to describe it. It scared the kids.

I can't be doing with this, I thought. Why did nothing ever go right? All I wanted to do was *live*, but my hair was going to ruin us. *He's gonna find us*, I thought, panic rising like bile in my throat. Desperate, I ran back to the bathroom. I pulled a Bic razor from my washbag … and I shaved what was left of my hair from my skull. Done.

We borrowed some hand-me-down clothes from the refuge; things that were 'new' to us, so he couldn't find us by familiar garments. They were far too big for us, all the wrong sizes, but I hoped that would help with the subterfuge too. I swapped pushchairs with my new friend, so I was using a different one. And, once I trusted her, I even asked her to watch two of my kids while I took Dan to school, so that I didn't have to walk down the street with all four children. That would have been a giveaway too. If I walked down the road with four kids, I was instantly Mandy, whether I'd shaved my head or not.

I'd got Dan into a new local school, within a few days of arriving, both because he had to have an education and because I hoped it would help him feel a bit more normal, to have a routine. Fat chance. How normal is it to have to answer to a different name on the register, wearing clothes that aren't yours, while all the time you've got half an eye on the school playground in case your crazy dad shows up? Added to all of which, Daniel was introverted, always had been. He wasn't like Jahméne, who would make friends within five seconds of meeting someone. Dan took much longer to open up. He was cautious. It was so difficult for him, being uprooted from everything he knew and dumped in a new school in a classroom full of strangers, who were all whispering about him behind his back. My heart went out to him.

With Dan safely, if not happily, at school, I went down to the social to try to get some money. I told the woman behind the counter what had happened: why I'd had to leave everything behind at my old address, and why I needed money that day. She said in response, 'You've got to wait.'

'Please,' I said. 'We need some money to live off.'

Eventually, she took sympathy on me – but then she started typing my details into the system to get me the cash.

'Stop!' I told her in alarm. Memories of the hours Dusty spent on his computers were fresh in my mind. He was a technological whizz, and I feared what might happen if our details were lodged on the system. For all I knew, this woman's innocent entry on the social-security system could act as bait to lead him to us. 'My ex is brilliant with computers. He might be able to find us if you do that. Please: you can't put anything on the system.'

She froze in irritation, and then turned back to me. 'Well,' she said, with an ingratiating smile, 'you can't have any money then.'

Everything was complicated. It was such hard work. I somehow managed to get some money to tide us over, and I hurried back to the refuge. I didn't like being outside its walls; it felt dangerous.

The next day, I went out on the school run again. We'd been at the refuge for just over a week by then and, despite myself, I was starting to relax. My checklist was all ticked off, we all looked completely different, we had different names, and we were over a hundred miles from home. I started to believe: *Maybe we've done it. Maybe we're free.*

A co-worker from the refuge had promised us a lift in her car that morning. As she was walking out with me, I took all four kids with us, splitting them between us as we made our way to the car, which was parked around the corner from the refuge. I carried Corice on my hip and she hugged me close, looking over my shoulder as I carried her in my arms.

I hadn't gone far when I felt her shift her weight against me, jerking upright, alert and excited.

And then I heard her cry out.

'Daddy!'

Chapter Three

Please don't be him, I thought, as I froze on the pavement, my fear making a statue of me and my little girl. *Please just let it be that she's said that by accident, that she's got confused, that it's not him.*

Corice was bouncing in my arms, in joyful recognition. Her daddy spoiled her, so at that age she was usually excited to see him. I turned around, my heart in my mouth.

There he was. It was the worst shock, the worst horror. I just wanted the floor to open up and take me.

Shit shit shit, I thought. *What do I do now?* I couldn't get a breath for what felt like forever.

The co-worker beside me panicked, and everything kicked off at once. It was like in the films, though, where everything feels like it's going in slow motion. I've had that happen about five or six times in my life, and this was one of them. I was trying to get the kids in the car and get away from him, but it was like we were moving through thick black mud. The girl from the refuge wasn't helping me at all, she was like a headless chicken, and the kids were yelling and crying, in a cacophony of shock and fear and hurt and noise.

And cutting through it all were his lying words: 'I'm not going to hurt you. Don't do this to me. Come home.'

His words were like knives going in my eyes.

My kids and I somehow made it through the mud and slammed the car doors. Just like that, time sped up again. The co-worker jammed her keys into the ignition and she drove off down the road at speed. We just left him standing there, crocodile tears on his cheeks and a dark, hard look in his eyes.

'Oh my God, he knows where we are!' I cried to the girl, turning to her in panic. 'What do we do?'

I can only think she was in shock, too. She said, 'Well, you have to take Dan to school … '

'Mum, I can't go to school, I can't!' my son sobbed in the back of the car. He was scared stiff. 'He's found us, oh, Mum, he's found us!'

'You're not going to school!' I told him firmly. I couldn't believe that co-worker: didn't she *think*? *Of course* I wasn't taking him to school.

I wasn't going to let him out of my sight.

We were all in such a state, I can't even remember what happened over the next few hours, but the refuge workers weren't dealing with the situation as they should have. From then on, my ex just sat outside the refuge in his car, watching and waiting. It even turned out that he'd been there for a day or two already, his car parked up in the shadows, but he hadn't made his move until he was sure that he'd got the right place, that it was us he was watching going in and out, clueless of his scrutiny.

'Do you know what gave you away?' he would say to me, later. 'Cos I see you've shaved your hair off, you stupid cow. I see you're wearing clothes that don't fit, that aren't yours. It was none of that. You know what gave you away? Your stupid walk.'

I have a bit of a bounce when I walk, some kind of buoyant energy; a spring in my step, even when I'm not happy. And he'd recognised that: the tell-tale lilt in my movements that I couldn't chop off or change the colour of. How was I supposed to change the way I walked? I felt a surge of failure as he taunted me: I thought I'd covered everything; I never dreamed in a million years that my walk would be my let-down.

It didn't matter anymore. It was too late now; too late for any evasive manoeuvres. He was parked outside, and he wasn't going anywhere.

As for how he'd tracked us down to Bath, so very specifically, he told me that later, too. He said he'd gone into the social security office, and he'd given them a whole sob story – shown them his Jekyll face rather than his Hyde – and he'd duped them into giving out our new address; which wasn't even supposed to be on any system, but was because the authorities had cocked it up yet again. 'I can't find my children,' he'd sobbed, begging them to help. He'd slipped them twenty quid as a sweetener … and the deal was done.

His constant surveillance was tough to cope with, but even worse was to come. The refuge workers soon came to me and said, 'He's applied for parental rights, so you have to do visitations with him, with the kids.'

'Are you being serious?' I said. 'Have you not read in my statements what he's done to me?'

'Yeah,' they said. 'But he's got rights because he's the father.'

And so they made me take my kids to this community room in a local church, so we could all meet 'as a family'. They organised chaperones to be there: these women who sat in on the meeting to monitor what was going on. I was absolutely terrified walking into the room. I just knew he was going to do something, say something ... something was going down.

He'd bought presents for all the kids; Corice got an enormous fluffy rabbit that was almost as big as she was. He was being all nice, chatting away with them and smiling his smile with his shiny white teeth, dirty lies pouring out of his mouth like sewage: 'You know, kids, I'm really sorry, I shouldn't have done all that.'

I felt like I was in an alien place, where black was white and everything was upside-down. As I kept a close eye on the children, I kept darting looks at our chaperones. *Are you watching this? Are you listening?*

After about half an hour of this senseless pantomime, I caught his eye by accident. And, immediately, he drew his finger across his throat as though to say: 'You're dead.' He went still and he said simply: 'Stop now.'

I knew exactly what he meant: stop messing about or you're going to die. He was telling me I was dead meat unless I left the refuge and went back to him.

I was scared, but I was also strangely pleased that he'd done it in front of the chaperones. *There's no way they didn't see that*, I thought. As soon as the meeting was over and my ex had gone, I turned to the one nearest me and said, 'So did you get all that then?'

I hoped the police would lock him up for good, now that he'd threatened me in front of independent witnesses.

'What?' said the woman, confused.

'All that,' I said. 'He just threatened me. Did you not see that?' She hadn't. So much for chaperones.

We went back to the refuge, climbed the stairs to our top-floor room. The one blessing was that we were so high up, and the windows so small, that he couldn't possibly see inside our space. The room was at the back of the building, away from the street, and it was some comfort that at least he didn't know exactly where we were inside, even if he was always watching the front door.

Within just a few days of him tracking us down, he got a message to me on my phone, through someone else. He told me that, if I didn't stop 'messing around', as he called it, he was going to burn down the refuge. He was going to burn down the refuge … because he knew we lived on the top floor, and he knew there was no fire escape. The floor below ours had one, but the top floor didn't. If the building caught fire, the kids and I would all be doomed, trapped by the flames and the heat and the thick grey smoke. He was going to burn us all to death.

How on earth does he know which room we're in? I thought, panicking. I was so, so scared … and so confused. *Has he got binoculars?* I thought. But the room faced the back and the windows were way above even my head; he couldn't have seen us in there even if he'd got round the back. *Has someone grassed us up?* I thought next. And that seemed to be the only answer.

I grew paranoid. *Is it the co-workers, or the other women, who have betrayed me?* I thought. I scanned the refuge, as though the traitor would be obvious.

The fact that they weren't made my anxiety ten times worse.

I talked to the co-workers about my worries – 'How does he know which room I'm in? Who is grassing me up?' I demanded – but they just seemed to think I was losing the plot.

'Calm down,' they said. 'No one's telling him anything. There's no way he can know which room you're in.'

'There was supposed to be no way he could have tracked us here,' I grimly pointed out. 'But he's sat outside *right now* – and you're not stopping it.'

My resolve hardened: I was *not* going back to him. I was determined to get through this, to make a clean break of it, no matter what he threatened. I insisted that the refuge workers call the police.

Two officers came out to the refuge and eyeballed me with faint disappointment. 'So how did he find you then, Mandy?' they said. 'Did you tell him where you were?'

I stared at them, my bald skull seemingly giving them no indication that I had tried my damnedest to get away – and stay away. I felt like they thought I was stupid.

The feeling was, quite frankly, mutual.

I told them what he'd said to me about the social security office, and paying someone to give him the information to find us. 'You write that down,' I said. 'You need to investigate that to see who's blagged. We could all have been killed by now and that person needs to know that.'

Then I told them about his threat to burn down the refuge, and I said, 'What are you going to do about him?'

'Well,' they said, 'you can get a restraining order against him, and that should keep him away.'

'How does that work, then?' I asked.

'We send him a piece of paper,' they explained, 'that says he's not to go within x miles of you.'

'Paper?' I said. 'He's not going to pay attention to a piece of paper.'

'That's all we can do, really,' they said.

They weren't going to charge him with assault. They weren't going to charge him with rape. They weren't going to charge him with buggery.

I wanted to take action against him – I wanted them to lock him up – but it seemed that no one was listening. It was a different time back then. The police officers didn't have the training that they do now to deal with it. The two officers – one male, one female – took a statement from me and I told them everything. They said, 'We're sorry for what you've been through,' but they didn't care. The fact my ex was blagging and apologising didn't help matters either. They fell for his story, and that made my story fall into nothingness.

The police officers closed their notebooks and stood up to leave. 'We'll go out there now and tell him to stay away from here,' they said. 'If he wants to see the kids, he can only go through the system, with chaperoned meetings.'

'He's already threatened me there once,' I said. 'You want me to go back there so he can do it again?'

But I didn't have a choice.

I took out the restraining order. If it was the only help they were offering, I would take it. But Dusty just threatened to eat it in front of me; that was how much stock he put in that. It was useless, anyway. I had to see him at the family meetings; feel his simmering anger as he sat inches away from me on a community-centre plastic chair.

It felt so wrong, but no one would help.

Months passed, and still we stayed in the refuge, forced to see him at these regular meetings in a cold church hall. He got angrier and angrier. If I went down the street, taking the kids to school, he would come right up to me: 'Stop messing about.'

When those bully-boy tactics didn't work, he tried being nice instead. 'I'm not going to hurt you,' he'd say, trying to charm me. He got people we both knew to contact me, to say, 'He was having "issues", love. He's sorry. He won't do it again.'

I didn't believe a single word.

But I couldn't stay in the refuge forever; I'd outstayed my welcome as it was. I asked them to let me stay – 'I need help,' I said, 'he's not all he's making out to be' – but other families needed our room; other women beaten to a pulp were lining up, needing the beds.

'Oh, but your chap is sorry,' the refuge staff told me, anyway. 'He's saying nice things. And don't your children love him!'

Some of them did, that was true. The kids wanted to see him at the meetings, and they enjoyed chatting with this smiley dad who turned up. They kept saying to me, 'Can we go back home now?'

They meant their home in Birmingham. That wasn't possible, of course, but what they really meant was that they wanted things to go back to 'normal'. They wanted to get out of the noisy, dirty refuge, with its lack of privacy and its watchful eyes, and its walls that stank of desperation and fear. And I couldn't blame them for that.

In April 1994, we moved out of the refuge: Daniel, Jahméne, Corice, Isaac and me. It didn't feel like a fresh start at all. It didn't feel safe.

If Dusty had the confidence to threaten me in the refuge, I thought, *and the arrogance to do it in front of the chaperones and the staff … then what will he do when there is no one else there?*

It wouldn't be long before I found out.

Chapter Four

We were moving to a kind of halfway house: a private housing-association home set aside specifically for families coming out of the refuge. We knew from the start it was only temporary accommodation, until they found us a longer-term property. It was in Combe Down, just behind the shops.

It was a topsy-turvy place, set over three floors: a tiny kitchen downstairs, with a coal-burner fire; a bathroom and two bedrooms on the top floor; and the final bedroom, and living room, set on the first floor. It was on an estate – a nice one, because Bath was a pleasant place to live wherever you found yourself in the city – and it was a small house, but the kids loved it. Daniel especially was relieved to get out of the refuge. He unpacked Danger Mouse and ET in his bedroom, and the place really did start to feel like home.

All the children had their own beds, and bathtimes and bedtimes became special again. I could read the kids stories and sing them to sleep without worrying about other people. I remember Jahméne used to pretend he had gone to sleep and then, as I tried to walk quietly out of his room, he would sit up and say, 'One more song, Mummy, *please*,' and then bedtime went on for another hour or so. Corice, meanwhile, loved books, so together we would act out the characters in the stories and give them accents. It all got so animated. It felt good to have our own privacy again, our own home. The boys loved having stairs to play on, on which they would act out their superhero games. Daniel had taught Jahméne his flying trick, and once, when I was in the kitchen, some kind of inkling told me to go out to the stairs. I got there just in time to catch Jahméne in my arms as he launched himself from the top step. I almost had a heart attack. I told both of them, after that: 'No more flying. I can't keep catching you guys all the time. You have to understand: there's going to come a point when I'm not going to be there to catch you.'

But while it was fun and games for the children in our new house, I was scared stiff at being alone. Bath was a strange city to me; there was no one I knew there, aside from the refuge people, and they all had their own battles to fight. And I knew my ex had an evil plan up his sleeve for revenge. He was just biding his time, choosing his moment. I would have to pay for taking the kids and running: of that I was absolutely certain. It was only a question of when.

I went to the police again and asked for a panic alarm. I was so determined to fight back this time, not to let him win, to use all the means I could to stop him. I begged them to help me.

'Please,' I said, 'I fear for my life. He's gonna do something, I know he is.'

They threw me a bone and agreed to supply me with a panic alarm. There was just one hitch. Just as they are today, resources for tackling domestic violence are criminally underfunded. I could have an alarm, the police said, but there was a waiting list. They added my name to the bottom of it, and then there was nothing more I could do but wait.

Wait for Dusty to turn up.

It didn't take him long. As though he sensed the police wouldn't stop him, he was soon sniffing round the house, worming his way inside; driving up to the house just as we were all getting home from school, for example, acting nice and saying he was only there to see the children. He wasn't supposed to just show up, he was supposed to go through the authorities, but he came with gifts the children could see, and I couldn't deny them the treats that made their eyes light up. And so he would come into the house, laughing with the children, and watching me all the while, his eyes drinking everything in. Over and over, he said in a voice I barely recognised that he was sorry and would never hurt me again. He was acting strange – it was such a false niceness. It was actually scarier than his evil side because it was confusing. I never fell for a word that left his lying lips, though. I just couldn't stop him coming in. I couldn't stop him … full stop.

As he got more and more confident, he took what he wanted from me. 'No' was not an option when it came to sex. How can you say 'no' to a man who holds your life in his hands? He was being nice, pretending to care, pretending not to notice when I stared in horror at him or stiffened at the slightest touch. And then he would rape me, holding me still as I silently endured his 'loving' caress. I think it was his way of 'marking' me with his scent, as though he was paranoid I would get another man. And because he hadn't beaten me, nothing was done. Rapes were never an issue to Dusty or to the police. It was like they thought I deserved it or asked for it or accepted it. No one stopped it.

Almost straight away, I fell pregnant. By the time I did a test I was around three months gone. It was a shock: I had gone from being told I couldn't have any more children to having one every year, even after using contraception. The timing was unreal; the situation was wrong. *Why has this happened now?* But, as before, I couldn't abort, I just couldn't. From the moment I found out he was on his way, I loved that little baby growing inside me with all my heart.

Dusty wasn't angry about the pregnancy; 'detached' would be more the word. Like I had done it by myself, to myself.

As spring turned into summer, I carried on in my strange new world – now with more reason than ever not to set Dusty off on a mad rage. I felt like I was living in a twilight zone, waiting for the sun to set fully and the dark night to fall – waiting for Dusty to take his revenge on me for running away. I knew he hadn't forgotten it. I knew he was just waiting for the dust to settle. He even said calmly to me one day, 'Don't think it's forgotten – you haven't got away with it.' He was just taking time to work out my exact punishment, which in his brain I completely deserved.

With the police not helping, I came to a stark realisation: *I need to get my act together. I need to deal with this situation differently.*

And so I changed. I stopped fighting or going to the police. Not because I thought I deserved what he was doing or because he'd broken me. Oh no: it was strategic. I had to try being friendly with him instead; bowing down to his whims. It was a funny time because it was almost as if Dusty too was playing by new rules – because he kept the 'nice' mask on for the longest time I had ever known him to; for the longest time since he had first shown me his true face, at least. As before, he didn't live with us full-time. He came and went over those months; he didn't ever stay long. It was like he just wanted to show that he was still in control, turning up uninvited and surprising us – but I was always on guard. When he did show up, he was in full-on 'happy Daddy' mode, nicer than nice. He was trying to fool everyone, but I was never fooled.

I relished the times when he'd go away, instead, and leave us to it. As they had always done, his absences marked our time for relaxation and fun. The minute he went out the door: freedom. Daniel later said the kids knew they couldn't relax when he was around, picking up on vibes of tension, and so they learned a certain way to survive. But when their dad was gone they could just be themselves – they could be children.

That was so important to me. I'd always felt my own childhood had been robbed from me, so I wanted my kids to be kids for as long as possible. Art became a part of our world, as my little family struggled to cope with so many emotions. I told my children to draw it out: release through art. Keeping hurts, confusion and anger bottled up can drive you crazy, and so we got quite creative to say the least. I got modelling clay and we'd sculpt and shape new worlds, making everything just the way we wanted it. Dan made a whole chess set of characters once, later on in life; the children's imagination was a wonder in itself. They made towns, houses, people, shops, right down to the tiny bits, like vases with flowers in, all made out of plasticine. They created endless masterpieces, and we did painting and messy play too. Their dad was strict but I'd let them run wild, streaking colours all over the paper and themselves, each brushstroke an act of defiance. We'd put on loud music – Whitney and Michael Jackson – and dance and sing, from Dan right down to Isaac, wiggling his nappy-clad bum on a playmat. Even the baby in my womb seemed to rock and roll with the lively melodies we would play. Laughter and song filled the house. If anyone was observing from the outside, they'd have thought two different families lived there. We were one family when Dusty was around, and a totally different one when he took off.

I started taking the little ones to a local church-run nursery group, and there, blessedly, I made two good friends: Kate and Juliette. I became especially good friends with Kate, as she lived on the school-run route so I would pass her every day. She was in her mid-forties, with soft brown eyes: a beautiful person inside and out. I didn't tell her exactly what was going on at home, but she just seemed to get it.

Dusty would still time me on the school runs, however, when he was there, so I couldn't dawdle en route, but occasionally I would stay to help out with the kids at the nursery and that gave me some breathing space. Sometimes, Dusty would turn up and spy on me, but the women understood his dominance somehow, and they would make sure to turn away from me, and make it look like we weren't close. Their friendship, and my faith, kept me strong.

I had always had faith, and my experience after the ectopic pregnancy, when I'd heard the voice that said, 'It's not your time yet', had only made me feel closer to God. My faith had deepened over the years since then; it had seen me through so many dark times. I knew it would see me through this strange waiting game, too, while I waited for the executioner's axe to fall.

My ex hated anything that gave me hope. When I started taking the kids to church services at Combe Down and Dusty saw us having fun there, he forbade us to go. But I didn't need a church to feel the truth inside me: my spirituality was something Dusty could not touch.

Life-on-edge went on. The police called me one day and said a panic alarm had finally become available for me. As they handed it to me, they warned me that I should press it only in the instance of a serious attack. Other women I knew from the refuge had told me that, too – the women said that if you pressed your alarm too often the police ignored it, as they then assumed you were using it for what they thought were petty arguments; as though they didn't believe attacks could happen every day, that domestic violence could be that frequent.

I took their words to heart, and I understood: I should use it only if my life were in danger. This wasn't for the odd slap, or punch, or for an unwanted sexual approach. They didn't count. I had to cope with those on my own.

'Don't worry,' the police said as they handed the alarm, strung on a necklace, over to me. 'We'll cover you. If you press that button on the alarm, we will be with you within three minutes. You'll be fine, we'll be there.'

With Dusty's punishment hanging over my head, I took the alarm with a certain amount of trepidation. I still didn't feel massively secure, knowing that I was totally relying on just an alarm with a button on it for my life, but it was better than nothing.

And the police reassured me. They told me over and over: if I pressed the button, they would be there within three minutes. I had nothing to worry about, they said. They promised me, in fact.

They had my back.

Chapter Five

July 1994 came around, hot and sunny. I remember hosting Isaac's first birthday party that month. Dusty came – something I never would have predicted a year before, when he was daubing 'SLAG' in red paint on my living-room walls and screaming that Isaac wasn't his.

But Isaac's pale looks were starting to change by then: his blue eyes were turning hazel and his skin was taking on a more olive hue as he aged. He looked much more like Daniel had done at that age, now.

He looked more like his father.

So perhaps it was guilt, too, that suddenly made Dusty change his tune about his third son. Before, it was all 'he's not mine, he's not mine', right in front of Isaac's face, but now my youngest boy suddenly became a favourite, like Dusty was trying to make it up to him. All of a sudden, it was as if Isaac was the world and all the other kids faded out of the room. As he grew older, Dusty would start to take him out on day trips, without the others, which rankled the kids, but to my children's credit they never made Isaac feel bad about it; with help, they understood that it wasn't Isaac's fault their father treated them all differently.

At Isaac's first birthday party it was really uncomfortable, though; mostly because we were all uneasy when Dusty was around. Even though he'd been 'nice' for a couple of months by then, we still didn't trust it. Whenever he was nice, we always knew we had cause for concern. If he was acting happy and overjoyed, it was always more frightening than if he was being his horrible self because we knew we had to wait for the twist; for the flip side that would inevitably come.

Every single day that summer, I felt the executioner's axe hanging over me. I was just waiting for it to fall.

That same month, I had my twenty-week pregnancy scan. All was fine with the baby, despite all the stress and fear. 'Hello, Junior,' I said to him merrily as I watched him move throughout the scan; Junior was what the other kids and I called the baby inside my bump. As I had always done, I was loving being pregnant: my kids were my life. As my new baby shifted on the black-and-white screen, moving healthily inside me, I sent him a message of love from the bottom of my heart.

A rare smile played over my face as I watched him move, entranced. He would be my fifth child, but I was as besotted as a first-time mum with my unborn baby. He looked fully formed in the grainy picture; at that age, they've developed all their limbs, and their fingers and toes and even their eyes, and from then on, they just grow bigger and bigger until it's time for them to be born. Junior was due in December: an early Christmas present for me. Almost reluctantly, I wiped the gel from my belly as the scan finished and I gave my unborn child a gentle rub at the same time. *I love you, Junior*, I thought, sending the message along my synapses and down into my soul. I waddled out into the summer sunshine, counting my blessings. Twilight zone or not, I thought I had a lot to be grateful for.

It was maybe a week or so later, as I returned from the school run, that I came home to find Dusty in the house. Alone. He wasn't here to see the kids this time.

A wave of heat hit me as soon as I walked through the door; for some reason, even though it was a hot summer's day outside, he'd started up a fire in the burner in the kitchen, and the burner door was open, blazing flames within. There were two chairs placed next to it, opposite each other, about four feet apart. He'd deliberately set them up that way. And as I walked into the kitchen he said to me: 'Take a seat.'

And I knew. Oh, I knew.

My executioner had arrived.

Oh my God, oh my God, oh my God … What's he going to do?

I didn't run; I knew he could catch me. He was still in his weird, false mood as I entered – acting all nice – but there was something about him that reminded me of a simmering pot of water: angry bubbles rising to the surface, quicker and quicker. It felt like he was going to explode at any minute. His feet were bare, I noticed randomly; he was making himself at home.

Not wanting to alert him, I meekly did as I was told and sat on the chair. But, as I did so, I fingered the police alarm, hanging on a loop around my neck. Something about his manner made me think that this was it: that the axe was coming down at last; my punishment was looming. I sensed he was evil, that day, and I feared for my life.

He saw me touch it, as he took the chair opposite mine.

'That's it, get the necklace,' he said, so sweetly; to my surprise. I could hear that laugh he sometimes had in his voice, tinkling like musical bells. He was amused. He thought the alarm was hilarious. And then he said: 'Go on, press it.'

And I did. I pressed it like mad, the skin on my thumb white from the pressure. There was a clock on the wall behind Dusty, and I glanced at it swiftly, noting the time. Three minutes, they'd said. I just had to keep him off me for three minutes.

My ex was grinning, white teeth shining in the firelight on his face. He was grinning at me; laughing at me, I realised.

'You actually think they're going to come and save you, don't you?' he jeered at me, after a minute had passed by. He gave a short laugh, more like a bark. 'They're not coming for you. You're not worth it.'

I tried to ignore him. I was watching the clock and I told myself, *They'll be here in a minute.*

He stood up and stoked the fire with a heavy iron poker. Two minutes gone. 'They're not coming for you because you're scum.'

I shut out his words. I prayed in the back of my head that he was wrong; I told myself that right at this minute a police van full of officers was tearing through town on its way to me.

Dusty sat back down on the chair opposite, his legs splayed wide. Confident, cocky, as he always was. I darted another glance at the clock. Three minutes.

They should be here by now, I thought. *Any second now they're going to blast through the door.*

My ex laughed again as he noted the time, too. 'Are you still looking at the clock?' he taunted. 'They're not coming. You're not worth it.'

The seconds ticked on by. We sat opposite each other, for what felt like an eternity. He was taunting and teasing me. He went on and on, 'You're scum, you're worthless, you're this, you're that …' He found it so amusing that I'd even entertained the thought they'd come. He was laughing at me, having a dig, glorying in his triumph.

Why aren't they coming? I thought desperately. *Why aren't they coming? They promised me, they said three minutes …*

It felt like hours passed as we sat there, but it was probably only thirty minutes. And still they didn't come. Throughout, Dusty taunted and jeered, teased and laughed. With every minute that passed, I could see him growing more and more powerful. He revelled in it. It was the ultimate game for him, I realised: I'd summoned the police, and they hadn't come. It was like he had the police in his pocket; they were just toy soldiers to him, petty and unimportant. They couldn't stop him.

They didn't even try.

Dusty and I sat opposite each other on the chairs, the fire growing hotter and hotter by our side. In time, his jeering stopped, and he just looked at me: a fixed stare that sent shivers down my spine. His eyes were locked on mine, drinking in my desperation. I couldn't break his gaze. *What's he going to do?* I thought. *When's he going to do it?*

All of a sudden, he made his move. He leaped to his feet and grabbed at my head. He tried to sink his fingers into a handful of my hair, to find purchase to force me to move – but it still hadn't grown back fully after I'd shaved it; there was no long ponytail for him to use to steer me this way and that as he pleased anymore.

That made him angry. He was annoyed. With a roar, he grabbed the back of my neck instead, and pushed me into the fire. The flames came closer and closer to my eyes as I screamed, feeling the searing heat of the orange tongues as they licked at the air, inches from my face. It was like a wall of heat, intense, overwhelming, every brick of it built with flames that blazed ferociously. And then he held me there as I sobbed and begged, to show me his power – so close to the flames, but not quite close enough to burn me, just the right distance to say, 'I can do this if I want to. One false move and your face is going to be a melted mass of fat and skin and bone. One false move and you will never be the same again.'

I thought he was going to push my face right in. I battled with him as hard as I could, but I couldn't shift him. And then … something moved inside the fire, and a piece of coal tumbled out – right onto his bare feet.

His grip slackened as he went to grab his foot, in pain, and I ran for it, hands around my pregnant belly, trying to keep Junior safe. Dusty was hopping about and I ran, ran, ran. I tried to get away from him. In blind panic, I ran for the stairs and darted up them.

He was right behind me. He chased me up the stairs and down the hallway and then he leapt on me in the bedroom. He punched the living daylights out of me, fists pummelling every inch of my body, and then he wrapped his hands around my neck and squeezed. I was choking, trying to scream at him, 'The baby, the baby!'

Only then did he release his grip; but just to tear my clothes off. Still beating me, he raped me in my home: claiming me, punishing me, telling me with every thrust that I was his, that I was nothing, that I was never, ever, *ever* going to get away.

Then he wrapped his fingers round my throat again. It was a ritual of his by now. It was a way for him to control my breathing, and that's the most powerful thing, isn't it? To control someone's breath … right down to their last.

But this strangulation was different from usual. I think Dusty lost control – he went too far. Enraged by my running away, energised finally to be dishing out my punishment, he strangled me so tight, with so much power, and for so long, that I started seeing dots flashing about in my restricted vision, and then black blurred blobs. I could feel my heart racing, thumping, loud and fast in my ears. I thought my eyeballs were going to explode, right out of my face. I panicked as I heard the crunching sound his grip made on my throat as he squeezed with both hands and pressed with all his strength. Blood filled my face until it burned with heat.

And then my chest went tight. I stopped breathing. I went limp, life ebbing slowly away as the minutes passed. My energy drained completely.

Then, as I had done after my ectopic pregnancy, I heard five words again, spoken clearly to me: 'It's not your time yet.'

In a rush, I suddenly came round to Dusty yelling, close up in my face: 'You made me do this!' He was shaking the life back into me. 'How dare you run from me! You can't run … You can't hide! I told you I would find you. I told you if you ran I would kill you. Do you think I can't kill you?'

He was spitting venom, his pupils slanted: he was in a rage. He slapped me left then right across the face to make me come round, again and again saying, 'Stop faking it!'

He was working himself up with his own thoughts of warped perception. He had to prove his manly control over me. All the while I was going in and out of consciousness. And still in the back of my mind, somewhere, I hoped and prayed, *Maybe the police will come and kick the door down and come and save me.*

But they didn't.

Dusty ranted over and over for hours. Who the hell did I think I was to defy him? And, oh, what trouble I was in now ... All he could go on about was revenge, and punishment. He paced the house, talking to himself about how he could torture me. There were so many ways, he said – and he went into detail. It was a new level of anger; a dangerous, unpredictable anger. In my head I was chanting to myself, *Just breathe, it's just scare tactics, you can get through this. Just breathe, think of the kids.*

Think of Junior.

That night I was sore inside and out. My throat was raw; it was hard to breathe. It was as though everything in my neck had been crushed to a pulp. My voice box and airways became raspy, lumpy, like I was breathing through coarse sandpaper. But I wasn't allowed to rest. His rants went on and on. He said that I had made him rape me and beat me. He said that I was the reason he burned his foot. I was meant to feel pity for his wound, to find cream and a bandage for him.

And still the police didn't come.

Three days later, I was leaving the house to take Dan to school when I finally saw a police car come round the corner. It cruised down our road and paused outside our home. As I shut my front door and Dan and I walked down the street, the officer inside casually rolled down his window.

'Are you all right?' he asked me. 'Because you pressed your alarm the other day ... '

I looked through him for what felt like twenty minutes. I just stared right through him, and then I gestured to my face. A black eye bloomed there, while red finger marks adorned my neck. He couldn't even see the damage inside, but he didn't really need to. It was clear that I'd been battered, and badly.

Because that's what happens when three minutes becomes three *days*.

But the officer didn't even get out of his car. He didn't do anything. Everything about his actions said: We're not bothered. All the things I'd been promised, by these people who were supposed to protect me, vanished in a puff of smoke: another magic act, another dark surprise. And there was my ex, like an evil MC at the heart of all the tricks, raising his finger to his lips, licking it, and holding it in the air. *I win again. One in the air to me*.

'They're not coming for you. You're not worth it,' he had said.

And in that moment, I thought, *Yeah, you're right: I'm* not *worth it. They're never going to help*.

It was the worst thing ever because I knew, deep inside, that we were now on a new level of danger; one that was totally unpredictable. In the next moment, I thought fiercely: *I've got to work out a strategy to keep us all alive*.

And then I realised, in a rush, as a massive, overwhelming feeling hit me: *I have to do it all on my own*.

Chapter Six

It was a cut-off point. I had tried and tried up to that moment, every which way, to get away from him. Going to the police, running to the refuge, pressing the alarm. I had told the authorities everything. What had they done with the information? Nothing. What had they done to help me? Nothing. What did I mean, to anyone? *Nothing*.

It was him and me.

And he was winning, hands down.

It was tough – so tough – after that. The hardest thing of all was talking with Daniel. He whispered to me, 'Why aren't the police arresting him, Mum? Why aren't they stopping him? Why is he getting away with this?'

His dad overheard him and mocked my little boy. 'I'm more powerful than the police,' he said to Daniel. 'I can do what I want and nobody can stop me.'

And what evidence was there to say that wasn't true? None whatsoever. So Daniel had to grow up thinking his dad could do anything and that there was no comeback. There was no point him telling anyone at school what was going on – even if he'd dared – or asking for help. He'd seen me ask for help; and seen where it had got me.

There was no way out.

The days passed, and the bruises from my punishment faded. But one pain didn't stop. I'd felt different, inside, from the moment I'd come round after the strangulation. My insides felt really strange, and I couldn't feel Junior anymore. I was so scared that something bad might have happened to the baby, but my ex wouldn't let me go to the hospital.

Over the next week, I felt sicker and sicker. It got so bad that, in the end, risking his wrath, I told him I simply *had* to get help – but it was still two weeks until he finally allowed me to go to the doctors.

He came with me to the hospital, not willing to let me go alone; perhaps for fear of what I might say. We all went: one-year-old Isaac, who was adorable at that age, with red cheeks and a cute face; bubbly two-year-old Corice; boisterous three-year-old Jahméne; and eight-year-old Daniel, who always seemed more mature than his years. The kids knew I wasn't well and they were worried about me, and the baby. Dusty didn't seem to care less, though: he was moody. 'There's only something wrong with you because you're a slag.' He said that all the way to the hospital, and even repeated it while we were in the waiting room, muttering his insults at me, putting me down while the kids played unnaturally quietly with the hospital toys on the tiled floor.

After a short wait, the nurse called me in for an ultrasound. I went in alone, while Dusty watched the kids. She smeared gel on my belly and ran the scanner over my stomach. She was looking at the screen, which was turned away from me, and then she said lightly, 'Oh, I've just got to go and get a doctor.'

She came back with one, and he picked up the scanner and had a look too. He mumbled something to the nurse, and then she turned to me and said, almost on her way out of the room: 'Your baby's dead. You've got to stay in and give birth.'

She closed the door behind her and left me alone. The room was spinning beyond fast. Grief, shock, pain, hurt: they assailed my senses, blew my brain. Through my utter devastation, I had just enough room left to think: *This is murder.*

He has murdered my child.

It wasn't like my other miscarriages, when my body had been scarred and physically unable to carry a baby to term. Just a few weeks before, this baby had been healthy. Just a few weeks before, I had seen him on a screen, perfectly formed and perfectly well. Now, they were telling me he was dead.

Tears streamed down my face. I wanted to scream and shout at my ex: 'You've done this! You've done this, you MURDERER!' But even then I knew I couldn't. He had got away with everything so far, and he was going to get away with this too. It broke my heart.

I was painfully aware that he was just in the next room with the other kids. I started thinking, *How am I going to tell him about the baby dying?* Because I was petrified he would take the other children away in a rage.

I heaved myself off the bed. I was wearing a hospital gown, and I felt so vulnerable in it, with its open back. I walked out to the waiting room, and the nurse came back and told my ex what had happened, just like that.

He had a fit. 'You're a slag!' he shouted at me. 'That's the reason for all this!'

Corice burst into tears. She didn't know what her dad was saying, but she knew what the raised voices meant: trouble. Dusty gathered the kids together and started storming out of the hospital.

'Mum! Mum!' cried Jahméne over his shoulder, as he was dragged away. 'What is it?'

'What's happened, Mum?' asked Dan. 'What's wrong?'

Dusty turned to them. 'Your mum's messing about again,' he told them bluntly. 'She's a slag, so the baby's dead.'

And with that, with him telling them nastily like that, they were gone. The nurse held me there, not letting me follow. 'You need to give birth,' she told me firmly. 'You come back inside, I've got to induce you now.' And even though I wanted to go after them, I couldn't: I had to go back into the hospital room, and deliver my dead son.

I think the only people who can truly understand what it's like to give birth to a lifeless child are those who have done it. It is indescribable. Because it's not just physical pain – it's the pain of losing a child. All the way through my labour, through each wracking contraction, I had to face that – and face the fact that my ex had done it; and that I'd been carrying this child and I hadn't *stopped* him from doing it.

I let him kill my child. I couldn't stop the thought that came over and over me, with every pulse of my womb.

Junior never got a chance – to come out, to breathe and fight for himself. That was taken from him. That was taken from him by his own father.

Afterwards, in the darkened hospital room, the nurse wrapped this tiny, tiny baby boy in a green tissue and placed him in my arms. This was Junior. This was my son. He had pink and red skin, and he looked so perfect, so small. Unlike my other babies, he didn't cry or make himself known. He lay unmoving in the cheap green tissue. It was a breathtakingly sad way to meet the boy I had been growing inside me for five months.

I can picture him now, in startling detail. I will never forget. He was pink on green. He had little fingers, with half-moon nails. He had his legs curled into him, like he was still safe in the womb. His eyes were closed, so I never knew their colour. He was flawless. He was beautiful.

He was dead.

I cradled him against my chest, and I cried like I had never cried before.

You were taken away from my warm embrace
As I kissed your cheeks and touched your face
The tears rolled down to a river of love
As I watched a light rise up above
I held your hand for a silent sign
As an angel whispered softly …
'This was your time.'

Chapter Seven

After a while, there was a knock on the door. A pastor came and sat with me as I held my baby close. He was trying to explain that these things happen and that Junior was in heaven now. I started telling him what had really happened, and so he stayed with me for a long while, and listened. He absorbed my tale into his black frock, and it stayed there, even as he blessed me and made his way out of the room. It never saw the light of day.

A bolshie nurse came in after that, tidying up. She saw the standard-issue green tissue on my chest and thought I'd been sick into it. She made to grab it, to throw it away, and the full power of my motherly instinct kicked in. 'This is my *son*!' I roared at her, cradling my precious baby in my palm. She backed away then and left me on my own.

All these emotions were going round my head. And as well as my pain about Junior, I was desperately worried about my other children. I told the next nurse who came in that I was discharging myself because I had to get home right away, but she told me there was no way they would let me go; I had to have things done, inside, and I couldn't go home until the morning.

So I stayed in, overnight. I held Junior for ages and ages; hour upon hour. I didn't want to give him to anybody else. I felt like his death was my fault; that I hadn't done right by him. And so I tried to do right by him now and kept watch over him for as long as I could, holding his little body in my hand, telling him over and over that I loved him so much.

All too soon, morning came. I told the doctors I wanted an autopsy done, hoping for proof that my ex had killed him. But the report just said that his heart had stopped beating. It didn't say that happened because his mother had stopped breathing, because she was being viciously strangled by the baby's dad. There wasn't a box on the form for that.

I went home. What else could I do?

Immediately, the children crowded round me: 'What's happened to Junior, Mummy? Are you OK?'

I bent down to their level and I gathered them in my arms. 'Junior stopped breathing so he's gone to heaven,' I told them, trying my hardest not to cry. 'He's at rest now. He's at peace.'

Dusty interrupted, looming above us all with his dark shadow. He repeated his refrain: 'He's dead because your mum's a slag and she sleeps with everybody.'

The kids knew by now not to listen to his lies but it was still horribly confusing for them. Some of them were far too young even to know what he was saying – they just knew it wasn't nice.

I arranged a funeral for Junior soon afterwards, organised with the priest who had sat with me at the hospital. I wanted poetry read out: special words for a special boy.

Dusty came to the funeral. The kids were at school and nursery so it was just the two of us, standing in a graveyard that was incongruously sunny.

Though I could hardly believe it, my ex slagged me off at the funeral, in front of the priest, while we were burying our son. He was saying it all out loud, not even muttering. 'This is because you're a whore and you deserve it.' It was bad enough that he'd strangled me in the first place, it was bad enough again that I then had to give birth on my own, to our dead child, but for him to do that over Junior's grave …

I'd thought, when the baby died, *Maybe now he'll stop and think about what he's done.* But he didn't, not for a second. He seemed to show no grief, only anger towards me. He was beyond evil: a cold, dark man with no heart.

The priest ignored him. He just carried on talking, giving the service. He read the special poem I'd chosen and my ex talked all over him, ruining the moment: 'You didn't deserve to be a mum, you slag.'

After the service was over, Dusty stormed off, and left the priest and me alone. I apologised for his behaviour, and the priest held my hand. He nodded at me, in recognition. But nothing else was said or done after that.

And so I just had to go back home.

As I knew he would, my ex got away with it. As always happened, the more he got away with things, the more powerful he became. Junior's death was a watershed: after that, he was back to normal – no more Mr Nice Guy. At night, in our bedroom, he would beat me and rape me, strangle me and choke me, and the system let him carry on being who he was. They gave him power. He would say to me, 'You can't stop me – no one can!' There was no let-up from his evil. I knew he would never stop, so I just had to do what I could to survive. And so I never fought back, anymore, not in any way.

If I had ever fought back, I would be dead.

Our time at Combe Down came to an end. In late 1994, we moved house again, to the longer-term property we'd been told the council would eventually find us. Our new home was on Sedgemoor Road in Bath – just down the road and round the corner from the house we were leaving. There was no point trying to make a fresh start; a secret new address hidden from my ex. We'd tried that when we went to the refuge – even when I'd first been at Combe Down he wasn't supposed to know where we were – but Dusty always found us. '*You can't run, you can't hide …*' He always knew things; and if he thought I was keeping anything from him, he would demand to know what it was. Then I'd have to tell him, whether I wanted to or not.

The police took the useless panic alarm necklace from me when I moved house; not that it had ever brought them running to my door. They knew Dusty was back living with me, off and on, by then, and so they said I was making that choice to be with him. I explained to them, in detail, what he had done, what he was *doing*, and that I didn't want him anywhere near me and the kids. I said that there was nothing I could do to stop him from being there because the police weren't stopping him – but as usual my words fell on deaf ears.

And so Dusty came with us to Sedgemoor Road.

Our new home was another three-bedroom council house on a big estate. It was a brick house with a large roof that came right down over the bedroom window at the front. We had a garden with a shed and, once I had cleared the usual council-estate rubbish from the lawn, we planted fruit trees – apple and cherry and plum – as well as rose bushes, and set up a rockery. There was loads more space so the kids could run around. In time, we even got guinea pigs and rabbits.

The younger ones shared a room – Jahméne and Corice, who were still as thick as thieves, slept in beds and Isaac in his cot – while Dan had a room of his own. I made the kids' room a proper nursery, child-safe so they could literally bounce off the walls and floor, and I painted Disney pictures on the walls, with all their favourite characters smiling down at them. It felt amazing to paint those murals because Dusty didn't let me do any artwork for myself. I was allowed to do Disney pictures in the children's room, though. It was decorated in bold primary colours: yellow, red, blue and green. The kids spent hours playing in that room.

As for the rest of the house, Dusty decided cork was going on the living-room walls again. He spread out his computers in there, where the hi-fi unit was, and set up the TV. Daniel's room, meanwhile, was a peaceful cream colour: quiet and lovely, just like him.

I didn't bother to decorate my own bedroom. Its dated flowery wallpaper and dark-red, heavy velvet curtains stayed just as they were when we moved in. The bedroom was where he hurt me, and no amount of primary-coloured paint could take away that pain.

And, for the next chapter of our lives, this was home.

Chapter Eight

To begin with, it was business as usual. Infrequent visits from Dusty; time to repair, to live. It was still stressful because he knew where we were and he would come and go as he pleased. But it was in that house that he decided he would now be spending more time with us – and he moved himself in. It didn't happen straight away, but over a period of time it fizzled into a situation where he was more often at ours than he was away.

That was very, very difficult in countless ways, but not least with trying to sort out my benefits. That gave him another power over me. I'd try to explain my reality to the social security office, that he just came and went and I never knew when he'd turn up, but they'd just say brusquely, 'You have to tell us when he comes to stay, and tell us again when he leaves.' If I didn't report any 'change in my circumstances' I'd get in trouble with the system. And they never ever got that I couldn't report it because I'd been beaten or forbidden to go out – even after I explained what had happened and said it wasn't my fault. They'd just say, 'We're going to stop your benefits,' and then they'd stop my money and I wouldn't have enough cash to feed the kids.

You would have thought that everybody – the doctors, the police, the social services, the benefits people – would have got their heads together and thought, *Hang on, this woman needs help*. Instead, they were making my life harder, adding to the stress. It was like it was me against the world, every single day.

As he had always done, Dusty would time me on the school run or when I went out to the shop. He would have his spies out, forever watching me. There would be threats if I spoke to anyone, anything from 'I'll lock you up for a week' to 'I'm going to rape you so hard you'll wish you'd never been born.' I always knew it was going to involve raping and punching and choking, so I tried to prepare myself for the worst-case scenario. And sometimes, I know it sounds sick, but I would have prepared myself for something awful, and when it was just a couple of punches or a strangulation that was over with quickly, I'd think, *I got off with that lightly today.*

To be honest, though, the threat alone was enough. It was a mind-control thing so I couldn't ever rest. Domestic violence is not just a black eye: it's an invisible gas that gets into your head and can poison your mind, if you let it. He wanted to control my mind and break me, so that he won his game. Yet again he'd lick his finger and hold it in the air: *One to me, Mandy – I win again.* He'd taunt and jeer, saying he would have me in a mental home by the time he was done with me. Every time it looked like I was flagging or was losing it, it would give him even more power. And sometimes I'd think, *Should I just let him think he's won this and then he'll stop?* But he was never fooled, he always kept on.

And it wasn't just my mind he wanted to control: his lust for power reached into every area of my life. Once again, he was dictating my clothes, my entire wardrobe. Some of the clothes I felt so uncomfortable wearing, but it was a power trip for him to force me to put them on. He'd pick out ridiculous things, black or blue skin-tight leggings and skin-tight tops. He hated my hair and would randomly attack me with scissors to cut off chunks of it, slicing off whole sections of a thick red plait. I could have nothing, not even my own hairstyle. I wasn't allowed to choose anything for myself. He decided everything. Where I went, what I wore, how I looked, who I spoke to … what I ate.

With him being at the house more, food was an area he now asserted much more control over. I had lots of stomach problems, partly from the ectopic pregnancy and my keloid scarring, partly from my childhood, and partly from his constant punching and kicking. The lasting damage meant I couldn't eat and digest certain things, including nuts.

So he'd put them in everything. And I'd either have to go without – the lack of food making me weaker still – or he'd force me to eat them, and enjoy watching me endure the crippling stomach cramps afterwards. He began to threaten that he would poison me, too, lacing the food or my drink, so then everything I consumed became fraught with danger as I wondered if this mouthful would be my last.

I was in a state of constant stress. And he delighted in it. The casual violence at home was unbelievable. He'd attack me randomly, poke and push, twist my skin, hit me with some implement he'd found around the house. He'd just punch me as I walked past, just reach out and do it, to see my reaction. He'd do all this while the kids were out at school and nursery, just the two of us left for him to have his fun at home.

My only respite was when he was on his computer; he'd get involved in whatever it was he was doing and I'd stay out of his way and think briefly: *I'm safe*. It was a false security, though, because what he was doing was playing games where he ruled kingdoms and killed people: dungeon-keeper death games, war games, evil games. I hated the sounds they made, and I feared his temper as he played them. And always, when the sounds ceased … that silence was a sound I hated more. Because as soon as his computer went off, he had nothing else to do. He was like a kid getting bored. *Oh, what can I do now?* And so he'd antagonise me, for his pleasure. Revelling in his power, poking and hitting and ordering me about. Eat this. Wear this. Take this. Raping me nightly. Beating me daily. It was a vicious cycle that went round and round and round.

Still, I didn't break. If the kids saw something, they might ask him, 'Why Daddy? Why are you hurting Mummy?' And he'd say, 'She's a slag and a whore and she deserves to be beat.'

I took many a beating to protect my kids. They were just being normal, in asking why, but sometimes it would set him off and I'd have to get between them, worried he was going to lash out. There was no way I was going to let him hurt my children. They were my world: pure, sweet innocents with hearts and souls of sheer, spun gold. They were not to be caught up in this madness; not directly, at least. I might not be able to get away from him or stop him, but I could try my very hardest to limit the damage he did.

Dusty was not a stupid man. He saw everything and mulled it over, and computed the emotions and reactions that he saw around him, working out how he could play things to his advantage. He saw how I was with my children. He learned clearly, over time, that the kids were the most important thing in the world to me. He took that little nugget and he stored it away, ready to use it in the future.

*

Bang. The front door slammed. Dusty was home.

It was late at night; the kids were all tucked up in bed. Everything was calm, but my heart started pounding as soon as I heard the door. Dusty would always want to pick a fight with me about something so immediately my brain began whirring, wondering, *What's he gonna have a go at me about this time?*

I tried to cover all bases so there was nothing he could complain about. *I'm breathing quietly*, I thought, moderating each breath to a volume I knew he'd be satisfied with. *The house is clean, the kids are asleep … I've done everything right.* I knew doing everything right didn't protect me because he would invent a new reason to hurt me if he wanted to, but I'd have been foolish if I didn't at least try to escape his beatings.

I waited for Dusty to come in to see me, but he didn't. *That's weird*, I thought. *What's he up to?*

Then I heard footsteps on the stairs. Lots of footsteps. The pitter-patter of tiny feet that I knew inside out and backwards. *The kids!* I thought. *He's got the kids!*

I wrenched the bedroom door open and ran downstairs. The front door was wide open and I pegged it outside. He was bundling the kids into the car, still in their pyjamas. They were blinking up at him, shocked out of sleep. He slammed the car door and turned to me with the most evil look I had ever seen.

'I'm going to kill the kids,' he told me, in deadly seriousness. 'I'm going to gas every single one of them to death.'

Oh my God …

I have never felt so much fear in my life.

We both heard the car door open then. Five-year-old Jahméne, rebellious as ever, had pulled on the handle to get out of the car.

Thank God, he hadn't heard what his dad had said, but he knew it wasn't normal to be dragged out of bed in his pyjamas to be thrown into a car in the middle of the night and, with the father he had, he knew something bad was going to happen. He started running of his own accord.

His father went and grabbed him, and put him back in the car. He turned back to me. 'I'm going to put the exhaust in the car and I'm going to gas them all,' he said again. 'I'm going to take them away from you … '

Jahméne scooted along the seats and ran out the other side. The other kids now picked up on the tension and started screaming their heads off. This had come out of nowhere. It was so random, so unexpected: we were all petrified. The fear was shooting through my veins like heroin, my heart hammering in my chest as I begged him, begged him, begged him to stop.

He ignored me – he just manhandled Jahméne back into the car, only to find that Corice had copied her brother and run out the other side. It was like a sick Benny Hill sketch for about five minutes, with him putting the kids in the car and them climbing out the other side to get out, over and over again, with the kids' high-pitched voices shrieking at top volume, crying loud into the night.

Down the street, curtains twitched. People were watching, but no one came to help. I was on my own with a madman, and it was up to me to make him stop.

I was trying desperately to think it through. I had to play it carefully – if I physically attacked him, I knew he would blow out of control. The adrenaline was coursing through me, high high high, my heart thumping as I had never known it.

As the kids ran and screamed and cried, distracting my ex, I ran round to the front of the car and threw myself on the bonnet, stretching my arms up to the windscreen. He would have to run me over, in full view of the neighbours, before I let him drive off with my kids. 'You're not taking them!' I yelled at him. 'I won't let you hurt them! You're not taking them anywhere.'

He said nothing, just slammed the car door after the children for the final time and ran round to the driver's side. And I thought, *He's actually going to do this.* He had hurt me so many times – why wouldn't he just drive over me and take the kids away?

I could not let that happen. I *would* not let that happen.

'Look,' I called out to him in a panic, my brain coming up with the only line I could think of. 'I'll do anything – I'll do whatever you want – you can do anything you want to me – just don't hurt the kids.'

Lives change in an instant. With a look. With a smile. With a stupid, thoughtless promise.

You can do anything you want to me – just don't hurt the kids …

He stopped, and he grinned at me. A weird smile, a crazy smirk, a grimace of pleasure and power.

And then he walked calmly back into the house.

Shit, what have I just said? I thought. *What have I done?*

I had given him permission to treat me any way he wanted. I had given him an inch, and I knew, with a horrified, sinking feeling, that he would take an evil mile. From now on, anything went. And I had signed the crazy certificates myself.

Life would never be the same again.

PART FOUR

THE DARKEST DAYS

I wish I was dead
I wish I was dead
Words spinning round in my head
I wish I was dead
I wish I was dead
Pain you inflict I dread
I wish I was dead
I wish I was dead
Head pushed down into bed
Words you heard said
But continued instead
Fuel fed
Tears of pain
and blood red
Oh, how I wish I was dead

Chapter One

Punching and kicking and choking became boring to him. He took it to another level.

I can't even repeat what he did; I haven't even been able to say it at counselling.

You can use your imagination to know what I could tell you. There is a way of degrading a woman if you strip her to her bare bones and torture every part that is woman. That's what he did. And he enjoyed doing it, too. It made him think he was a bigger man. Tears would roll down my cheeks – but it wasn't crying; my body would just do it. That would make him torture me harder and worse. 'Feeling sorry for yourself, are you?' he would sneer. He knew he was stealing the very essence of my soul each time he inflicted those tortures ... and he revelled in his glory, his win, his power.

It all took place in the bedroom, with the door shut. The kids would be in bed, asleep; or if it was daytime, he would send them to their bedrooms to play. It wasn't every day, every night. It was every now and then because he wasn't there all the time. He would torture me and then leave. Like he'd done what he needed to do.

I think he got his ideas from somewhere. Websites, maybe, or sadistic chat rooms. Because the stuff he'd do ... you'd think, *How would he even think of that?* I think he tried out stuff that he'd been looking at or talking about. I watch horror films now, movies where women go through rapes and stuff, and I think,

That's nothing. That's how my brain works when I'm watching it. Other people around me are crying and thinking, *God, that's bad.* But he was worse than any movie psychopath you can imagine.

His new tortures and their infinite variety made it impossible for me to predict what he was going to do next. I'd actually try to prepare myself for a certain kind of torture, but it would turn out to be something else, something far worse than what I'd thought, something I would never even have been able to imagine. He was an animal; he was sick in the head.

And it wouldn't be a punishment for anything I'd specifically done or said, anymore; not that that was ever really the reason for him hurting me. With a 'normal' wife-beater, the woman would have done something 'wrong' in the perpetrator's eyes, so that something would kick off. It wasn't like that with him. Everything could be fine and then he'd just flip, in an instant, and the only thing that would give the change away would be his eyes slanting. The blacks of his eyes would slant, like a cat's. I knew shit was going to happen when his eyes changed.

He would lock me in the bedroom. It could be the middle of the afternoon. And then it would start.

'You're taking your clothes off; you've got to sit there.'

We had a telly at the end of our bed, and he'd make me sit in front of it, nude, while he sat next to me, still with all his clothes on. I can't tell you the humiliation that puts you through, at the beginning. But worse is the fear: the fear of what he's going to do to which part of your body, of how he's going to do it, of how much pain you're going to be in afterwards ... all the while knowing that you have to cook the dinner at five o'clock. I'd start running through the hours in my head, thinking through what was going to happen and how I'd have to act. *If he's done something really bad, and I've got to cook the tea, how am I going to do that and not show the kids I'm hurt?*

I'd look around the room and think of random everyday objects: *What could he do with that? I don't want him using that so I best move it.* But he would always surprise me. The stuff I'd left in the room, that I'd thought was safe, he'd use and prove me wrong. Bottles. A drinking glass. He would break the bottles; break the glass. He would call me a whore and say that this was what I was worth. And then he would hurt me inside, and my back passage as well, so that I'd bleed.

When you're cut, inside, it stings. It smarts like hell. Every time I went to the loo I was reminded of what he'd done. It seemed in those years that I was bleeding constantly. I spent a fortune on pads to soak up the blood. Pads galore.

He'd revel in the blood. If he injured me so badly that I was maimed, he would find that really amusing. He'd rape me, afterwards, in that state. The amount of times I got raped in a condition where you'd think, *What the hell, how could you do that after that?* But he wouldn't just do it, he'd enjoy it.

It wasn't like he was aroused, like a normal person. I don't think 'aroused' is the right word. His face … it was sadistic. I wish I could paint it, but then I wish I couldn't. It wasn't a normal sexual arousal, like when you're in love with someone and you want them sexually. It wasn't that kind of thing. It was: 'I'm gonna inflict pain on you and you know I'm gonna do it and I'm gonna enjoy doing it to you.' Sadistic arousal, stoked by power.

I would try not to look at him. I kind of made my vision straight, staring into nothingness; I wouldn't even be watching the telly, even though it was right in front of me. I don't know how I did it. I was zoning out so I didn't focus on anything – hoping it would all have gone away by the time I returned. I would go somewhere else in my head during his attacks: up into somewhere white, a pure whiteness. It wasn't peaceful, though; it was like a blocking wall. But sometimes his words and his actions broke through.

He would tell me over and over that he didn't want anyone else having me, that he'd make it so another man would never want me. He'd cut me, a world of pain on sharp edges, and he'd say, 'No man will want you now.'

I didn't understand why *he* wanted me … just to 'play' in his sick torture game, I guess. He complained about me all the time. He would blame me for being dry and hurt me for being dry. What did he expect? He was my torturer, not my lover. What did he want me to say, 'I'm sorry it's not doing it for me, you trying to peel the nails off the ends of my fingers'?

He concentrated all his efforts on hurting me down below or on my body where it couldn't be seen. By now, he'd worked out that if he hurt my face I couldn't really go out, not unless he wanted people asking questions, and now he had me where he wanted me, he didn't want anything to spoil his fun. Most of my injuries became bodily ones that could be covered up. Internal and stomach and chest and head, bruises beneath my thick red hair.

He still hated my hair. It was very strong – he used to lift me up by it and throw me across the room, but it still wouldn't come out of my head. He liked the idea of ripping it out of my scalp and having it in his fingers, like that was an achievement. He got a great deal of pleasure when that happened.

When he first changed, after I'd promised him he could do anything as long as the kids stayed safe, my reaction was simply, *Shit … Shit! This is a whole other level, but I can't stop it from happening!* I was in fear of my life; more importantly, of my children's lives. It may sound strange – though it won't to any parent – but I didn't fear for myself in the way I feared for my kids. My love for them was all-consuming. I had told him I would do anything to keep them alive.

I would keep my word.

I went to the doctor and got myself put on Depo-Provera injections to prevent pregnancy. It was a different world I was living in now – there was no way I could bring a child into this. The injections made me put on weight and I piled on three stone.

I didn't care.

One afternoon, in the summer of 1996, while the kids were in another room, Dusty attacked me in the kitchen. At first, he was trying to smash my head through the back-door glass but it was toughened and to his frustration it wouldn't break. I kind of wriggled sideways along the wall. But getting away wasn't an option; his face said that clearly. He was riled up, fuelled and ready to take the attack to a whole new level.

He lunged forward, real fast, with his mouth open. He went to bite my nose. I quickly put my hand up to protect my face, instinct kicking in. But, as usual, my 'fighting back' only enraged him. So he clamped his teeth onto my hand instead. He bit through to the bone like a dog, like a rabid dog: hanging on and not letting go. As I cried out in shock and pain, he changed the direction of attack and bit my nose, leaving two small puncture wounds from his teeth either side of the bridge of my nose. He did that to say, 'You're not going to stop me doing what I want.' Then he dropped me and walked away.

Over the next few days, I gingerly inspected my wounds. My hand had got the worst of it by far. It went green and black, but I wasn't allowed to get it treated, as usual. So I just carried on with life, doing the washing and cleaning, driven by fear. *What's next? What can I do to protect myself?* I remember my heart just thumping so fast and loud, it was crazy in my ear. And always, always, his threats to kill the children hung heavy in the air, deadweights dragging me down.

A bit of time passed, but even after a couple of days my heart was still pounding. I was in the grip of my fear and I couldn't control it. Everything was coming to a head and I felt so overstressed, pressure building up in every blood vessel in my body.

I went to hang out the washing. As I put my arm up to peg something on the line, a pain shot right down my arm and into my chest. I went to move and found I couldn't. I felt the blood go to my head, felt dizzy … Our next-door neighbour asked me if I was OK from over the fence, but I couldn't reply. Then the pain twisted a knot in my chest, and it felt like a huge elephant had sat on me, squashed me and wasn't getting off.

My neighbour ran round to my side of the fence and said he was taking me to hospital. I was panicking because I knew my ex didn't want me to go to the doctors and my hand was still all manky, but I couldn't really argue with my neighbour about it as I could hardly catch my breath …

The next thing I remember is being strapped to an ECG machine by lots of wires. My heart was racing, then stopping, then going off the chart, then flat, over and over. A doctor came in and said he thought I had suffered a heart attack. He started to ask if I had been under any stress recently to bring it on – and then his words trailed off as he looked at my hand.

'What happened?' he asked.

'I banged it on the stairs,' I lied. I knew there was no point telling the truth; my kids and I were in danger if I did.

He picked it up and examined it. 'Those are clearly teeth marks. That looks like a bite.' He stared hard at me.

I felt the truth weighing on my chest, as heavy as the elephant from that very afternoon. *I'm in a hospital*, I thought, *Dusty won't do anything here* ... But before I could even think anything more than that, Dusty himself stormed in and threw back the curtains around my bed.

'What are you playing at?' he shouted at me. 'Get up, get out, stop messing about! You're going home now, you've got dinner to cook.'

He yanked me off the bed and pulled the wires from my chest. Dragging me along, he pushed past the doctors and nurses with me and the children in his wake. None of the hospital staff even tried to intervene. I'd thought my surroundings would stop him from doing anything – but he did it anyway. And he got away with it! The staff just looked terrified; they didn't help.

Before I knew it I was back at home in the kitchen, preparing dinner. I was being called names. My ex was raging: 'How dare you do that, don't *ever* do that again,' like I had suffered a heart attack on purpose. I kept my head down and peeled the potatoes. Everything felt surreal, like I was acting.

Then there was a knock at the door. Dusty went to answer it and I heard him say hello to whoever it was in his charming, velvety voice. He ushered them into the kitchen and stood behind them, smirking. It was my GP. I didn't know her well because I was never allowed to go to the doctors for treatment; I only knew her from taking the kids for their shots and sniffles. *I bet she's come to tell me I have to go back to hospital*, I thought. But I knew I didn't dare leave my kids with their dad when he was in this mood. *I'll have to tell her I can't go to hospital tonight because of the children. I'll have to tell her that I'm staying here.*

But she hadn't come to check I was OK or insist I got treatment. Instead, she had come to have a go.

'I've just had a message from the hospital that you signed yourself out!' she cried at me. 'Just what do you think you're doing? It's stupid, discharging yourself and leaving like that. What have you got to say for yourself?'

My heart started going into overdrive again. I couldn't speak. My ex was almost grinning at that point, just standing behind her, drinking it all in.

'You're a time-waster. I don't want anything to do with you anymore. I've had enough,' she said then, spitting the words at me like venom. 'I'm striking you off my books for being so irresponsible. You can find yourself another doctor.'

And off she went, the door slamming behind her. By which time my ex was in full-grin mode: job done. I was now down a hospital and a local doctor, all in one fell swoop, after a suspected heart attack. I felt all that stress through the highest levels. Standing there in the kitchen, watching my ex smirk broadly at me, I had never felt my heart thump so fast. As it had done in the hospital, it would stop and then start, like I was being tested: *live die live die live die*. But I had to carry on, do the dinner, smile at the kids and … well, just cope and get on.

I felt like crying inside, though. Instead of punishing me, why did they not help me? How many signs did they need to see what was going on? How many severe injuries? No doctor, no police, no social services, no questions. That was just the norm – and it stayed the norm, no matter how many injuries I had. It became a pattern I had to tolerate, a pattern which fed my ex with untold power that he laughed and gloated over.

Worst of all, to my mind, was the effect on my poor children of incidents like that. They bore witness to them and were probably programmed subconsciously not to speak about what went on at home because they could see for themselves it didn't work: Dad got away with everything … simple! If the authorities couldn't stop him, who could?

Dusty did his best to make sure they didn't speak out, too. He would threaten me in front of them now, saying if you tell so-and-so, if you do this, I'll kill … (he'd pause and decide on a name) … Jahméne. He'd say things so the kids would have that on their minds and they'd think, *I can't say anything*.

After the heart attack, I had to come off the Depo-Provera injections. I got a cap fitted, instead. I had thought that coming off the injections would make my weight go down, but it didn't. I got heavier and heavier. *Why am I putting on weight again?* I wondered. I did a pregnancy test, but it came up negative. I did about three tests and they were all negative.

But on the fourth test, the result was unmistakable: I *was* pregnant again. A new little innocent soul was about to enter our hellish world – and there was nothing I could do to stop it.

Chapter Two

By the time I realised I was pregnant, I was many months gone. But I don't agree with abortion anyway. There is no way on this earth I could ever kill a child of mine. Whatever you may be thinking, maybe that I was wrong to give birth to his children, judgement should not be passed until you understand 100 per cent why, through a shared experience of emotions. So my only thought, right from the start, was that I just had to do my best for my unborn baby. I knew it wasn't going to be easy. I was scared, knowing what had happened with Junior. I didn't want to bury another child because of my ex.

When I told him I was pregnant, though, he went away, as he used to do at Nechells. *Thank God.* It was like a weight being lifted. He only came back from time to time, and when he did it was clear he was starting to struggle with his dual personality. Before, he'd do all manner of sadistic tortures to me and then, calm as you please, he would step outside as though nothing had happened. Now, even a simple trip to Pizza Hut could set him off on one. They served a burnt pizza at one family meal and he went mental, grabbed a mop from somewhere and shouted his head off. It was as though he couldn't control his temper; or couldn't be bothered with the Mr Nice Guy act anymore.

Another time, someone cut us up in the road and Dusty launched into a full-on car chase with the kids in the back, screeched in front of this other car to make it stop and then dragged the driver out to hit him on the road, while all these other cars were rushing past. Then he got back in our car, turned to the children and said, 'Don't let anybody walk all over you, kids. Don't let people cut you up.' As though he was imparting advice!

I had long talks with the children, trying to help them understand our situation, and teaching them how to survive, given we couldn't get out. I would basically drill it into the kids: 'Stay out of his way as much as you can.' If he called for them, they obviously had to go, but I went through a protocol with them of how to breathe, how to stand, what to wear, how to move their hands. I had to – because this was all stuff he'd pick holes in otherwise, and then it would all kick off.

Especially important was not to look him in the eye because I think he saw that as a sign of impertinence. Who were we to look him in the eye? So I told the kids: 'Don't look at him, just keep looking straight ahead or focus on something you can actively do, like your colouring or reading a book.' Jahméne was still a rebel and he'd stand up to him a few times, but as he got older he learned that what I said meant something, and he learned to keep out of the way.

The kids were so excited I was pregnant. We were a clan and to them this was another little member of the crew. I know I shouldn't have brought children into that world, and many will question why I did, but until you are faced with a life such as this you simply cannot understand. We had our happy times and the happiest moments were when we were all together. The kids were all really close and they were very protective of the baby. They would talk to him in my tummy and they'd play him music and stuff, putting the headphones on my burgeoning belly. They were all very caring children. I am proud of them. Our normal family times were what gave us hope.

It was during this pregnancy that I had a chance to be proud of my kids not just as a mother, but as a teacher. Due to various complications, their school places were no longer suitable so I decided to home-educate all the children for a time. It actually turned out to be a blessing, in many ways, because my teaching became a survival mechanism that kept me sane. I think if I hadn't been doing that, I would have been pulled down into my ex's pit of craziness. But it made me switch off from the violence, as I had to concentrate on $2 \times 5 = 10$, and *Washington, D.C. is the capital of the USA*, and *Bonjour, je m'appelle Mandy* five days a week.

The Local Education Authority (LEA) came out to the house to tell me what I had to do and I said, 'OK, that's fine, I can do that.' We got hold of second-hand computers for the kids to use; they weren't the latest models but you could put a CD-ROM in them to learn from. We got Dorling Kindersley books to teach history, art and human biology. I was teaching them German, French and Spanish, too. *Sesame Street* was brilliant for the younger ones because they picked up so much without even knowing it. I loved doing every single lesson because it was so rewarding. The kids were like sponges, soaking up knowledge; I could give them anything and they'd learn it. They were all bright kids.

But, as you'd imagine, the responsibility had its own stresses, too. The LEA would often spring surprise inspections on me, to check up on my work, and when combined with my ex's abuse that was very hard to deal with. I always did well and they were impressed – the kids were three or four years above their age for what I was teaching them, the inspectors said. It was a welcome compliment when all I was getting from Dusty was: 'You're useless, you're nothing, you're a slag.' To achieve made me stronger mentally, more determined to stay alive.

In the spring of 1997, when I was over halfway through my pregnancy, we were all in the car one day, with Dusty, when he suddenly flipped. He was driving down the motorway and he just turned to me and said, 'Get out.'

'What do you mean, "get out"?' I said – warily, because he didn't like me asking questions. 'We're on a motorway,' I told him, in case it wasn't patently obvious.

He didn't respond – just started kicking me in the side to get me out. He was trying to push me and kick me and I was fighting to stay in the car, and all through our struggle he was speeding down the road at 70mph. The kids were screaming in the back, Corice yelling as high as she could.

'I'm pregnant,' I was shrieking at him. He just redoubled his kicks.

'OK, OK,' I said, begging him to stop, the memories of Junior fresh in my mind. He screeched to a halt and kicked me out, and then drove off, leaving me there by the side of the road.

I stood still for a while, realising how unsafe it all was, the cars flashing past me in a fast-flowing metal river that could kill me, and my baby, if I so much as stumbled. In the end, I just had to start walking down the side of the motorway. I had no idea where I was or where to go. It was before the days of mobile phones so I couldn't call anyone. I didn't have any money and I was petrified what he might do to the kids.

I walked and walked. And after I don't know how long, I sensed a car slowing behind me and then coming to a stop.

It was him. He'd driven round and come back, and now he demanded I got back in the car. The kids were still screaming, worried silly. He was laughing; he found it all very amusing. Just another one of his games.

Those 'games' of his weren't just played with me, either. As he had always done, he brought trouble to my house. I was about eight months' pregnant when I got up to answer a knock on the door one afternoon. As I opened the door, I heard a metallic click and then a cold ebony gun was pressed to my forehead. I thought I was going to have the baby there and then, my heart was racing so fast. I was in shock.

The gunman didn't push me into the house. He just stood there. He pressed the gun harder into my head, ignoring my enormous stomach, and he told me: 'A message for your partner. I wanna see him.'

Later, a whole gang turned up and started throwing rocks at the house.

'He's not here! Go away, go find him somewhere else!' I shouted at them from a window, scared out of my wits.

But then my ex came home. He grabbed a big curly pizza chopper, like a machete, from the kitchen and he ran off after them down the road.

Then it was like one of those surreal Benny Hill moments again. One man ran one way, pursued by Dusty with a machete. Then you saw Dusty running back the other way, with three thugs now hot on his heels. The police turned up, sirens wailing round the streets, but the gangsters all scattered so nobody got arrested. Later that night, my ex came back to mine, fuming, and took it all out on me.

The police still turned up to mine, regularly; not surprising given incidents like that. Sometimes they'd be after him; other times they'd have been called out because someone might have heard him attacking me, even though I tried to stay as silent as I could. If they saw that I'd been beaten, they'd quiz me about it.

But they'd ask me their questions in front of Dusty. What was I supposed to tell them? That's all changed now, by the way; they've now got the training to know that they have to take both parties away and question them separately to get anywhere close to the truth. But back then, in front of my ex, they'd say to me: 'Have you got anything to say? What's been happening? Why have we been called out, what's he been doing?' And I couldn't say a single thing. You can't speak out in front of your torturer, not when they've threatened you on pain of death not to breathe a word. I might have been stupid, according to Dusty, but I wasn't *that* stupid.

The police coming to the house and doing nothing made my ex even more powerful. Every police let-down only fuelled his powers. He became like the devil on drugs. The more he got away with, the worse his tortures became – more sadistic, more calculated, more weird. And he would say, over and over, 'I can do this and nobody can stop me.' It was another one in the air to him.

On 5 June 1997, I gave birth to my baby. I named him Darren. He looked like Daniel and Isaac, but he had darker hair. I felt especially protective over him; I felt protective over all the kids, but I felt like I had to watch out for this one in particular because he was tiny. The others had sort of learned how to survive, by now, but this little one still had to learn the ropes.

I remember he used to like playing in this red washing basket I had: he'd take his toys in there and play. All his baby photos show him sitting in that, and he says to me now, 'Did I just live in a bowl, Mum?' But he used to like crawling in there and playing. I'd let him do it, happy he'd found a safe sanctuary to call his own.

I only wished I could have done the same. After Darren was born, Dusty came to visit more and more regularly. And his vicious, sadistic abuse continued in the bedroom upstairs, behind closed doors so the kids couldn't see. Just as he'd done on Christmas Day 1993, he gloried in whacking me on the arse in front of the kids after a brutal rape, taunting me. Even his casual violence stepped up a gear. We'd sit watching telly in the bedroom and he'd just grab my breast and squeeze and twist it to cause me pain. He'd poke me in the face and say, 'You whore!' I wouldn't have 'done' anything but I couldn't say anything, so I'd just sit there and take it.

My lack of reaction then became a new game for him, though: she didn't flinch from that, so I'll try this instead. I'll pull her arm up behind her spine. I'll bend her fingers back.

Coping with a new baby, home-schooling the kids, walking on eggshells around my ex, enduring what he dished out ... it was like one long torture that never stopped. Day-to-day life was intolerably hard. Days and weeks would go by with no conversation because we were all too scared to say anything. It was so weird. I never knew what to say and what not to say, and he'd just twist my words anyway, so in the end I found it was easier to say nothing at all.

Dinnertimes round our table would be deathly silent. If Dusty had cooked dinner – his usual nut dishes, engineered to cause me pain – then we all had to eat it and look like we enjoyed it. We became expert actors, playing our parts to perfection. But that was never, ever good enough for Dusty.

About a year after Darren was born, the kids finally all got places at school and my home tutoring came to an end. I was back to being timed on the school run, but at least I got to go past Kate's house again and take some comfort from her friendly face.

There was no way I could tell her what was going on now, though. It had gone too far for that. I was too scared to tell her anything for fear of what might happen to the children if he found out I'd blagged – and I was also too ashamed of what he forced me to do. He'd tied my tongue with his depravity as surely as if he'd physically knotted it with his own filthy hands.

The kids enjoyed school, I think, for the most part. Isaac was coming up to five, in his first year, and he settled in really well. He was naturally sporty and always a joker – he was quite a character and made lots of friends pretty much straight away. Daniel was about to become a teenager, and was at the top of his class for maths and science so I knew he would do well when the time for formal exams came round. Corice and Jahméne, aged six and seven, were still inseparable. They used to go everywhere together, holding hands. Maybe they did it to look out for each other, I don't know – four eyes are better than two, kind of thing – but they also had fun. They would record made-up radio shows on tape, singing all the jingles. I loved hearing them do that. Corice was excited to go back to school. She loved our pets, especially our baby rabbits, and she told me proudly, pushing her glasses up her nose, that she was going to be a vet one day.

In time, we got the loft converted, a cheap DIY job, and the kids' sleeping arrangements changed. Dan, for privacy much needed, got the room up in the new loft, which you accessed via a staircase in Jahméne and Isaac's room. Corice and Darren shared, sleeping in bunk beds, in the old playroom.

That sounds so ordinary, doesn't it? A loft conversion. But this was our ordinary life. We went to school every day. We went on days out to the beach.

Dusty always spoiled those day trips, though. He hated going on holiday, he hated the beach, he hated sand, he hated happy people. All those things would make him angry, and he would always take his frustration out on me when we got home. But do you know what? I would rather them had a day at the beach and I be tortured for it, than them not getting to go at all.

We went to Bournemouth Beach loads of times. Dusty would park the car next to the beach … and sit in it while the kids and I played on the sand. He wouldn't get out; he'd just stay in the car all day long, watching us through the windscreen. He would put a dampener on any day out. Even if we just went to another town, all together, to do some shopping, Dusty would ruin it. A queue in a shop would be taking too long or something, and he'd lose his rag and go off on one. You'd think, *Control yourself …* but he couldn't. Then I'd get the flak for it at home.

I think the hardest thing of all, though, was coping with no sleep. Like an expert torturer, Dusty would keep me awake for hours on end. It was another form of control, see, because if I was exhausted I was less likely to fight back or find the wherewithal to run.

It used to be, back when Daniel was born, that Dusty would stop me from sleeping himself, poking me and pinching me, but he'd upped his game since then; he'd honed his skills.

Now, all he had to do was make threats.

'If you fall asleep,' he'd say idly. 'I'm going to knock you out with chloroform and take you to a cellar run by these people I know. They hold people there, Mandy. They make them sex slaves. You'd never get out. If you fall asleep, that's what I'm going to do to you.'

And he'd actually show me the bottle of chloroform and this cotton wool he'd bought specially for the purpose, and he'd say, 'All I have to do is stick this over your mouth when you're asleep … and you wake up and you're in a sex cellar somewhere.'

There were about fifty threats that loomed over me if I slept, any one of which could happen. He said he would inject my arm with drugs; and once, when I'd slipped up and let myself slide into sleep, I woke up with a red dot on my arm. *Has he done something to me?* I wondered, in a panic, confused and paranoid – but not knowing if the paranoia was justified. I rubbed at the mark. It didn't come off, but it didn't hurt, either. I tried to reason with myself, *Surely I'd have felt it.* But how did I know for sure?

I couldn't sleep with those kinds of threats hanging over me so I developed a new way of resting. If I 'fell asleep', I wasn't ever properly asleep. My senses would be alert even when I had my eyes shut. I would still be listening and smelling, all my senses working, scanning, just in case he was going to do something to the kids or me.

Unsurprisingly, I couldn't keep it up forever. I'd try to time my 'crashes', when my body would just shut down and force me to sleep, for the times he was away – but as he came more and more often to Sedgemoor Road, it got harder and harder to control. And so there were times when I'd pass out and come to, only to find his hands around my throat.

Or he'd just be standing over me, staring into my eyes like a crazy man.

Or I'd wake up and he'd be sitting next to me on the bed, humming his own little tune: *'You can't run, you can't hide …'* The summer I fell pregnant with Darren, the Fugees, with Lauryn Hill, had released 'Ready or Not' and this was now his absolute favourite. He would croon it to me over and over.

It was one of the scariest things he did.

When you don't sleep, you're dizzy all the time. You can't even see properly. Perhaps inevitably, I started having accidents at home. On top of being beaten up and raped and buggered and bruised, I would do things like burn my arm on the cooker element. I'd drop things – and literally bump into doors.

One afternoon, in 1998, when I hadn't slept for about a week, I was in the midst of doing chores, my eyes burning from lack of rest. Dusty was being particularly menacing and evil at that time, and my mind was shot. Struggling to get through the day, I heaved the washing basket into my arms and started down the stairs.

I didn't see one of the kids' book bags, abandoned halfway down. As my foot stepped on it, I skidded.

I went hurtling down the stairs and plunged headfirst into the sharp corner of a wall that stuck out at the bottom of the stairs.

In an instant, my skull exploded in a sea of crimson blood.

Chapter Three

It wouldn't stop bleeding. I thought I was going to pass out. I grabbed a white bath towel from the washing basket and pressed it to my head. Within seconds it was dripping with blood, sodden and red.

My ex was out the front. The stairs were right by the front door so I opened it and stuck my head out to get his attention.

'I need to go to hospital,' I said, trying to speak through the throbbing pain in my skull. It was the headache from hell – and still the blood poured out.

Dusty ignored what I said; ignored my injury, and the river of blood. 'I need some cider,' he told me. 'Nip up the shop and get it.'

Dusty was drinking more these days, choosing stronger and stronger lagers and ciders, consuming them more and more quickly. It worried me because the drink fuelled his temper, but who was I to stop it? Now, he fixed me with a gaze that I knew meant business. He stared at me till I gathered my shaky legs under me and staggered to my feet. The world swam before my eyes; I was so dizzy. I clutched onto the bannisters for dear life, my other hand holding the wet towel to my head. Blood pooled under my fingers: the towel was full of it.

'Go,' he said. He raised his arm, looking down at his watch. Timing me.

I hurried down the path as fast as I could, each step an effort. The white towel was now red, not an inch of it untouched by the still-streaming blood. I managed to get to the shop and pulled his favourite cider off the shelf. The woman behind the counter stared at me as I plonked it in front of her with trembling hands. It was a struggle to stay upright.

'What have you done to your head?' she asked in horror.

I can't even remember if I answered her. I probably said: 'It's nothing.' The biggest understatement of the century.

The next day, I was still in agony: my head pounding, my skull still bleeding and my balance shot. Every time I had to stand up – to lift Darren down from his high chair or to do the dinner for the kids at the stove – it was like the planet lurched on its axis. I was so, so dizzy. In the end, my ex gave in and drove me to the hospital. He literally kicked me out of the car at A&E and zoomed off, leaving me on the pavement outside. My body was covered in bruises from his beatings and he wasn't about to help me get seen.

I staggered into the waiting area. The blood was still coming. One of the nurses came over and handed me a massive thick pad to press to the gaping hole in my head. 'When did this happen?' she asked, alarmed.

'Yesterday,' I muttered, not able to meet her disapproving eye at my response.

They took me into a cubicle and examined me. They wanted to stitch it – but they told me they couldn't. Because I hadn't sought treatment right away, the wound had started to clot deep inside and they couldn't do what they needed to. I remember having a banging headache and this doctor just shouting at me, telling me off for leaving it so long.

It's not my fault, I thought, *why are you shouting at me?* But there was no point in saying anything.

In the end, they stuck a line of medical glue down there and sent me home. It took months to heal because it had started closing up incorrectly so deep in the wound.

They never even looked at the rest of my body; not that I was expecting them to. As they always did these days, my bruises stayed hidden, concealed beneath the skin-tight clothes that Dusty chose for me.

His power grew stronger; his control seeped into more and more areas of my life, like poison travelling along a victim's veins. If I went to the loo to have a wee, I'd be sitting there and the door would suddenly burst open and he'd drag me out. Or if I was having a shower, trying to wash off the blood from his latest attack and have a moment of peace, he would rush in and stop me. I don't know what that was all about. You're vulnerable, I guess, while you're naked in the water or sitting on the loo, and he loved to exploit vulnerability. I found myself changing my life pattern. When he was around, I'd go to the toilet less and I wouldn't wash so that I wasn't so vulnerable.

He always found a way to humiliate me though. As the years passed, he started ripping my clothes off in front of the children. It was like he knew it affected me more than if it was done behind a closed door. I'd run away – no child should see that – and he'd chase me, which he delighted in too. I got chased around the house a lot. He loved running after me and hunting me down, trapping me in the bedroom. Then he'd rape me excitedly, while I bit down hard on my cheeks to stop myself from crying out loud.

I don't know how I survived it all. Sometimes I would sit crying, asking God what I had done that was so bad to deserve all these tortures. Living in fear eats out away at soul; it destroys everything. It gets so that there are no sunny days, no warmth, no hope, no silver lining. His constant abuse was so horrifying. But when the people who are supposed to help you turn out to be on his side ... it becomes even more paralysing. It becomes unstoppable. I felt like I was trapped in an invisible prison, with no way out. All I could do was live each day, surviving from one hour to the next. Faith, hope and the will to live for my children saw me through the worst tortures I had ever known.

Only once in those Sedgemoor Road years did I try to fight back. On that afternoon, he was in the bedroom strangling me. Taking me to the edge and bringing me back, playing the game he so adored. Playing God. *Will I live or die today?*

He decides.

And for some reason, I just thought, *I'm not having it*. Every time he strangled me, I couldn't help but think of Junior. The pain of burying my child was always just beneath the surface, more agonising even than the pressure of Dusty's strong slim fingers on my throat. This time, though, the agony of grief bubbled up inside me and boiled over, and I thought, *No, it's not happening again. He's not going to stop me breathing again.*

I brought my hands up and I pushed him off me.

It was like I'd pushed a red button.

His eyes slanted and he jumped back off me, and ran straight out the room.

Oh my God, what's he doing? I thought. *Where's he gone?*

I heard a smash and a crash in the bathroom and then he came back in with the shower pole in his hand. And he just rammed it into my face, the metallic circular end of it driving straight into my mouth. And then he gripped his hands on the pole and he ragdolled me around the room, dragging me every which way by the pole in my mouth. He pushed me against the wall, adjusted his grip and drove the pole deeper inside. It was in my mouth, cutting my cheek – and then he shoved it hard down the back of my throat. I gagged, choking on the metal. He was pushing me into the wall and there was blood everywhere. And he was just going round, round, round with the pole, revelling in his new toy.

I collapsed in a heap on the floor and he yanked the pole out of my mouth and started whacking me with it, thrashing me hard. His words ran over the staccato beat of each *thwack*.

'Don't you *ever* push me off again! Who are you to fight back? Who are you to fight *me*? Nobody stops me. Nobody tells me what to do.'

He went on and on and on. I pressed my face into the carpet, trying to avoid the hail of hits from the pole, my body curled into a ball as he just kept striking me, over and over. And I thought, *You stupid cow.*

From then on, I took every beating silently. Every torture. Every rape. I knew what happened if I fought back now. From then on, it was always: let's just get this over and done with.

Chapter Four

A new year, a new century, a new millennium – and still the tortures continued. In the year 2000 I remember the time Dusty strangled me then punched me in the left eye hard, straight after, and I felt it burst. All the white just turned to blood, and I was blind in that eye for a couple of days. That scared me so bad. For even if he wouldn't let me paint, in every nuance of my being I was an artist: I saw the world visually. To lose my eyes, I thought, would be to lose my soul.

I thanked God when the sight came back.

Around a week after that attack, a druggie stormed into our house, hunting my ex, swinging his nunchucks round and round. My ex had done something to a neighbour, I think, and she had sent this guy round to sort him out. I remember those nunchucks being inches from Isaac's tiny, precious, seven-year-old head as he was caught in the crossfire. I remember sticking my hand out to take the blow. If I hadn't, he would be dead; my hand went black with bruising. The guy was high on drugs; he didn't care that my children were in the room. Again my life went into slow motion, like in the films, as I reached out to grab every child out of harm's way, taking the blows from the spike-edged metal bits that were on the end of what looked like lumps of wood on a chain. He and Dusty fought like dogs – but hours later they were sat on my front doorstep, chatting like mates; another character brought under my ex's sway. Dusty didn't care that he had brought this danger to my home; he didn't care that my kids got caught up in it. Luckily, none of them got hurt.

In the same year Dusty developed his repertoire of evil. He already used his teeth, his fists, his feet, his fingers, his cock. Now, he brought a new player to the table.

Knives.

He used to stand in the kitchen, going through the drawers, choosing the best blades to use on me. We had a knife sharpener, like chefs use, at Sedgemoor Road and he would stand there for ages sharpening each of his selections, talking to himself, and all the while there would be that *swish swish* sound: the swipe of the blade going back and forth. I would hear him doing it, knowing that he was going to use that sharp knife on me … knowing, too, that he knew I was listening. That's why he did it: to frighten me; to build the tension. And he would talk all the way through, too, about how he knew the knife was going to work better if it was sharper, and about the injuries he was going to inflict. He would talk normally – it wasn't a shout, or a whisper. He would just talk evil calmly, like he was making a shopping list: all the things he wanted. And he was going to tick them all off, one by one.

I can't listen to the sound of a knife sharpener anymore. It's a trigger for me: it takes me right back. Right back to Sedgemoor Road. It makes me cower in fear. Just the sound of it, the swipe of a blade … that *swish swish* cuts me inside out.

He bit me more and more often, clamping his teeth either side of my nose and savaging my hands if they got in the way. When he lost control, and forgot about keeping my face unmarked, he liked to push his thumbs into my eyeballs, push them right in, so it felt like my eyes were going to disappear into the back of my head. More than once, I thought he'd actually popped them and made me blind; it was that painful. I can't explain that pain: it goes down your cheek, behind your cheekbones, as the force pushes down hard on your eyes. Some agonies you can switch off from – you can go to the white zone – but that wasn't one of them.

If he did ever mark my face, he kept me in the house; he'd take the kids to school himself and forbid me to go out until the bruises and the bloodshot eyes faded. I took to trying to protect my face as much as I could, letting my arms and hands take the brunt of his beatings, so that he wouldn't keep me in. Going out into the world reminded me of what normality was. It kept me ticking. If I lost contact with it, *I* was lost.

I started to drink his cans of beer when I was with him because I worked out that if he drank over a certain amount I was in serious trouble. It was all about watching what he was doing, monitoring and observing his behaviour, and then calculating what I had to do to save myself. He used to drink Tennents Super, a really strong lager, and I figured out that he was all right – for him – if he had two, but if he had more than two then he'd start changing his character, and if he had four then I was done for – because at four he didn't know what he was doing and that was when it got really dangerous.

So I started saying, 'Oh, can I have some of that?' And then I'd drink some of his stash so there would be less left for him to imbibe.

There were a few times, I will admit, when I drank to get drunk, to not feel pain: the battered woman's anaesthetic. I'd think, *Do you know what? I'll just have another one, to block it all out* ... I know a lot of women who have gone down that road and not been able to get back – but I was lucky enough to be in control of it. I would do that maybe two or three times a year, just when I knew it was a point where I wouldn't be able to cope with the pain without it. But I resisted its temptation most of the time.

Over the years, I had built up my resistance to Dusty's attacks too. I have a very high pain threshold; thank God, because otherwise there is no way I would have survived. But like anything in life, there is a flip side. And the flip side to my ability to endure his torture was that my unbreakable spirit enraged him. There was nothing he wanted more than to see me broken. He tried every which way. His words – 'you slag, you whore' – his threats – 'I'm going to kill the kids one by one and make you watch and then I'm going to kill you last so you suffer' – and his tortures ... they were like hundreds of hammers designed to chip away at me, chip away at me, right down to my core, but still I struggled on.

As Dusty took things to darker and darker depths of depravity, each new level was like his brain was calculating what he could try that would break me. He kept upping his game. During each attack, if something wasn't breaking me, he would get frustrated and try something else. So it would start with a slap – a slap not dissimilar to the one he gave me all those years ago in Rugby. Then it would be a punch – like the ones he doled out in Moseley Road. Then he'd try the kick, or the bite, or the rape, or the buggery, or the sadism, or the knives, or the broken glass or or or ... Or the children.

In the year 2000, Daniel turned fifteen. He was studying for his GCSEs and doing brilliantly. He was even featured in the local paper for his exemplary academic achievement. I would praise him to the heavens, so proud of my boy, and he'd dip his head modestly and push the glasses he now wore up his nose in a nervous gesture. His dad never praised him, but Dan didn't really try to seek his approval anymore. Instead, on the increasingly rare occasions his dad was away, he would say to me boldly, 'Mum, when I am older, I will train and get big and I will stand up to him!'

I always shushed him, and stroked his hair, this boy-man who was growing taller day by day, but who still seemed so fragile inside, like a willow tree bending in the wind. 'Dan,' I would say, 'you know your father can't be attacked. He would never stand for that – it would end in death. Please, don't put yourself in danger. I couldn't bear it if you were hurt.'

One afternoon, after the kids were home from school, Dan and I were in the kitchen with his dad. I don't even know what prompted it – perhaps fifteen years of his father's abuse was enough – but Daniel spoke back to his dad. I was a little way away from them and I turned round as the barb of Dan's words hit home.

In an instant, Dusty was on top of him, the back of his hand powering across my boy's cheek. He slapped him, and Daniel's glasses flew off. My child stood there in shock. For though my ex might threaten horrors to me about the kids, he and I had done a devil's deal that the children were not to be touched and, in the main, Dusty kept his side of the bargain. He pushed Jahméne about; he would call him Thomas after me, my surname, because Jahméne took after me so much. I think evil can spot God and fears Him: Jahméne's faith must have shone out of him because his father didn't like him, never had. I saw Dusty launch towards

Jahméne once with a plastic spatula. There were times he would deal with him roughly, Jahméne told me in later years. Generally, he kept his venom limited to putting the children down verbally and teasing them in his own cruel way. Dusty would show his authority and demand respect through fear; he did that with pretty much everyone he came across, including the children. He wanted to be the boss, the leader, the ruler, the king – a bit like in the computer games he played. But he would assert himself above the kids through threats and innate dominance. This physical attack on Daniel was unprecedented.

I felt a roaring anger inside me when I saw him hit my child and I went absolutely ballistic. I went right over to Dusty and I squared up to him and I said, in a calm and level voice, 'Don't. Touch. My. Kids.'

He balled his hand into a fist and punched me hard. I absorbed the blow and pushed him off me. His eyes slanted and he punched me again. I was *never* allowed to push him off me. He started beating me in front of the kids. They couldn't do anything, and I didn't want them seeing any of this. I ducked the next blow and ran away, legs pounding like pistons.

He followed me. He hunted me down. He chased me to the bedroom and he raped me in there, while the kids stayed silent downstairs.

It was agony, of course. But I would rather that than Daniel be hurt. Anything for my children.

Later in the year 2000 Darren turned three and I got him a place at a local nursery. The days stretched in front of me, then, without him to care for 24/7, suddenly, I had time to spare.

I went often to the post office in those days; it was where I picked up the child benefit. You had to go to the counter to collect it, and my exchanges with the woman behind the Perspex screen were rare opportunities for me to talk to someone. I liked to chat to her as she stamped my paperwork and counted out the money. Our conversation was always on a deadline, of course, because Dusty would be timing my outing to the shops, but even that brief connection with another human being was precious.

One afternoon, in November 2000, she happened to mention that a job was going at the post office – a cashier's job, where you stand on the front desk serving the general public. She encouraged me to apply and even handed me an application form. In two minds, I took it home.

Immediately, Dusty mocked me, 'You won't get that job. You're too stupid for that.' But, to my surprise, he didn't stop me filling in the form. He didn't stop me from attending when they invited me to an interview. He didn't even put his foot down when they offered me the job. All he said was, 'You won't be able to keep it because you're stupid. They'll get rid of you.'

I think it freaked him out, though, that I'd been chosen from the applicants as the one they wanted. He got frustrated and lost his temper a lot. And as I started in my new role – at first shadowing the manager, Karen, to see how she worked, and then being let loose on the public myself – he started sending spies in, to be a pain, to ask impossible questions. At first I thought I was being paranoid about that, but it was clear over time that people were reporting back to him. He'd come in himself, too, and just watch me. Mindful of what had happened at Techno Cameras back in Birmingham, when he'd strangled me because he'd heard me laughing with a colleague, I was careful never to look as though I was enjoying myself.

I was, though. Oh, I loved it. It got me out of the house: it was the only freedom I had and I made the most of it. It was so liberating, pretending that I was normal, that I was part of the world. Uncomfortable as it was to have him and his spies watching me, I was on a mission to prove that I was worth more than he said I was; to prove to myself that I wasn't just some battered wife who couldn't do stuff. I worked really hard.

Karen gave me a thick file to take home, about five inches deep, full of information and protocol I was supposed to learn – because working in the post office is not just about weighing items and sticking on stamps: you have to do banking, and passports, and travel money, and benefits, and social security; all kinds of paperwork and accountancy. Our post office was part of a shop as well, so I had cashing up to do and that sort of business-led admin. My ex refused to let me study the fat file at home, so I had to take it all to work and try and learn it on the job. It was intense, to say the least. Starting in November, too, meant that I'd only just begun when the Christmas rush hit. Talk about being thrown in at the deep end …

But I counted my blessings every day. I was shocked Dusty was even letting me go to work; even if he was spying and making me come straight home after my shift. I honestly thought he was going to stop it. Every day that I went to work I thought, *He's gonna stop it today; he's gonna turn up and do something stupid so I'll get the sack, or he'll just stop me from going in.* That was always looming over me. So every day that I got into work without a mishap was a bonus that he hadn't stopped it.

Within just a few months, Karen came to me and said she was promoting me. The post office had been taken over by an agency and my immediate supervisor had left – Karen wanted me to have her job. She also started talking about her retirement, and how she wanted someone that she could trust to take over her position. She said she wanted that person to be me. She started training me up so that I wasn't just doing the day-to-day banking, but learning how to do all the accounts and the bookkeeping for the whole operation.

Crikey, I thought, *first I got the job, and now I've been promoted … I must be doing something right.* Yet I felt overwhelmed by her trust in me. *Am I ready for this?* I wondered. *Am I really the right person for this?*

I spoke to Karen about my worries. 'I don't know if I'll be up to this,' I confessed.

But she brushed away my insecurity like it was nothing: so many cobwebs, spun by my ex. She said firmly, 'You'll be fine.' She was so confident I could do it – and that gave me an internal power in my mind: *I've actually achieved something here.*

Dusty hated me being promoted. He never said anything specific to me about it, but it obviously grated on him that I'd done well after he'd said I wouldn't. He started making my life even more of a hell than it already was – stopping me from sleeping in the hope I'd miss work, or beating me on my face so I'd have to go into work battered.

I'm proud to say I never missed a shift. I'd cover up what he'd done the night before, or even that same morning, before I came into work. I'd have strangulation marks and bruises, and my mouth would get cut a lot; either because of me biting it to stay silent as he raped me or because of him punching me in the face, so that I got my cheek or lips caught on my teeth.

Occasionally, members of the public might say to me, 'What happened to your face?' There was one old lady in particular who was really friendly, and as she chattered away to me she would ask me what I'd done. I'd just say I was clumsy and had banged it. I think most customers genuinely thought I was clumsy.

But it was one thing for me to get away with lying to the strangers behind the Perspex screen. It was another thing entirely lying to my manager, who saw me day in and day out.

I remember Dusty had split my lip once. I did my make-up real clever so no one would spot it and tried to breeze into work as though nothing had happened.

But straight away Karen said to me, 'What happened to your lip?'

So much for clever make-up.

My manager was a warm lady, really lovely. She was short, even smaller than my five foot three, and she had dark brown hair silvered with bits of grey. If she didn't believe me when I said, 'I banged it,' she didn't say anything then.

The following week, I had a mark on my neck from Dusty strangling me.

'What have you done to your neck?' Karen asked, her kind brown eyes looking levelly at mine.

Over time, she worked it out. It wasn't even just the bruises and the strange marks she saw. I was often jittery at work – Dusty would terrorise me before I left the house so my heart would still be pounding in fear as I took my place behind the counter. I'd come in shaking, on edge and uneasy, and Karen picked up on all those vibes and figured it out.

As our friendship deepened, she did broach the matter with me and she said, 'You've got to get out, Mandy. You shouldn't stay there.'

I had to explain that I'd tried to leave before, but that it had never worked; that the police didn't help and I couldn't stop him. 'I just have to put up with it until he decides to leave,' I said to her, more brightly and with more hope than I felt inside.

I didn't tell her that Dusty had been at ours for so long now that I feared he was never, ever going to leave us alone.

Chapter Five

The one-year anniversary of me starting work came around. Somehow, Dusty had allowed it to continue for 365 whole days. As I threw myself into tackling the Christmas rush at work, I also steeled myself for the holidays at home.

Christmas for normal families is a happy time of year. But I always used to dread it because it meant we were stuck in the house for a few weeks with Dusty around, with all the doors shut tight against the cold. Christmas, birthdays and holidays were always the worst times for tortures because Dusty seemed to get extra stressed. I would be raped frequently, buggered and beaten. He spent most Christmases with me and my children, and always made the atmosphere horrid. I don't recall laughter and happiness.

The only small plus about Christmas was that it was in winter. And in winter, it looked less odd for me to be dressed in long sleeves and scarves, which I'd have to wear all year round to cover up the bruises. I could feel more part of the world, then, and not like a woman with a shameful secret.

That Christmas of 2001, I remember Dusty being caught up in an *EastEnders* storyline that was gripping the nation. Each night the soap was on TV, he'd summon me to the bedroom to sit next to him on the bed, naked, while we watched. If I ever took too long putting the kids to bed beforehand, he would stick his head round their bedroom doors and order me: 'Come on, leave them.' And I'd have to give them a quick sweet kiss goodnight and follow him directly to the torture chamber, where the familiar soap theme would be coming from the telly.

On the screen, Trevor would be attacking Little Mo, raping her in her bathroom, building up to the big storyline on New Year's Eve where she would fight back and hit him with an iron. There was a lot of violence. I hated that programme; it used to wind him up so much. He used to sit there, like he was learning, getting ideas, but at the same time he'd be saying, 'Oh my God, Trevor's really bad. She needs help.' It was just like when he'd watched the Tina Turner film, as though he couldn't see himself in the psycho role, as though he didn't do those things himself at home. It used to confuse me: he couldn't see he was that man.

He'd make me sit next to him and watch it, but I'd be watching him. I could see him getting adrenaline as the violence escalated on screen, and when it finished I knew something was going to happen to me because it would spark him off. It would fire up his anger – and then I'd be the target.

I couldn't even try to save myself by drinking his beer anymore. As the months had passed, I'd tried to keep pace with him, but he kept drinking more and more. And then I think he'd cottoned on to what I was doing because he'd switched his drinks. Now, he'd gone on to these spirit drinks, 90 per cent proof, and I wouldn't touch that stuff. I saw what it did to him, and it was dangerous.

The New Year began. I kept on with my life: working in the day, caring for the kids, keeping up with the housework … being tortured at night. I tried to play my ex; I would come home from work 'stressed' so that maybe he would think, *Oh, she's not having much fun so I won't pick on her about it.* It was a weird psychology but I knew if I ever showed any kind of happiness or enjoyment he would stop it right away. In time, though, he'd started to think that maybe my job, with its access to thousands upon thousands of pounds, could be useful to him. I remember him making comments about me robbing money from the safe. And I thought, *You got no chance. This is my job.*

The job freed his time up, too, of course. With me out all day, he had time to plan his tortures. He had time to sleep, so that when I came back shattered from my shift, he'd have loads of energy, ready to torment me all night long. He started to tell me about the tortures he had planned, telling me what he was going to do to me, like he was running the ideas by me to see what I thought – and then he'd laugh. Sometimes, he'd carry out his threats; other times he wouldn't and would simply say, 'I'm saving that for tomorrow.' So I never knew what would be coming that night when he shut the bedroom door behind him and turned to face me, with a sick, sick smile on his face.

The ideas wound him up and they'd spill out of him at all times, even just around the house. I think it was a mind-control thing with him, as though if he saw he'd left a half-hour space where he hadn't done anything to control me, he'd have to throw a line in to remind me that he was in charge of my life.

Sometimes the kids would hear stuff and come to me in a panic when he was gone. 'I heard Dad say that, is he really going to do that?' they'd ask. And I'd have to reply, 'No, no, he's just saying it.' I think he saved the really sadistic threats for me, but they'd overhear him saying things like, 'I've got to teach your mum a lesson.'

He would still tell them I was a whore and a slag and was going round having sex with different people. I wasn't doing anything; I was too scared even to talk to another human being, so doing that would be like, *what on earth* … But he used to come out with these excuses to say that that was why he was hurting me. The kids weren't stupid; they knew they were lies. I remember Jahméne actually saying to me, 'Well, *when* did you do that?' Because I was always either at home or at the post office; I was never allowed time on my own. It was confusing for them, no matter how much I tried to explain.

With me being out at work, Dusty now had more opportunity to sit with the kids and talk to them, too, telling them mush to sully their minds. He used to sit and talk to Dan about stuff for hours on end.

I wouldn't find out till much, much later what he'd said.

The tortures went on and on and on. It felt like I hadn't slept for about four months, but still I didn't break. That was frustrating Dusty, more than ever. He would walk around the house pacing, angry, like a pent-up animal prowling his lair. He was a walking bomb, ready to explode at any second.

Along with the strong spirits, he started dabbling with over-the-counter drugs. I have no idea what he was on, but it made him more and more vicious. He was picking fights with everyone. He had a row with a woman down the road and threw her cat heartlessly at the wall. It was like he just didn't care about impressing anyone anymore; Dr Jekyll was dead, long live Mr Hyde. He spent his days holed up at home, studying on his computer, honing his skills, reading book after book about how to beat the system. More than ever, he was revelling in his power over the police, calling them an ass as he swotted up on all sorts of computer wizardry. He would do all that, and he would play his violent computer games too, surfing the net for sadism, seeking inspiration for his sick tortures.

Summer came, and as the temperature outside rose so too did the tension at home. One day, he Bic-shaved his head and whole face including eyebrows. I have no idea why he did that, still to this day. His mood was flippant and dangerous and very unpredictable.

On Friday, 5 July 2002, to my amazement I was promoted to manager. I was going to be in charge of the whole place. They gave me the keys to the building and the safe as I finished my shift: a big bunch of keys on an old-fashioned loop. It was overwhelming, the level of responsibility I'd be taking on from Monday morning, and I was bowled over that the bosses had enough trust in me to do the job. I was excited, too.

Coming home, the keys heavy in my bag, I was torn between that excitement and fearfulness. I was scared to tell my ex about the promotion, especially given what he'd said about robbing things, but I had no choice. Yet he didn't really say anything, not that I recall.

As with everything I did, though, he stored it away, as though it was a jigsaw puzzle piece he was slotting into place; as though it was the timer on his bomb, now all wired up to the explosives in his mind.

From that moment on, the clock started counting down.

'Mum, look at me, look at me!'

I glanced up at Isaac, who was just a couple of weeks away from his ninth birthday, doing a cartwheel in our back garden.

He was the sportiest of all my kids; he loved anything athletic. I'd adored doing gymnastics as a child myself so I had taught all my children how to do handstands and stuff; we kept our lawn cut nice and flat so they could run about on it. They would all see who could stay upright the longest, upside down. Jahméne had it down to perfection and would normally win. Watching them play happily in the garden were moments when I would actually feel lost in normality.

We also had a family-sized paddling pool and when the weather was nice, as it was on that sunny Sunday afternoon in July, two days after I'd picked up the keys, we often put it out on the lawn and spent long lazy afternoons out in the garden. All the kids loved being in the water – from Darren, who had just turned five, through to Corice aged ten and Jahméne aged eleven, all the way up to sixteen-year-old Dan. Today was one of those days: family fun in the sunshine, the musical ring of the kids' laughter a symphony for my soul.

The shadows started lengthening as the day drew on to mid-afternoon. It was maybe three-ish when all of a sudden Dusty turned to me and said, 'Go upstairs now.'

Ten … nine … eight …

It was the kind of tone he used when he ordered me to the bedroom: an angry demand, though never a shout. I thought, *Oh no …*

Seven … six …

It was the middle of the afternoon, so I tried to strategise. 'I've got to sort the kids out,' I began, hoping to buy myself some more time.

'They're fine,' replied Dusty, curtly. 'They're going in the nursery to play. Aren't you, kids?' He fixed each one of them with a look.

We all got up and traipsed our way obediently indoors, leaving the sunshine behind. Kids can be masters of intelligence, and mine were experts at pinpointing mood swings by then. They knew something was going to go down – but they couldn't do anything about it.

That must have been its own hell for them. I can't ever understand their version of events because I was in my own twisted story. But they were upset as we took them inside; Dan went straight up to his loft room, while the others were going into the nursery to play. I tried to calm them down as they scurried up the stairs, murmuring reassuring words, but I doubt they worked.

Five … four …

I went up the stairs then too, with Dusty behind me, closing off any escape route – not that I'd have ever dared to run. He'd been drinking. He'd got this bottle of spirits from somewhere, some mega-strong blue alcoholic drink from a foreign country. He had the bottle in his hand as we entered the bedroom, but then he put it down and cracked open two lagers for us instead. He poured mine into a half-pint glass and handed it to me. Then, as we settled down on the bed in front of the TV, he put on a film: *Gladiator*.

Three …

I was wearing a red tube dress. He flashed his scissors and cut the dress in half, down to a skirt. I felt awkward sitting there with my breasts bare, so I pulled it up, over my chest.

He pulled it down.

I dragged it up again; he yanked it down. *He's in one of those moods*, I thought. He had made his message clear: I was not to have anything on my top.

I let him win, a small victory that I hoped would appease, and sat rigidly still, feeling uncomfortable and ashamed. I sipped my lager as my eyes darted round the room, like those of a caged animal. Dusty sat back and watched the movie.

Two …

He started to get riled up, becoming angry about what was happening in the film. My heart rate instantly sped up, keeping pace with his agitation. I heard my heartbeat pounding in my ears, like thunder heralding a coming storm. I canvassed the room, plotting and thinking, analysing and assessing. *I need to move stuff*, I thought. My eyes alighted on things close to me: combs and pens and anything with sharp edges. *I need to push that out the way*, I thought, *I need to cover that up with something so he can't use it.*

Yet there was nothing immediately nearby that rang alarm bells for me. I went to take another sip of my drink, raising the glass to my face.

One …

The glass … I didn't even think about the glass.

As I lifted it, he suddenly smashed it into my face. It exploded on impact, driving razor-sharp shards straight into my skin.

Boom.

Chapter Six

All these months, up to now, his torture had been calm and controlled, planned and premeditated. This felt different. This was out of control. *Oh my God*, I thought, *what's coming next?* I could tell that he had flipped, beyond anything I had previously known.

Most of the glass was embedded in my mouth, sticking out of my face. I was so shocked by what he'd done, I couldn't even feel it. My hand held the fractured base of the glass and I carefully put it down on a cupboard next to the bed.

Then he just turned into this wild animal.

He jumped on top of me and I was trying to get away. Everything was happening so fast. In the struggle, shards of glass fell to the floor. Somehow, I managed to get off the side of the bed. I stood straight up onto a two-inch fragment, but my senses were numbed, everything focused on fight-or-flight, my heart pounding *live die live die* in my chest. I didn't realise I'd been wounded; I had no time to – he leapt at me and grabbed my hair, scrunching it up in his fists. He yanked me by my hair round the side of the bed, ripping hair from my scalp as he dragged me round against my will, holding his prize in his fists: bloody red strands with flaps of skin attached to the top. As he threw me to the floor beside the bed, he started kicking and punching me in the head, saying over and over, 'Who do you think you are? Who do you think you are?'

He was kicking me for a long, long time, but then he suddenly bent down and yanked me upright by my hair. He lifted me up and then punched my head into the wall, pushing me up against it so I was trapped. His gravelly animal instinct kicked in then; ever since the attack in the kitchen in 1996, when he'd bitten my hand, he'd had this instinct to attack my face with his teeth if he was getting frustrated. And he was getting frustrated. He used to bite me and let go, bite me and let go. So when he raged towards me with his mouth stretched wide, like a hound from hell, his teeth vicious pinchers set to clamp down hard on my skin, I thought I knew what to expect. I thought we'd covered this. I thought I was prepared.

I should have learned by now: you can never prepare for my ex.

He lunged at my face, and his teeth went right into my nose, both sides. He grabbed my nose in his jaws – and he lifted me off the floor with his teeth, growling at me as he did it. It was like he had some sort of superpower, like he'd charged himself up, and he lifted me all the way off the ground and then dropped me. I instinctively lifted my hands to my face as he lunged in again, and he took a chunk out of two of my fingers, biting right through to the bone. He spat out the skin as he snarled at me, and then drove his teeth into the flesh of my raised arm as I cowered beneath it.

He got bored with that, or perhaps he was annoyed that I still wasn't broken, because then he pulled me onto the bed and jumped on top of me, pushing his knees against my splayed elbows to pin me down. I was trying to wriggle my legs on his back to get him off me, but it was useless. He was too heavy for me, too intent on his mission. He was only about 10.5 stone to my 7.5, but I was weak: weak from shock, blood loss, sleep deprivation, food deprivation, years and years and years of abuse. I didn't stand a chance.

He began punching my head, from side to side, side to side. Then, ages after, he started punching my chest. The chest hurt more than the head because I'd blocked out the pain; he'd kicked and punched me in the head so much that afternoon it had gone completely numb. But when he started punching my chest it was a new pain, a new method of attack. It was what he always did: *If A isn't working, try B. I will make this whore break, I will destroy her* … As his fists pummelled into my breasts and ribs, I could feel my breathing was being affected. I couldn't breathe. I started to panic – *live die live die live die* – trying to breathe with him punching my chest.

Then he went back to my head. He was punching my ears. He was punching my eyes. He was punching my nose, my cheeks, my chin, my whole entire face. My ears were bleeding; my eyeballs, my nostrils. Blood streamed around me in thick coppery rivers, and my face swelled up to ten times its usual size. Both my eardrums shattered under his blows, so then I couldn't hear the mindless words he was raining upon me, slagging me off, putting me down, abusing me with every strike.

And still he kept on hitting.

A break: a clearing in the clouds around my head. Cutting like lightning through the smog: pain, pain, pain. He pressed his thumbs to my eyeballs and *pushed*. Pain sliced through the white space in my brain and brought me right into the moment. Agony behind my eyes, all down my cheeks, my eyeballs feeling like they were bursting at the back of my head. Pure blood everywhere, eyes swelling, swelling, swelling. When my eyelids peeled back, a black cloak had been cast over everything. All I could make out was a dark shape above me: him.

Him raising his fists and hitting me hard in the head, over and over again.

For around four or five hours, that part of the attack went on – then he suddenly jumped off me. I was drifting in and out of consciousness. He was mumbling to himself, but I couldn't hear what he was saying. The black shape ran out of the room and I thought, with blessed relief, *It's over. He's finished what he's doing.*

He started singing then. Weird words: something like 'I'm gonna get you …' Because I was going in and out, I wasn't altogether there, and I don't know exactly what it was. But the kids could hear. The kids could hear everything.

They heard him run downstairs and rifle through the drawers. And then they heard: *swish swish. Swish swish. Swish swish.*

He was sharpening knives in the kitchen.

He did it for ages, over and over, knife after knife. Then he came up the stairs, clutching his booty, mumbling to himself. Mumbling about how he was going to cut my body up.

He came back into the bedroom. I was barely with it, but my survival instinct somehow kicked in. My eyes were so swollen I could only see through slants, and as I tried to look out through them, I could just make out through the black cloak of blindness that he was coming towards me. He was swiping the knives towards me, left to right. They were long knives: meat cleavers and twelve-inch bread knives. He had about three or four in both hands and he was wielding them in front of him, like in the psycho films. I was trying to edge backwards but I wasn't really with it, so he kept catching me, cutting me on my arms, which I was putting up to protect myself, as I tried desperately to dodge out of his way. He just went on and on and on. He'd got my clothes off at some point in the attack on the bed – I have no idea when – so I was naked, fighting this knife-wielding maniac with nothing more than my bare hands, hardly able to see the blades he was cutting me with. Left to right, left to right: over and over again they came.

Then suddenly, whip sharp, he grabbed me by the hair and sliced off chunks of my plaits, laughing, saying he was giving me a new hairdo. Then he pulled me out of the bedroom, taking the knives with him. He dragged me naked down the corridor by what was left of my hair – and together we burst into Corice and Darren's room.

The kids were sleeping – or, rather, pretending to be asleep. As he chucked me into their bedroom, into a heap on the floor, Corice sat up on her top bunk and started screaming her head off. And no wonder. I was an absolute mess. Stark naked, bloody and beaten: my whole body was just a battered ruin. Chunks had been taken out of me. My hair had been ripped out of my scalp. My face was swollen, my eyes two bruised plums with blood trailing down my cheeks like tears. A nightmare vision come to haunt their dreams.

I don't remember Darren crying. He was on the bottom bunk, my five-year-old boy. There was no time to reassure either one of my children – though what words I could have used to salve them, I have no idea – because Dusty lifted me up off the floor then. He grabbed a scrap of my hair in his fist and yanked me to my feet. I wobbled in his vicious hold, swinging as though on a hangman's noose … facing the same fate.

He stuck a knife in my throat, right underneath my chin. I felt it prick there, kissing my neck with its cold metal tongue. He leaned in close and spoke into my shattered ears, loud enough for the children to hear. This message was meant for us all.

'You are all gonna die,' he said. 'And it's your fault. Because you're a whore. It's your fault that they're all gonna die. I'm going to have to kill *everybody* because of *you*.'

He dropped me to the floor and as my heartbeat thundered in my ears – *live die live die live die* – I couldn't cope with any more. The blackness swallowed me whole, and I faded clean away.

My last thought, as I saw my ex start towards the bunk beds with the knives in his hand, was: *Not my children, dear God, please God, not my children …*

I thought I had blacked out. It was Corice, later, who told me differently.

I was in a broken heap on the ground. Dusty went to walk across to the bunk beds. He had the blades in his hands, and he was going to get Darren first. He thought I was out of it. *I* thought I was out of it. It was only Corice, watching in terror from the top bunk, who saw what happened next.

The bloody mess in a heap on the floor crawled across the bedroom on her battered hands and knees. She laid her hands on the madman with the knives. Somehow, she found the strength to clutch at him and pull him to the ground, before he got to the kids. I did that. I did that without even knowing it. He was not going near my children.

He tumbled to the ground in a tangle of limbs and razor-sharp weaponry. And Corice said that he then jumped up, like an animal, and charged out of the bedroom and down the stairs, like he was on a mission to do something.

I staggered to my feet.

'Stay in your room,' I told the children. 'Stay in bed. You lock yourselves in and you stay in here. Do not come out of your room.'

I thanked God I'd fitted locks on the children's rooms, on the inside, so they could lock themselves in. Perhaps I knew that one day they would need them.

That day had finally come.

And then: darkness. All the lights went out, suddenly, as though the power had stopped dead. It was pitch-black. Alarms started going off, loud, loud, our fire alarm piercing through even my ruined eardrums.

As Corice and Darren locked their door, and I hobbled back to the bedroom, I saw another door opening down the hall. It was Jahméne, coming out of his and Isaac's room to see what was going on. Daniel was just behind him.

'Go back to your bedroom!' I shouted at them. 'Lock your door!'

Then we all heard their father coming up the stairs. A light came with him too. A blue light; a blue flame. He'd been out to the shed and got the blowtorch. He'd taken the time to put a new gas can on it, so the flame was huge and powerful: two to three foot long and an inch wide.

I had pushed him to the floor. He was going to make me pay.

'We should call the police …' I heard Jahméne say.

'Just stay out the way – *please*, kids!' I told my boys.

Still their dad kept coming, burning things as he went. I later found out that he'd been testing the flame outside; he'd caught an electric wire with the blowtorch and that's what had tripped the lights and the alarms. He was burning stuff as he made his way through the house, playing with the big blue flame.

'I need to phone the police but I *can't* phone the police,' I heard Dan say to his brother. They were getting frustrated about what to do. They were only kids, and all their lives they had seen their dad dominate and rule – not just our world but every authority that we ever came into contact with. Their dad had told them he would kill their siblings if they ever spoke out. How could they risk it? They didn't know what to do.

Their dad was at the top of the stairs now. He started towards me in the bedroom.

'Stay out the way!' he screamed at his sons as he went. 'Stay in your bedroom!'

And then he came charging towards me, with the blowtorch on full beam.

Chapter Seven

As he entered the bedroom, he was waving it from left to right, laughing. Like: 'I'm gonna get you.' Proper psycho.

I jumped on the bed. I had nowhere to run to. I was on the bed, half upright, naked. And I just thought, *Crap*.

He stopped by the door. He had something to show me. He started burning the door slowly, going up in a line with the flame. 'Oh, look how quick that burns.'

He moved into the room, found something metal. He burned it. 'Oh, it burns metal, too.'

He was trying it out on things as he came towards me, showing off its power. I could only watch through my cloaked eyes, petrified. I could feel its heat even from a distance. A blowtorch flame is thousands upon thousands of degrees hotter than normal flames. It's the hottest searing flame you can have and it was melting everything in its path.

How can I protect myself from this? I thought desperately. My natural reaction was always to put my arms up, to protect my face, but I could see that he was boring holes through things that were far, far tougher than me.

Still, he came towards me. He was talking aloud about maiming and melting and disfiguring, working his way around the room, left to right, left to right, for ages, like a game. Every time he caught something with the flame, it disintegrated instantly.

I screamed. In fear, in blind panic. My cries chimed with the alarms that were still going off. Noise and chaos all around.

I went further and further back on the bed, until I ran out of space to move anymore. He had hemmed me in, like I was a sheep he was preparing for slaughter. I pulled a pillow in front of me, by my knees, for what little protection it could afford, but he aimed the torch straight at it, laughing. The flame bore right through the pillow and a rotten stink filled the room. Burning feathers. It was a gross smell, and it fermented with all the other odours in the room: burned wood, burned metal, blood and sweat and fear. It stank. He aimed between my legs, just below my stomach, and as the flame tore through the pillow he caught me, for the first time, down below. I screamed again, choking on the pain and my own tears. I was sobbing and sobbing, on my knees on the bed, while he stood in front of me with the flame, wielding it left to right, left to right, taunting and tormenting me.

'Just do it,' I said, in a stupid panic, not thinking correctly. He had already burned me, and I could think of nothing but the agony of my searing flesh.

I brought my arms up to defend myself, and he directed the flame at them as I shifted on the bed. He caught my arms and my hands in the blazing heat. I could feel myself melting … but I couldn't do anything about it. I could feel the intensity of the heat, those thousands of degrees concentrated on my bare freckled skin. Even after the flame had gone into me and come back out again, it felt like it was still there. The burning went on and on and on …

My ex sniffed. 'Smell that burning flesh,' he snarled loudly, with an evil laugh.

I remember thinking, *Oh my God, he has completely lost his mind*. He was like some ravaged living-dead creature, spitting venom and acting out the worst nightmare yet. The thing was … THIS WAS REAL.

He caught my stomach again with the flame. Searing heat. I turned around on the bed, trying to scramble away – from him, from the pain, from the flame – so he burned my back. He burned my hair. There was a point where he was trying to bore a hole in my leg, mid-thigh, aiming the flame deliberately, watching his trail of destruction with his eyes all slanted, a crazed animal let loose.

And then … I saw Daniel. He was kneeling on the floor in the hallway, by the bedroom door, with his hands on his head. Time stood still for me and him as we locked eyes. He couldn't move. He was frozen in fear.

I barely had the strength to scream, but I tried to tell him, 'Get the police, now!' I thought his dad was going to kill me, kill us all.

But Daniel didn't move. He couldn't: he was powerless. That memory stays with me; a memory I now have to live with, every day. I felt tears run down my cheeks with sheer and utter sorrow that my first-born had to witness such a horrific sight. And I am left with this vision of my boy for eternity.

Out of everything, it haunts me more than the actual flame itself.

Dusty turned around to Daniel then, the blowtorch still burning brightly in his hand. I summoned all my strength, fuelled by fear, and I yelled at Daniel at the top of my voice: 'RUN! GET OUT!'

Daniel stumbled to his feet then, blinded by what he had seen and couldn't forget, and he ran into Jahméne and Isaac's room. He barricaded it behind him, so his dad couldn't come in after them.

Safe. He was safe.

But I was not.

Dusty turned back to me. I began begging him to end it, to kill me, because I couldn't play this game anymore. I was in absolute ... *beyond* agony. *This needs to stop*, I thought frantically. Alarms were still sounding out ten to the dozen and, despite everything, I actually thought the police or fire brigade might turn up. And then another thought struck me: *If he kills me now, the children will be free of him. He won't get away with this.*

There and then, I experienced this strong urge to die that was so emotionally overpowering.

I felt I had to sacrifice myself for my children's freedom.

Everything moved in slow motion, like speed had been sucked out of the night. In between my staggered heartbeats, marking the tempo of his torture, I suddenly thought, *I can't actually die because I need to be here for my kids.*

My kids ...

I had this overwhelming rush, like I was coming back into my body: *I need to stay alive. I have to stay alive.* I changed my tactics. I sort of went towards him, and he stepped back suddenly and dropped the blowtorch on the floor. Then he ran out into the corridor and sat down upon the stairs. Jahméne would later peer cautiously out of his bedroom door to see him sitting there, biting hard on his own arm, and crying. Crying like he knew he'd gone too far.

I didn't know where he went; I knew only that he was gone. As my body still burned from the flame, from the holes bored right through my skin, I blacked out.

*

Blinking. My eyes were blinking. Why couldn't I see properly? What had happened?

It was early on the Monday morning – maybe six, seven o'clock. I was lying on the bed. I was alone.

I looked around me. What I could see of the room through my swollen eyes was like a war zone. The bed had been burned, holes in everything: the pillows, the sheets, the hard wooden frame. Everything around it was melted. There was blood all up the walls, on the fixtures and fittings: on the TV, the carpet, the bed. There was smashed glass. He'd melted the wall and there were patches of burned bits and blood, and bits of my scalp stuck fast to it from where he'd punched my head into the wall. The sheets were sodden with blood, red stains marking where I'd bled straight out onto the sheets. It was like a bloody massacre, everywhere I looked.

I was trying to think what had happened, but my brain was protecting me. It was still in that shut-off state, the place I went to so I couldn't feel pain. I had sore bits, but my brain wouldn't let me focus on them. I'd tripped a switch in my head and all I felt was an eerie, cold numbness. I'd tricked my mind to stop feeling pain in order to get me through it. There was just a numb dead feeling. A numb, near-dead woman, lying in a heap upon the bed.

My brain tripped the switch for me this time, and I passed out into unconsciousness once more.

When I came to the next time, Dusty was there. He was shaking me, angry, saying words that reached me dully: 'You need to drink.'

The curtains were shut, but there was light in the room: July sunshine, fighting to get through the thick red drapes.

My ex had a glass of water in his hand. He was trying to make me drink.

I couldn't drink. My face was swollen, my mouth mashed up. Shards from the half-pint glass he'd bashed into my face at the start of the attack were still studded in my skin. His hours-long beating round my head had smashed up all my teeth. My lips were pointing every which way, torn asunder by his fists and the broken glass and the fragments of my teeth. My mouth was just a mess; I couldn't even get the water in it. It was dribbling down my face and I had no energy even to help him give me the liquid.

I flaked out back onto the bed. That whole day, I drifted in and out of consciousness. I remember it through a haze.

In the distance, through my broken ears, I remember hearing ringing bells, over and over: the telephone. It was Monday – my first day as manager of the post office. The keys to open up were sitting in my handbag. Perhaps they were ringing to find out where I was.

I could hear other things, too: the children, playing in the next room. I listened as hard as I could to their voices. I was counting them all, counting them in: *That's Daniel; that's Jahméne. That's my Darren. That's Isaac's voice; that's Corice.* I was counting them to see they were safe. *The children are all alive,* I thought, *they're all OK.* Relief flooded through me, freshwater swimming through my broken veins.

At some point during the day, when I came back to my own mind after blacking out, he was there again. I was very aware that he was still angry and that he was still on a mission. And as I lay there, not able to move, bloody and broken and battered, he got on top of me, and he raped me.

I can't even think how he could do that in the state I was in.

It wasn't working for him, actually, because it went on for ages and ages. He couldn't get what he wanted to do right. And I could feel myself, even when he was raping me, going out of consciousness – but when I came round, he was still there, doing what he was doing.

I used to have a cross on a chain on the end of my bed: a present my old friend Shania had given me, long ago. Sometimes I'd hide it, but it was there that day. It was a rosary, much treasured; a crucifix about three inches long. I focused on it. It gave me strength.

He saw me looking at it.

'God won't save you because you're not worth it,' he said, derision heavy in his voice. 'Why do you think God's gonna save *you*?'

He grabbed the rosary and looped it around my neck. He pulled it tight, strangling me with it, as he raped me deep inside.

'Where's your God now, huh?' he jeered. 'You're not worth saving.'

He threw the crucifix to the floor, like it was rubbish, and he kept on thrusting.

'Does that hurt?' he said, enjoying it. 'You deserve this.'

I stared up at the ceiling. I was crying, not from upset, but because I couldn't stop the tears that ran down my cheeks. I was in so much pain they flowed uncontrollably from my swollen eyes. You would only know those kinds of tears from experiencing this level of pain: saltwater running with no emotion attached, just running endlessly; there was no stopping them.

But the tears burned. The salt in them stung my wounds as they trickled out. They were like acid, dripping into all the cuts, hurting me all over again.

I looked up at him, at his evil face looking down and watching me, not wanting to miss a moment of my suffering. I was just thinking, *How can you be doing this, when I'm like this? How? What* are *you?* And his face ... his face was just like: 'I am going to inflict the most pain on you that I possibly can, but not actually kill you ... yet.'

He kept on rambling, talking to me, to himself, like he was convincing himself that it was OK, what he was doing; that I deserved it; that he was doing it right.

I stared back up at the ceiling, all hope gone. For a minute, again, I begged God to take me. I said it so deep in my mind.

But a voice came back to me: 'It's not your time yet.'

Why? Why? I thought. But the voice didn't say anything more.

So then it was just the two of us, and him raping me, over and over.

Inevitably, as time passed, I needed the toilet. I told him, but he said I wasn't allowed to go.

'I don't want the kids seeing you like this,' he said, his eyes raking over my naked, bleeding body. 'This is all your fault. It's your fault you're in this state. I don't want the kids to know what you look like right now.'

So I had to wait until they were all out of the way, tucked up in bed sleeping – or trying to. I remember crawling along the corridor to the toilet. I hauled myself up to sit on the loo, and he stood watching me. It was a small cubicle, with just the toilet in there, and he banged the door into the wall and simply stood there with his hands on his hips, not letting me out of his sight.

I tried to pee, but I couldn't. I couldn't even push; I couldn't do anything. So I was just sat there, nothing coming out. After a few beats, he dragged me back up and said I was wasting his time. He threw me back in the bedroom.

We went through that routine three or four times throughout that long night. My bladder kept telling me I needed to go, but when I got there, I couldn't; his scrutiny rendering my body useless. On the third or fourth time, I managed a slim trickle of urine, and I burst into tears.

Because it stung like crap to pee. Yet it stung like crap to cry. Everything … everything hurt *so much*.

I think I tried to lean on the wall or something, barely able to stay upright by myself, and suddenly his fist came powering into my face while I was sat on the loo.

'Stop feeling sorry for yourself,' he said in disgust, annoyed by my weakness and my tears. He pushed and pulled me, then dragged me off the loo and along the corridor … and back into the bedroom.

That was Monday, 8 July.

Tuesday came around. And Dusty decided I should eat something.

I remember him coming into the bedroom. I'd been going in and out of consciousness, but I struggled to sit up as he came in, not wanting to be on my back anymore, all vulnerable. I was a tiny bit more with it, and I found the black film over my eyes had lifted a little bit. That was such a huge, huge relief, because I'd thought I was never going to be able to see again, but on the Tuesday a little more vision filtered through the black smoke. I still couldn't see normally, but I could see a touch more than I had the day before.

I could see well enough to notice that Dusty had something in his hand as he came towards me. 'You need to eat,' he told me.

Through my shattered eardrums, I heard the pop of a bag of crisps being opened. It was like he'd gone out and thought, *What can I give her to make her suffer even more pain?*

And he'd found his answer: salt and vinegar crisps.

He held the bag in his hands and dug his fingers into the silver packet. He lifted a handful of crisps out. 'Eat them,' he ordered.

My mouth was like a horror film. Broken teeth embedded in my cheek. Broken glass studded in my skin. Lips split every which way. One side of my mouth even had a hole in it, all the way through. I can't even word it properly, what the inside of my mouth was like.

'I can't,' I said, in a gravelly, unused voice that didn't sound like mine. 'No.'

You could never say 'no' to Dusty.

He shoved the crisps into my face, their salt stinging in my wounds, ignoring my protestations. Classic, isn't it, salt in the wound? Works every time. It stung like mad. He grabbed another fistful and shoved more at my ruined face. 'You need to eat,' he growled at me. 'Eat.'

I was trying to spit the crisps out.

'Trying to starve yourself to death, are you?' he jeered.

And I thought, *He's gonna get really angry if I don't eat.* And then: *Oh, just do it, Mandy.*

But I found I couldn't, even when I tried. I couldn't actually move my mouth to chew or make it open and close because it was that busted up. I couldn't even feel the muscles that I wanted to use. Dusty got angry, and stormed off …

Stormed off to be with the children. I listened closely. I could hear him laughing, as though he was playing happily with them. The kids told me later: he was. He was making them breakfast and cooking them dinner, getting their clothes out and getting them dressed, and playing games with them, like nothing was wrong.

They hadn't seen me since he'd attacked me with the blowtorch. They thought I was dead; they thought he'd killed me. They weren't allowed to ask about Mummy in the next room.

They were so, so scared.

But he was laughing and playing Happy Daddy in front of them. They had no choice but to act happy for him because he was acting like a psychopath. So they all laughed together, while I lay on the bed in the bedroom, drifting in and out of consciousness, barely keeping it together.

Dusty suddenly had a surge of energy. He started going round the house, moving things about. I remember him coming into the bedroom and fiddling around with books and papers, and sitting down at the computer and tapping away on it.

What's he doing? I thought. *I need to be alert to what he's doing.*

He was ranting and rambling, and I forced my ears to tune into his words.

'Right,' he was saying, as though he'd come to a decision.

And then he said: 'It's finally come to the time when you're going to have to die.'

Chapter Eight

What? I thought, my brain not willing to process it, not after everything I'd been through. *No ...*

'This is it,' he then continued, in a completely normal tone of voice. 'We've got to this point and it's gone too far now, so you've got to die. And what I'm going to do is chop your body up into bits.'

No no no no no ...

'But I'm *not* going to bury you in one place – because the police will cotton on to that. So I'm going to put your head at the bottom of the garden, and then I'll put your arms somewhere else. So that it takes them years to find your whole body.

'I might put your legs under the stairs,' he said reflectively. 'I'm having a think.'

I started panicking. I was having a panic attack, right there on the bed, my breath catching in my throat till I thought I was going to pass out.

He paused in his rambling, scarily thoughtful speech. I was panting hard, and the rhythm and volume of my loud breathing was annoying him.

So he left the room. Got a hammer, and started ripping up the carpet and the floorboards on the landing outside ... so he could check how much space there was between the floors. I heard him talking to himself again.

'I'm going to put her legs there – or her arms, because either of those will fit there.'

I couldn't breathe, I was panicking so much. And I just kept thinking about the kids. I was praying and praying to God to keep my kids safe and alive. *Please let them be safe*, I begged Him. *If anything, take me, because nothing's going to stop Dusty doing what he wants to me, but please save the kids. The kids need to survive this.*

Dusty came back into the bedroom. He was as calm as anything. He looked at me lying on the bed, as though he was sizing up a cow's carcass.

'I'm going to cut your head off first,' he said, 'and then I'll bag that and I'll take it to the park. I need to get some black bags. If I put your leg in a black bag … '

He was mulling over how to do it all. He looked at my feet.

'Well, that knife won't do,' he said, shaking his head as though imagining he was sawing into my shin with a specific blade. 'I'm going to have to sharpen the bone chopper. I'll have to chop your feet off with that.'

We had a bone chopper in the kitchen downstairs. A ten-by six-inch blade. It was what the butchers used for meat. That's what he was planning to use on me.

He left the room again. I heard him banging about, going through all the cupboards and drawers and dragging things out. He was building a big bonfire outside in the garden, and he was throwing anything that was connected to me into the flames. Books, writing, art, my knitting … anything to do with me. He was burning stuff and breaking stuff and binning stuff – throwing it into these big, strong black sacks that weren't the normal ones we used for rubbish.

Everything was engineered for just one purpose: he was trying to erase my existence.

I lost all sense of time. He was very busy all day long, that was all I knew, with the burning and the breaking and the thinking about how best to chop me up. It took him hours: taking up the floorboards, throwing stuff out, typing away for ages on the computer; a constant tapping that punctuated my lapses in and out of consciousness. Once, when he was banging away downstairs, still muttering to himself, I gathered my courage and forced myself to hobble off the bed, trying to ignore the agony of every step. In the corner of the room, the computer glowed: he had left it open, unwatched. I thought, *I need to get help from somebody*. I managed to drag myself over to the machine and I emailed his sister, just one word: HELP.

I don't know why I chose her; perhaps I thought she, out of everyone, might be someone who could talk him down. She tried phoning my mobile, later, but I wasn't allowed to answer it. A lot of people had been ringing, in fact, but no one came to call.

At last, I guess, the sun set and it was night-time. I had no idea what the time was. I had been trapped in the horror house since Sunday afternoon; it was now Tuesday night. I hadn't been cleaned or been given permission to clean myself, so I was still covered in blood: some of it dried; some of my injuries were still oozing red, while others were tacky as my wounds tried to close themselves up. I must have stunk to high heaven. I still couldn't see, couldn't hear at all properly. I had no strength to raise my head. I couldn't even bear to look at my body; I didn't want to see the damage he had caused. I kind of detached myself from my physical body, in order not to feel pain.

He came back into the bedroom. He dragged me off the bed and hung me over its wooden edge. That was deliberate, so I'd get pain from both sides: from the hard wood of the bedframe on my hips, and from him, raping me from behind. He was laughing, like it was funny, what he was doing. I was crying and crying. He was thrusting and smirking.

And then … he took it up another level. He kept me bent over the bed. My feet were on the floor, but I wasn't really standing; I had no strength to stand. He kicked my feet apart and then positioned me on this spindle of wood at the edge of the bed, and he stood up behind me. He pushed my head down into the mattress. Then he held me steady, and he buggered me.

It was the ultimate humiliation. And he knew he was giving me ultimate pain on top of everything else he'd done. This was it: the final degradation.

He had tried to break me for so, so long. I had withstood him for so, so long. But as he thrust inside me, driving me against the bed – each movement agony for me, from inside out – I felt myself hanging on by only a single, fragile thread.

I wish I was dead, I thought in my head. I thought it in time with his thrusts. *I wish I was dead I wish I was dead.*

Words spinning round in my head.

I wish I was dead I wish I was dead I wish I was dead.

I heard him laugh in delight: unknowingly, I was saying it out loud.

'I wish I was dead, I wish I was dead.'

He seized my head by the remnants of my hair and twisted it round to make me look at him. He was desperate to see my face. He drank everything in, getting off on the fact I wanted to die.

He gritted his teeth and smiled, and thrust into me even harder. He pushed my head away from him, and then kept pulling it up and forcing me to look into his nasty slanted eyes. With each thrust he could visibly see that he was causing the utmost pain. He smiled because he knew he was doing that.

'You want to be dead, do you?' he panted. I could hear the smile in his voice. 'Death's not good enough for you.'

I was hanging on by a single thread, but he wouldn't cut me free.

I felt guilty, then. Immense guilt. Even as he took me, raped and buggered me, even as I begged to die, I thought, *My kids are in the next room. They need me. They need me to survive.*

I told myself: *You need to snap out of that thought. Right now. Right now, Mandy. Stay alive.*

He finished, and let me go. I crawled back onto the bed. I was bleeding from every orifice, and I collapsed in a heap on the red-stained sheets.

And then: I felt the mattress move as he climbed into bed next to me. He climbed into bed next to me … and he fell fast asleep.

Wednesday morning. I opened my eyes slowly. By degrees, my vision was coming back. As the light poured more openly into my eyes, I winced: too bright. I had the biggest headache on the planet that morning, the migraine from hell. It made my skull feel like I couldn't even lift it up because it weighed a ton; it was hurting that much.

It was hurting … Bit by bit, I was starting to feel again; I was coming back from my numb, dead state.

I began to touch my wounds gingerly as I lay there on the bed, trying to catalogue where I'd got injuries and holes, cuts and burns. I thought frankly, *I stink, and I'm covered in crap*. My eyes scanned the room around me, but I couldn't see any mirrors. There were no mirrors anywhere. I don't know if he took the mirrors away but there was nothing I could use to see what I actually looked like.

I was alone, I saw; Dusty was off somewhere else. I forced my damaged ears to listen. I could hear a kerfuffle from inside the house: the kids going up and down the stairs, like they did every morning before school. I listened to the fading patter of their feet, and then I heard the front door slam.

I heard a car starting up outside, and driving off.

The kids … he's got the kids!

Panic rose in my chest. What was he planning to do?

I remembered, with crystal clarity, his words yesterday: 'You've got to die. And what I'm going to do is chop your body up into bits … '

I have to get up, I thought. *I have to get out. I have to save the kids.*

For I remembered his words over the years, too: 'I'm going to kill the kids. I'm going to gas every single one of them to death … I'm going to kill the kids one by one and make you watch and then I'm going to kill you last so you suffer.'

Now he had them, God knew where, in a car that could quickly become a killing machine. *Is this the day?* I wondered helplessly. *Is this the day he's going to snuff them out forever, my five bright candles burning against the dark?*

Not if I had anything to do with it. With difficulty, I dragged myself to the edge of the bed, my head reeling, feeling sick and unsteady. Every time I moved, pain wracked through my body.

I concentrated solely on the sheer effort of getting to the edge of the bed.

I concentrated so hard I didn't hear him come back. I didn't hear him come in.

'What are you doing?'

I glanced up at him, fearful.

'Where do you think you're going?' he sneered.

'I need the toilet,' I said. 'I need a wash.'

That was true, at least.

He came over and helped me up. He got my arm over his shoulder so he could drag me along the floor. My legs wouldn't work properly. It was like I couldn't operate any of my muscles. It was weird: I'd go to use something, assuming it would just naturally work, and it wouldn't. I had no control.

He plonked me down on the loo and I managed to go, every drop stinging me down below, running raw into the wounds he'd made last night.

'I'll run you a shower,' he said then. 'Get in there and clean yourself up. You look a mess.'

He helped me into the shower – I was so shaky I couldn't have managed it by myself – and then he disappeared; went off out somewhere. *The kids must be at school*, I realised. *Safe.*

I couldn't stand up in the shower, so I curled into a ball in the base of the white tub, my knees drawn up into my chest. The water was hitting me. And with every drop of water that touched my skin, it was like being burned and stabbed all over again. It hurt so much: sheer pain.

I sat in there for ages and ages. And, eventually, the water ran cold. I liked that feeling. Everything went numb.

I opened my eyes. The water was splashing off me: splashing blood all up the walls, red on white. I watched bits of my body float down from my head as the shower pulsed on my skull. Chunks of my scalp, with hair attached, just fell off my head: parts of my body falling into the bath. Each and every wound bled into the tub, until it was full of blood and skin tissue.

I was looking at the mess, and thinking numbly, *Am I ever going to recover from this? Or am I going to die?*

I remember thinking, too: *Why am I even having a shower? He's going to chop me up and kill me.*

I couldn't rub myself to wash; it was too painful. I just sat there, in the cold stream of water, in the bloody tub, watching my body fall to pieces before my eyes, for what seemed like hours and hours and hours.

I heard a voice.

I raised my head from where it was bowed on my drawn-up knees.

'Mandy … Mandy,' it called, as though from a great distance.

I thought I was hearing things. *He's gone out*, I thought. I was in the house on my own; I must be cracking up.

'Mandy … Mandy,' it called again.

I gingerly placed my hands on the edge of the bath and hauled myself up. Dusty's dressing gown was hanging up in the bathroom, so I grabbed it and wrapped it round myself, not bothering to put my arms in. It smelt of him, and I nearly gagged.

'Mandy … Mandy.'

What is *that?*

Bang! There was banging on the bedroom window. *What on earth …?*

The shower room was next to my bedroom. I opened the door and peered out.

Through a gap in the curtains, I could see there was a man at the window, two storeys up, banging on the glass and shouting my name.

'Mandy! Mandy!' He spotted me. 'Are you OK?'

I stared at him in disbelief. I saw the uniform he was wearing.

After eighteen years, the police had finally come to call.

PART FIVE

THE RESCUE

I wish I could free my mind
Leave everything bad behind
With just enough room for things
That are kind

I wish I could live my life
Without the fear
Of a torture that's near
A day without shedding a tear …
To let me see clear.

Chapter One

'Are you OK?' the policeman at my window said. 'What's the matter? Where's your partner?' He was bombarding me with questions.

'I don't know anything,' I said. I felt so many mixed emotions it was impossible to process them all at once. But one feeling rose to the surface, learned by heart through years of hard lessons: *You shouldn't be here.*

'He'll think I've called you,' I said to the copper, the realisation dawning on me. The officer was up a ladder outside my house, for anyone in the neighbourhood to see. 'He'll think I've called you and he'll kill the kids. You need to go. You need to go right now and find my children. If he's got the kids, he'll kill them. You need to go get my kids. Go! Now!'

His head disappeared from the window and he ran off. The urgency of the situation gave me newfound strength. I got myself downstairs, just in time to hear a loud banging on the front door. I opened it up and a guy from down the road was there, a gangster-type who was 'frenemies' with my ex.

'What's going on?' he questioned me at once. 'The police have been going up and down the street … '

He trailed off. He took a good look at me: at my plum-like eyes, at my ruined mouth, my strangled neck, my battered face. 'Oh my God … '

Then, just like that, he ran off. I didn't know where he was headed, I just knew, more than ever, that I had to get to my kids.

I grabbed the phone and with shaking hands I dialled the younger children's primary school. As soon as they picked up, I started talking. 'Are my kids with you? Have you got my kids? Where are my kids?'

'Calm down,' said the teacher. 'Calm down, Mandy.'

Then she said words that drove five wooden stakes deep into my heart: 'I'm sorry, but your ex has got them.'

She was sorry for a reason, too. A bloody good reason. In fact, it beggars belief that the school let him take them. Because the reason the police had come to my window that morning was not because a neighbour had called to report the blaring alarms and my cries for help in the middle of the night. It wasn't because someone had seen the bonfire and my ex's crazed activities preparing for my murder.

It was because my scared little girl had spoken out.

That morning, as soon as she'd got to school, Corice had gone up to her teacher and whispered, 'I think my dad's killed my mum.' She only spoke out because she thought I was dead. For three days, she'd been living with that horrible secret, and it came out of her like vomit, desecrating the sunny summer day.

Her teacher told the principal, and the principal rang the police. The copper at my window had been sent to the house to ascertain if I was alive or dead. All thanks to Corice.

And yet, with the school knowing what she'd said, they thought it was perfectly reasonable to let her go when my ex drove up and demanded to take all my kids.

'What?' I screamed down the phone at the teacher. I didn't know then what had happened, but I knew my ex was a nasty piece of work. 'Why have you let him take them?' I sobbed. I went absolutely ballistic, crying and yelling, delirious, driven mad with suffering, screaming down the phone at this teacher.

A noise outside: a car. I heard it pull into our drive and a car door slam and then the sound of rushing feet coming to the door. I dropped the phone. As I limped as quickly as I could to leave the kitchen, the front door flew open and my ex came storming into the house. He pushed past me, ranting to himself. And then the kids followed him in. I watched them, one by one, traipsing past me, white-faced and terrified. *Darren, Isaac, Corice, Jahméne.* I counted them in. I thought with relief, *They're alive.* It was just the younger ones; Dan was at a different school. And my ex had gone to collect the little ones for a reason.

Somehow, he'd found out it was Corice who'd 'blabbed'. And so all the way home from school, he'd been threatening them, telling them they were all going to die *because of Corice.* Telling them it was *all her fault.* So much blood had drained from her face she looked as white as a sheet. She was so, so scared. The kids looked relieved – inadequate word – to see me standing there, but they couldn't run to me, not when their dad was around.

Not while we still weren't safe.

Dusty was pacing the kitchen, that prowling animal again, going backwards and forwards, tense energy growing like a fireball with every stride. He had his fists clenched by his sides and he was muttering to himself, with his head down, 'What to do, what to do, what to do …' He knew he was in trouble. He was trying to figure out a way to get out of this one.

While he was distracted, I silently pointed upstairs to the children. I wanted them to go up and get out of his way.

After they'd gone, Dusty seemed to have a brainwave. He ran up the stairs too – but he wasn't after the kids. He grabbed a hammer and he started nailing the carpet back into the floorboards, trying to cover his tracks.

The children had heard what he'd said, though, about how he was going to kill me and chop me up and put me in the floor. So they thought he was preparing. They thought there was going to be a bloody massacre. They all started screaming, in absolute terror, absolute fear.

I was stranded at the bottom of the stairs, without the strength or the muscle control to climb back up. I couldn't see what was going on. There was just the screaming and the hammering, ringing in my ears.

Bang! Bang! Bang! A knocking at the door to add to the chaos. I could see through the kitchen window that it was the police.

I called up to him, quietly, mumbling through my sore mouth. 'You need to hand yourself in. You can't carry on doing this. You've got to stop.'

He ignored me. He was pacing like a crazy man. I thought I knew what he was thinking: *No no no, I can't do that.* He started banging the carpet with the hammer again.

'I need to do it properly,' he was saying. 'Yes, I need to do that.'

The next minute, the front door was rammed in, and my ex started down the stairs. A load of coppers – about ten of them – swarmed in and he assessed them, coolly, from his lofty position on the stairs.

He came down slowly, then. He put out his hands to be arrested: calmly, ready for the cuffs. He smiled at them, as though to say: 'Take me.' As though he wasn't worried. As though he was going to get off, to get away with it: as he had in London, as he had in Birmingham, as he had in Bath.

And I thought, *Yeah, I bet he will get away with it.* Nothing seemed different this time round to all the times before.

As the police arrested him, Corice and Jahméne came pelting down the stairs to stand beside me. Dusty heard them and he turned, ever so slowly, and fixed his eyes on Corice. He gave her an evil, evil look. She was ten years old, and she cowered against me at her daddy's malicious gaze.

'This is all … your … fault,' he told her, quietly at first. Then he shouted: 'This is because of YOU!'

The police manhandled him out, not reacting at all to him threatening a ten-year-old girl. As soon as the door closed behind them, Jahméne burst into tears. It was the first time the kids had seen me in three days.

'We thought you were dead,' he sobbed, '*I* thought you were dead.'

Corice was trying to hug me, they both were – but I couldn't hug them back because I was in such a mess. My ribs were bruised and swollen from being beaten; my arms were burnt and cut. I couldn't touch the children without it being agony, all along every inch of my skin. All I wanted to do was hug my children close, but he'd taken even that away from me.

All I could do was put my bitten, charred hands on their shoulders and say, over and over, 'I'm sorry, I'm sorry, I'm sorry.'

Chapter Two

The police might have taken him away, but they'd done that in the past – and then just let him out, without telling me. I was still as scared as hell. I was expecting *more* shit to happen because in my mind he was going to get off. I'd been down this police route before and every time, only one thing was certain: like a terminator, *he comes back.*

I wanted to be sure the kids would be safe. But the coppers' reaction to that was: 'So we're going to take your children into care.'

'You're not taking my kids anywhere,' I retorted. 'They've just had three days of hell.'

These coppers had just turned up to do a job; they had no idea of the situation they'd walked into.

'You're not taking my kids away from me,' I told them.

Jahméne, who was listening to the adult voices above him, joined in. He hung onto my leg when they tried to take me elsewhere to give a statement, 'Don't take my mummy!'

In the end, we all got piled into a police van and taken to the station together. Some police person helped me get dressed before we left, easing trousers and a top over my injuries, slipping trainers onto my feet. As we rode in the back of the van – it was still daylight, a strange journey in the summer sunshine – each of the kids' faces was etched in terror; every single one of them. Dan had been collected from school at some point – I have no memory of him arriving but he was there at the station – and all five kids were scared stiff. They'd all seen this before. They knew what happened next. They were all wondering when their dad would be back; this time, bent on revenge.

At the station, a female officer came over to us.

'Mum's got to write what happened on her own,' she said brightly to my children. She was trying to be nice about it.

'I don't want to be parted from my kids,' I said. Her eyes narrowed a touch, like I was being awkward. 'Don't take my kids, please don't take my kids.'

I didn't want to let them out of my sight.

They got a couple of female chaperones over and they said they would sit with the children.

'Come on,' said the woman officer. 'We need you to write a statement now.'

She took me into an interview room. There was a pen and paper on the table, chairs around the desk.

'Take a seat,' she said.

But I couldn't sit down. He'd buggered me so violently the day before that I couldn't sit down on the chair; my bum hurt too badly.

'I can't do this,' I said.

'Here's the pen,' she said. 'Sit down and write your statement.'

I couldn't pick the pen up. He'd bitten chunks out of my fingers, burned them with the blowtorch: I was too badly injured to hold the pen. The officer gestured at the chair again, not understanding why I wasn't 'co-operating'.

'I can't sit down on the chair,' I said, wanting to cry.

She lost patience with me then. 'You need to do this now!' she shouted. She stormed out of the room. I could hear her moaning about me to someone, saying how I wouldn't write the statement.

And then a new policeman came into the room. He was about fifty, about my height, with greying hair and glasses. He seemed professional, yet compassionate at the same time. He had more patience and understanding than his colleague.

His name was DC Bob Eames. And he was the man who changed *everything*.

We'd never had a policeman like him before. We'd had brash people who didn't do their jobs properly but made out they knew what they were doing. We'd had chauvinist coppers who didn't even think it was wrong when a man raped the mother of his kids, because they were 'together'. We'd had arrogant people who'd refused to listen when I told them what had gone wrong in the past, trying to help them learn from mistakes. But Bob Eames was none of those things. In a corrupt system, overflowing with errors, you do get the odd person fighting for truth, peace and justice. DC Eames was one of those people.

He is rare, I might add. For every 100 DCs I have met in my life, he was and is the only one who was in the job for the right reason. I think he should be decorated with honours.

On that Wednesday, the very first day I met him, for the very first time in a police station I was *listened* to. I was *believed*.

When he understood it was the kids I was most worried about, he kept reassuring me by opening the door to show me they were safe. He helped me understand why I needed to do the statement there and then: 'If you don't write the statement, they're going to take the kids into care because you can't go back to your ex.' He listened when I said, 'I didn't ask to be with him. I don't *want* to be with him. But you lot have never stopped him before; I bet you're gonna let him out … '

He turned to me then and said, with a steely grit I thought I might just be able to believe in, 'I'm *not* going to let him out. You need to tell me as much as you can now, Mandy,' he continued. 'If you only tell me a bit of it, we can only charge him with a bit of it. If you tell me as much you can, we can hold him for longer; he'll be put away for longer. So try your very, very hardest.'

And I told him, and he wrote it down for me, word for word, because I couldn't hold the pen. I had to do a squiggle at the end to sign it. I missed out loads of stuff, that first time. I was rambling and my brain wouldn't let me remember, and more than anything I just wanted to be back with my kids, so I wanted to get it over with as quickly as possible.

I kept interrupting my statement to ask about the kids, to say things as their mum that kept popping into my head. 'They need to have dinner; they need to have a bath.'

The DC told me he wanted to take me to the hospital – and really, the arresting officers should have taken me there first, but as I was in the station we were doing the statement – and I just kept saying, 'But where are the kids gonna go when I'm at the hospital?'

Bob had thought of that. 'I don't want the kids going to the hospital with you,' he said gently, 'because you're in a bit of a state. I've got a lovely lady here' – and he brought her in to show me – 'and she'll take your kids to a safe house.'

The lady's name was Maggie and she was a social worker. I started panicking about what would happen next because I knew my injuries were bad and I was petrified about what would happen to the kids if the doctors forced me to stay in the hospital overnight; I didn't want strangers looking after them. Maggie asked me, 'Is there anyone we can ring to help out?'

It was Daniel who said: 'My grandparents.'

So they phoned Dusty's parents and his mum and sister came down. They must have gone like the wind because they were in Birmingham and we were in Bath, but they were there, right away.

I didn't speak to his mum. We didn't say anything. She was horrified and upset, and his sister was too, crying as they gathered round the kids.

Then the DC took me up the hospital. My legs were still like jelly and my foot had started to hurt, so much so that I couldn't put any weight on it, so Bob literally carried me into A&E. They rushed me through to a private area in a wheelchair, so that a special nurse there could examine me and catalogue the physical evidence from my wounds.

The nurse was tall and thin and beautiful: a blonde woman in a white gown. She helped me up onto the hospital bed and then turned to her computer to bring up my medical records.

'What did you say your name was again?' she asked, after a moment.

I told her, and she said, in confusion: 'You're not on our system.'

'I must be,' I said. 'I've had six kids, I've been in and out … '

'It's a blank page,' she said. 'There's nothing on here.'

The DC heard her and went out to investigate. Later, he told me: my medical records, my hospital records – they had all been wiped clean.

Like I'd been erased from existence.

With Bob gone to investigate the missing files, the nurse said she was ready to begin the examination. She started at my head and worked her way down, listing all my injuries, saying how big the cuts were and what the wounds were from: his teeth, his fingers, his fists. I didn't really pay attention to what she was doing as she wrote it all down, but from time to time she would say bits aloud, and I'd hear, and remember. I was surprisingly matter-of-fact about it all, though. I just wanted to get through it as quickly as possible so I could get back to be with my kids. I just thought, *I'm alive, I've survived – now I just need to do this next bit properly.*

It took the nurse hours upon hours to write it all down – there were so many individual injuries, layered one on top of the other. The more things she found, the more upset she became, though she was always professional and kind. Bob returned at some point, and stood considerately to one side, giving us both privacy, watching as the nurse worked her way down my body.

'That looks like a burn,' she said at one point, probing a yellow, gooey sore on my arm.

'He had a blowtorch,' I explained.

She nodded, with a pained expression on her face, and wrote it down. I could see her getting upset with what I was saying so I tried to say the most minimal explanations I could.

She got down to my feet, and paused. 'Are you aware you've got glass in your foot?' she asked.

'No,' I said, surprised.

'It's quite a big piece.' She pulled it out to show me. It was two inches long, and covered in blood, because it had gone all the way into my foot.

'I didn't know that was there,' I said. It had been there for four days and I hadn't felt it once.

Bob left the room then, crying. Of all the cases he'd done, he later told me, mine was the worst.

When she'd finished listing everything on the outside, the nurse turned to me and asked: 'Is there anything I haven't found that you need to tell me about?'

So I had to tell her about the buggery and the rape. She examined me then, internally, apologising all the while if she hurt me, and apologising too that it was taking so long, as she charted every cut, every rip, every tear.

I was almost delirious by that stage. I was panicking about the kids. 'This is taking too long,' I told her, 'I have to go; I need to be back with my kids. Please can you hurry up?'

She tried to persuade me to stay in, saying I had wounds that needed further care and they wanted me to stay in overnight, but I was adamant. God only knew what my children had seen and heard and witnessed over the past few days. I was frantic about their suffering. They'd gone from thinking I was dead to knowing I was alive but injured, and they'd seen the state I was in. And just when they'd got me back ... I'd been taken from them. I didn't want them to be scared that we would be separated; to think that they'd now be taken into care and never see me again. I just wanted to be with them to say, 'It's going to be OK. We'll get through this.'

The DC totally got me. He said, 'I get it, let's just sort out your major injuries and I'll take you straight there.'

So the nurse patched me up as best she could. The blowtorch burns were deep, so they took a lot of cleaning, which stung.

They gave me an X-ray on my skull because it was fractured or something. They padded up my foot. They cleaned the blood and the pus and the scabs off me. But there wasn't much more they could do. We were four days on from when the attack began and many of my wounds had started to heal over so they couldn't be stitching me up anyway.

At last – at long last – I was free to go. Bob helped me into his car and then, bless him, he drove like a racing-car driver to get me to my kids. We flew across the city in the middle of the night. My children were being cared for in this massive old detached house in Bath, in some safe house that the police had organised. I got out of the car and Bob helped me up the steps and into the house.

As I stood in the hallway, the kids charged towards me like bolts of lightning, all five of them running into me for hugs. I gritted my teeth and I wrapped my bandaged arms around them all. We were safe. And I couldn't help it: I cried.

It was time for us to go home.

Chapter Three

The safe house wasn't one we could sleep in, so we returned to Sedgemoor Road that night. Hell though it had been, it was still home for the kids, and what they needed now, more than anything, was a feeling of security. I could see they were still terrified, though they had calmed down a bit by the time I got to the safe house because their grandma and their aunt had been sat with them.

It was dark outside; it was late. The roads were empty as we were driven back to our house; Dusty's family members following in the car behind. I limped up to my familiar front door and opened it. There was a weird stillness inside; funny smells that I didn't want to think too much about.

We sat in the kitchen for hours, talking. They all fired questions at me at the same time, all upset, scared and frantic. Corice and Jahméne kept saying they'd thought I was dead, over and over. Daniel was stressed and concerned, and very deep about how he felt. He cried and hugged me. He said, 'I'm sorry for not helping you, Mum.'

This tore at my heart, as I relived the memory of him curled up on the floor, helpless, watching, as his dad came towards me with the blue flame on full from the blowtorch.

'You have no reason to say sorry,' I told him. But there was no consoling him; he was beyond upset.

Isaac, to my mind, seemed angry at me. He had his own reasons, being young and confused. I think he chose to shut me out as his father had poisoned his mind against me. Even on that night, only hours after their father had been taken away, I could tell it was to be a long road ahead of healing and repairing the damage done to all of us.

'Come on, kids,' I said quietly in the end, not wanting to speak loudly because of the constant pounding in my head. 'Time for bed.'

As they pulled on clean pyjamas and brushed their teeth, I tried to make time for each child, one on one: to hug them, to give them security, to say, 'This is it, he's not coming back.' I didn't believe my words myself, but I lied to give them peace. 'This is the end. You're free now. You're fine. He's not gonna get out this time.'

I tucked Darren into bed first. He was so tiny, my breath caught in my throat just to look at him. I think he dropped off to sleep almost straight away, he was so exhausted. And there was another reason, too. When you live with domestic violence, as he had done ever since he was born, you can shut off to things that other kids would think were horrifying and would keep them awake for days on end. Instead, you get used to sleeping when you know you need to sleep, whatever might be happening around you. Darren had always been able to sleep in the worst situations, and tonight was no different for him.

Isaac was next. I couldn't even kiss him goodnight because my mouth was a horror show – I couldn't even give him a reassuring smile. He turned away from me in his bed and pulled the covers over himself.

I wanted to speak to Dan alone next, but he'd already vanished up the stairs in Isaac's room, up into his loft bedroom, and shut himself away.

'Dan, come down, I need to talk to you,' I called out softly. I couldn't physically climb up to get to him.

'I'm fine, Mum,' he called back. Then there was silence. I knew he wasn't fine at all, but he'd withdrawn into himself and he wasn't coming out tonight.

Jahméne came into Corice and Darren's room with me, wanting to cuddle up with Corice: his 'twin', his friend. As he had always been, he was full of questions. He wanted to know what had happened. He could obviously see I had serious injuries on my face and they upset him.

'What happened in there, Mum?' he asked me. 'What went on?'

'Shh, Jahméne,' I told him, as I urged him to close his eyes and go to sleep. 'You don't need to know everything.'

I lay down on the floor next to Corice's bed. I didn't want to go into my bedroom; in fact, I'd told Dusty's mum and sister they could sleep in my room. I obviously wasn't thinking straight; it was covered in blood and broken-off bits of my body. I don't know where they ended up sleeping. I just knew I was staying with my kids.

'You shouldn't be lying on the floor, Mum,' Corice said to me, concern in her high-pitched ten-year-old voice.

'I'm fine, Corice,' I said to my daughter. 'I just want to be with you.'

She nodded, sitting up in bed. She was upset, and scared. I looked her straight in the eye and I told her what I needed to.

'Well done,' I said to her. 'That was *so* brave of you to speak out to your teacher. I know how hard that must have been.'

'It wasn't brave!' she cried out. 'I actually thought you were dead. I really thought you were dead, Mum ...' She started to cry again, sobs shaking her shoulders. 'He's going to kill us all now because of *me*.'

'Corice, sweetheart, don't!' I told her. 'Come here.' I beckoned with opened arms, wrapping them round her as best I could. 'He's not going to do that. We're safe now. And all this is *him*. It's his own mind. It's nothing we've done; it's nothing we've caused. You did the right thing.'

'He threatened to kill me,' she sobbed. 'He said it's all my fault.'

'But that's not true. It's no one's fault but his. He's not going to hurt you, Corice, I promise. You're safe now. We're all safe.'

I held her until her tears ran dry and sleep stretched over her like a blanket. Then I lay on the floor, next to my sleeping children, and I finally had a chance to think.

I don't know how I'm alive.

It was nothing short of a miracle, again. Everything whizzed round and round my head, from the broken glass to the blowtorch. I couldn't stop seeing his face ... those evil eyes. The harder I tried to stop thinking, the more it overwhelmed me. Tears flowed uncontrollably till they could no more.

I didn't sleep. I had the biggest banging headache ever, and everywhere in my body ached and burned, inside and out.

God saved me for a reason ... again.

I remembered blacking out as Dusty raped me, hearing the voice that I had now heard three times in my life: 'It's not your time yet.'

I am here for a reason. The reason is the kids. I need to help them through this.

It was a long, dark night – but there was a sunrise at the end of it. A new day. A new dawn.

Our first full day without him in our lives.

Life became a whirlwind, then. Our feet barely touched the floor. CSI and the police were in and out; they spent hours in my bedroom, photographing everything. They took swabs, they drew round blood patches; they were labelling every piece of the war scene. With them dressed in white clothes head to foot, it was like a scene from a horror film … but it was real.

I hovered in the doorway of the bedroom as they worked; the investigators were strangers, and I wanted to keep an eye on them because of the kids being in the house.

My eyes were fixed on the ground, though, not wanting to look into the room properly. Any time my eye caught a glimpse of something I got vivid flashbacks to the attack; flashbacks that took my breath away. It was unbearably upsetting to see bits of my body stuck to the walls, the furniture, the sheets. He had torn chunks out of my head, my hands; half a red plait would be lying randomly on the floor. The investigators were asking me questions all the time so I'd have to answer. 'What's this bit from? What's this?' And then I'd have to look.

On the first Thursday, the day after the police had stormed the house, I finally checked my phone and realised I had a stream of missed calls from work. Why they hadn't come round to the house or phoned the police when I didn't open up on the Monday morning, or the Tuesday, or the Wednesday, I didn't know. I went down to the post office that afternoon, with the bunch of keys they so desperately needed, intending to apologise for everything

– for not turning up, for the shop being shut for so many days – even though it wasn't my fault.

But the area manager wasn't having any of it. He didn't even ask me how I was, despite the bandages and bruises and cuts that were clear to see; he just went on and on about how much trouble I'd caused.

Back home I went. The DC came round to see how we were getting on. I had to go back to the station and give a more detailed statement – it was fifty-seven pages long in the end. Bob kept reassuring me that things were different this time, that they would put my ex away, but I was still sceptical.

'I don't trust anybody,' I told him bluntly.

'I'm not surprised,' he said.

So he tried his hardest to make a difference, to make us trust him. My kids were almost as wary of coppers as I was, so he had a massive job on his hands. He approached the children like a family man, like a grandfather, almost; I remember him bringing videotapes of cartoons round to the house for them to watch, to show he wasn't all bad and that he was there to help. Dan was the hardest to persuade, and I think he even had an outburst with Bob about his dad getting away with it. Other than that, Dan was unsettlingly silent. He spent long stretches of time in his room and he didn't want to talk.

Bob reassured me he was keeping my ex locked up and he also said firmly, 'There will be no contact, direct or indirect. He won't be able to ring you; he won't be able to write.'

A few weeks after the attack, a lady came out to photograph my injuries; apologising, saying it should have been done straight away. She took me into the bedroom to ask me questions and then I had to strip. It was horrible. I didn't want it to be done but she told me it had to be, for the court case. We were both upset by the end. She said she'd been in the job so many years and she'd never seen anything like this before, where so many things had been committed in one attack. Never before had she seen a blowtorch being used.

'He's not going to get away with it,' she told me.

That's what they all said.

I had to go up the hospital countless times, for days and weeks and months afterwards: getting treatment or having new scans and X-rays. My teeth were shattered so the dentistry alone was a painful slog. The hospital was many miles from our house and I had to walk every single mile of it, battered and bruised, because I didn't have enough money for the bus anymore – there was no way I was working when I had the kids to look after and with my body in such a state. Darren was refusing to walk anywhere since the attack, though, so I had to carry him on my hip every single mile I walked, which was excruciatingly painful, but I just had to get on with it.

I went to the social security office to try to get some financial help. I remember going with all the kids, who were all being interviewed by the police at that time, so they were stressed from all the questions, and remembering. We were all tired and starving hungry. We had no money, no food. We sat in there for four hours until I got my chance to speak to someone.

When I did, it wasn't worth waiting for. According to the system, I'd left my job by choice. Even though I'd come straight from the hospital, and had a police report as to what had happened, I didn't fit in a neat box and so they told me, without a hint of compassion, 'You have to wait eight weeks for money.'

Eight weeks. With five kids to feed. Darren was just coming out of nappies at night, we had no food and I couldn't pay the bills. In the end, we went *twelve* weeks waiting for the money to be sorted because they stretched it out due to 'complications'. The police and social services tried to help, and they got us some boxes from a food bank; they all said it shouldn't be happening, that the system was wrong, but their frustration didn't open any doors. I felt I was being punished twice over; that I was being punished for being a victim of abuse. I will be forever grateful for the charity of the food banks and others who gave gifts to the children. We would not have survived without them.

And if it hadn't been for the generosity of my friend Kate, from the school run, I don't know what I would have done. She kindly lent me £1,000 to tide me over. I made it last for nearly four months, living off the bare minimum; you learn to make the pennies stretch. Kate started coming round a lot, now the coast was clear. She was a true friend. She'd turn up with cakes and games for the kids: an angel with beautiful, warm brown eyes.

She was so shocked at what my ex had done to me; horrified and upset. We'd never been able to talk about the way he treated me, before. She asked me now why I'd never, ever told her how bad it was.

'Because nobody could stop it,' I told her honestly. I'd spoken out before and it had never got me anywhere.

Yet this time, almost to my disbelief, Dusty was still locked up. The police didn't let him out and he didn't get bail because of all the evidence CSI had gathered, and so he was shipped off to a prison after a day or so to await trial there. I almost couldn't believe it when I heard. Could I really trust the DC? Was this really happening?

Bob told me bits and pieces of what was going on in his interviews with Dusty. My ex had started off not saying anything at first, then Dr Jekyll appeared, all velvet-voiced and polite, reasonable and intelligent. He acted in that manner all the way up until a certain point – until it was clear the DC hadn't fallen for it; until the DC said, 'You're not getting out, you're going down, you're going to go to prison for what you've done.' Then he flipped and Mr Hyde showed his ugly face, and the DC said to him, 'And there you go: *that*'s the real you.'

Then Dusty started saying he had acted in self-defence. I had bitten his arm, he said in his statement; I'd been punching and kicking him, and he was defending himself. He showed the police a vicious bite mark on his own arm, as evidence. It was the one Jahméne had seen him make himself, while he'd been sitting on the stairs on the Sunday night, after he'd burned me with the blowtorch. The police took a print of the teeth marks, and of course that proved that it was *Dusty's* teeth that had clamped down on his own skin, and not mine. The DC was pleased with that result. 'I can't believe he did that,' Bob told me. 'The more lies he tells, the deeper a hole he's digging for himself.'

Next, Dusty said the whole attack was just a one-off incident. That he hadn't been hurting me for eighteen years. Because he'd never gone down for hurting me before, he calculated that the attack would be viewed as an isolated incident. He'd just flipped, this single time; it was temporary insanity; it wasn't his fault.

And all the while, I was living in the house where he had tortured me.

That was beyond hard. I don't even have the words. Every time I stepped through the front door, I relived everything. I heard his voice in the corridors and in the bedroom. I didn't want the bed in the house, blood-stained horror thing, whispering its dark secrets to me even behind closed doors. Everything lingered: a smell, a memory; it was impossible to block things out. I was being triggered into reliving the attack by everything around me, constantly. And so, even though I was still bandaged and sore, I went around stripping and painting over everything as soon as CSI were done, trying to change everything so nothing looked the same as it did before. I painted over the walls and the furniture. I was painting over things I shouldn't even have painted over but I just didn't want to have a visual of anything from before. I begged to move, but was told an exchange with another family would be the only way, which could take weeks, months, years. After all, who would move to the house of horror knowingly?

I couldn't rest. I couldn't sleep. It was like being alert 24/7. The fear fuelled me, my heart constantly pounding fast. I couldn't hold down food. I look back now and wonder how on earth I managed to do the daily routine running on complete empty. Trying to stay sane for the children, act happy, act as though everything was OK now, when inside I was beyond broken, mentally and physically. The social workers said all the time I was doing fine, though.

The kids were having nightmares so I'd be up and down all night trying to soothe them. We were going to child counselling at the hospital weekly, but I didn't think that it was helping much.

The kids drew pictures in their sessions. Isaac was shy and quiet; Jahméne and Corice spoke openly but only in short bursts and stunted sentences. Darren smiled when he spoke, almost unaware that what he was saying was sad. Dan sat quietly. His counselling was not compulsory as he was older, so in the end he opted out. Though I told the officials that out of all the children he needed the most help, and that he wasn't in the right frame of mind to be able to make that choice, there was nothing I could do about it. Later, he went to a teenage place to speak, but he said it didn't help him: reliving it was worse than not talking, he said, even though his head was always fit to explode with everything built up inside. For me, Dan's experience was another let-down by the system, the law; the stupid law that didn't make sense to me.

As it was, the kids weren't the only ones who were having nightmares. I stayed downstairs in the living room during the nights now, avoiding my bedroom at all costs. Eventually, I'd get exhausted and crash on the sofa, but I never slept properly. Night terrors chased my own dreams away, and my senses were still on full alert. I would never be able to relax in this house where his voice still haunted every room.

And then one day, while my ex was still in police custody, not that long after the attack, I came home to find a flashing red light on my answerphone machine. Not thinking anything of it – *maybe it's Kate; maybe it's the DC*, I thought – I pressed play.

Heavy breathing panted malevolently through the hallway.

And then my ex's voice echoed through the house for real. I froze at the sound of it, heart pounding in my chest. He had a message for me: no remorse, just anger.

'You're all gonna die.'

Chapter Four

I was terrified. *How is this possible?* I thought. I remembered Bob's words: 'There will be no contact, direct or indirect.' And yet here was Dusty, again defying all rules, making his threats right inside my home, violating me all over again, as he always did. *You can't run, you can't hide …*

I phoned the DC immediately. He couldn't believe Dusty had done it, that he'd gotten past all the rules and regulations – until I played him the message. Then he took the tape as evidence and stormed off to have it out with his colleagues. No one knew how he'd managed to beat the system. I repeatedly reminded them how clever he was and how evil he was, and that nothing could or would stop him from getting his own way.

Still the calls continued, even when Dusty was locked up in prison. Heavy breathing down the telephone. Threats spoken aloud in a horribly familiar voice that sent creeping shivers down my battered spine. The police were reluctant to believe it was him, at first, but when they investigated, they found out I was telling the truth: it was him, phoning me from inside the prison, trying to scare me into dropping the charges so he could walk free. 'Witness intimidation', I think that's what they call it. It doesn't do justice to the fear and sickening dread it makes you feel.

The coppers were saying over and over, 'How is he doing this? How is this still happening?' They told me that inmates in jail have phone cards that are pre-programmed so specific numbers are blocked; the restrictions on Dusty's card meant that it should have been impossible for him to ring my house phone. I raised my eyes wearily to those of the police, tired of having to do everyone else's job for them in this 'game' of trying to stay one step ahead of my ex.

'What if he swaps cards with another inmate?' I asked simply.

I was right: that was what he had done. A simple swap; a flaw in the hole-riddled system.

So the phone calls stopped … but then the letters started. A prison-issue white envelope landed with a nauseating whisper on the mat at Sedgemoor Road one morning. There was no stamp on it, so I think he'd posted it to someone else and they had put it through my door; I think he got round the fact that my address was blocked that way. I think it may have been a neighbour with whom my ex had a weird relationship who put it through my door. She actually told me to 'drop the charges as your injuries aren't that bad', before telling me he was a 'good dad' and asking 'how could you do this to him?'

I recognised his writing straight away, though, however he'd gotten it to me. So I didn't even give him the time of day to open it; I just called the DC and handed it to him. I did the same thing with the next letter that arrived the following morning. And the one after that.

And the one after that.

'Don't open them,' Bob warned me. 'He's mind-bending. Just give them to me and I'll put them in the file.'

So I did – letter after letter after letter. With each one that got through, I knew Dusty was on the inside licking his finger and holding it to the air. *I win again. I'm still in control.* The DC was trying to find out how on earth he was beating the system, because even if he was sending the letters to someone on the outside to post through my door, *all* letters from inmates were supposed to be read and vetted, but in the meantime they just kept coming. One afternoon, after I'd come back from yet another visit to the hospital – this time having my broken teeth fixed, if I remember rightly – curiosity got the better of me.

With a shaking hand, I slid my finger underneath the gummy flap of the white envelope and ripped it open. I wanted to see what he had to say for himself. Maybe, just maybe, he was trying to say sorry.

I unfolded the letter. He'd used a ruler so all his words were neatly aligned. He'd taken his time with it: he'd got hold of coloured pencils and used them to go round certain letters and words, reds and yellows and greens to highlight his message to me.

And his message could be summed up in one sentence: don't you dare say anything, Mandy, don't you dare speak out.

He threatened me in the letter, reiterating threats he'd made so many times over the years. *If you ever get me arrested, I'll have you killed, and the kids killed too. If I get put away by the police, it won't be me doing the killing, but I'll pay someone to do it. My mates. If you speak out, there are people out there who will come and sort you out. I know people who can do atrocities. I know people with blacked-out vehicles who will snatch you off the street and torture you. I know people who are keeping girls in cellars in Birmingham for prostitution, where they're chained up so they can't escape and they can't kill themselves. I'll make sure those same people come for you.* He went into detail about how they would do it – a scary level of detail. How would he know all about it if it wasn't all completely true?

At the end of the letter, he wrote breezily, 'We'll sort all this out. Things will be fine when I get out. I won't do it again.' It beggared belief.

I relayed everything back to the police. Even though his words terrified me, it never crossed my mind to back down. Even when an unfamiliar car with blacked-out windows – just like the one he'd described – prowled down our street, loitering where I had to walk as I took the kids to school, I was determined to go through with the court case, in the hope that there would be justice. I phoned the police when I saw that car, and they did a car chase: they sent the illegal immigrants they found driving it back home, but we never found out anything more about it. I don't know to this day what it was about, whether it was innocent or not. All I knew was that I'd had a bad feeling about that car and, over the years, I had learned to trust my instincts.

The letters kept coming, no matter what the police said about 'no contact'. I kept passing them to the DC, without reading them; I'd read enough. And then, one afternoon, after I'd been up the hospital again, maybe getting my burns seen to (which, weeks on from the attack, still burned anew every single day), I came back home to find Daniel sitting at the kitchen table – with one of his dad's letters in his hand. His face was green.

'What's the matter?' I asked him, though I could see for myself.

He didn't say anything, just pushed the opened letter across the table at me. I felt my heart sink. I'd kept so much away from him; none of the kids even knew their dad had been getting letters through. But now Dan knew the truth: his dad could still touch us, and hurt us, even from inside a jail.

I looked down at the letter and bile rose in my throat. I hadn't read the words yet but my ex had drawn a picture on the envelope, and that alone was enough to make me retch.

It was a crude drawing of Junior's grave in Bath, with a sharp knife sticking into the soil that covered my dead baby. It was sticking down into the grave, with blood dripping off it. He'd coloured it all in neatly. He'd taken his time to make sure it hurt.

'Can you explain what that is all about?' Daniel asked me, in a choked voice. 'We really need to sort him out, Mum, he is dangerous. He is angry. No one can stop him. What are we going to do?'

Dan was really upset and irate. He was panicking. He was afraid. And all I could say was 'sorry', over and over and over.

As I read the poison-tinged words in Dusty's letter, I knew that every single one of them would be etched in Daniel's brain forever. That he would visualise that his dad had said those things, planned those things.

Dusty had written about a fork, this time. About getting a fork, and gouging my eyes out with it. He went into great, loving, laboured detail: how he would stick it in my eyeball, and twist it, and pull it; describing what it would look like and how it would happen. He went into graphic detail about the torture, a whole page detailing exactly what he was going to do to my eyes.

Then he wrote at the end: 'And when I get out we will get married.'

What the …? It was his most disturbing letter yet. And it told me that he must believe he had so much control over me that his words alone would break me, even from inside the prison. He must believe that he had overpowered me with so much fear in the past that I wouldn't give the letters to the police.

He was wrong. When I gave *that* letter to the DC, the messages finally stopped. But it was too late. The damage had been done – to me, and to Dan. You can't unread words burned into your brain. I had a few emails too, which surprised me the most because it meant that my ex had online access. They gave online access to a computer whizz! But he was studying, they said, so it was allowed. I just kept reiterating how clever he was and that he would use any means to scare us. They didn't seem to get that if the system gave him the resources to do it then he was winning in first place: finger in the air, no one can stop him.

The authorities were obviously not taking me seriously. I had to go through lengthy procedures to block any means of him contacting us, which infuriated me. Why couldn't the system just not give him the resources in the first place, given they knew what kind of criminal he was? He was clutching at every straw given. He even used people in the area to try to talk me down and scare me into dropping the charges so he'd be released. He was desperate; he'd never been locked up this long before.

The letter was one thing for Dan to read, horrifying in itself. But my kids had to go through so much – all of them. It breaks my heart just thinking about it; it was a *million* times worse to witness. Because Dusty was pleading not guilty – by reason of temporary insanity; 'I'm going to go to Broadmoor and walk,' he taunted in his letters – the kids were caught up in the Crown Prosecution's attempt to build a case. What their father put them through that year – on top of everything else they'd already endured at his hands – makes me so, so angry, even to this day. And the system let him!

I had no control over it; it was the law. The kids had to go off and be videolink-interviewed individually. All of them were so young; Darren was only five. They were saying to me, frantically, 'What shall we say? If we say what Daddy did, will it get us into trouble? Will they split us all up? Will we get taken away from you, Mummy, if we say what happened? And will *he* know we spoke out? He said he would kill us for speaking!'

I told them all: 'Just tell the truth. Because that's all you can say. Just say the truth: everything that you've ever remembered or seen or heard, just say it. Don't worry about the consequences. Say whatever you need to say. Speak out. Have a voice. Because it's *your* story: what you saw, what you felt. Just say it. And it's also OK if you don't want to speak. They can't force you to do anything you don't want to.'

I don't know, even now, exactly what they said; the only thing I know about is what Corice said about me pulling Dusty to the ground as he walked towards the bunk beds with the knives in his hand, because the police used that in court. I do know that the team told me how incredibly articulate the children were; they said they couldn't have asked for more from them. A lot of children in that situation clam up and go introverted, but my kids didn't. They stepped up. They spoke out, no matter how hard it was. How brave, how sad, how awful, how heartbreaking. It still eats at me now that they went through that because of their selfish father. Goosebumps spread fast across my body, head to foot, as I write these words; tears still fill my eyes. There is no pain on earth that matches the mother-root connection, when your child is suffering. You feel every ounce tenfold; it tears at your very soul, it wrenches at your very core that you can't take it away. You can't kiss it better and make it all go away. I have to take that with me to my grave. The deepest, most damaging pain.

I felt physically sick every time they had to do interviews – because I knew they were in a room, away from me, alone, scared and so young, having to relive horrors that adults would have trouble not being affected by. Pure evil horror. They would come back to Sedgemoor Road upset – and upset further by the fact we were still living in the same house where it had all happened – and we'd talk through their emotions: their fear, their guilt, their hurt. I was so angry at my ex for putting them through it, because the only reason they had to do it was because he was pleading not guilty. Every single one of his children had to go to hell and back, repeating everything they saw and heard, because he wouldn't admit responsibility for what he'd done. To me, it was the ultimate indication of his evil. The final piece of sharp glass in my heart, twisted till I could bleed no more.

It was a blessing that the children had their uncle to help them through the interviews. Dusty's youngest brother was like a rock to us. My heart bled for their suffering each and every time the kids were forced to relive the tortures they had heard or witnessed. They were shaken and ill, stressed and beyond upset. Their uncle was the tower that held them strong as I was broken and could not give them strength in that way. He was the opposite to his evil brother: he genuinely cared for my children.

Dusty actually threatened him for helping us – and my ex wasn't the only one who didn't support the relationships we had with his family. Bob Eames advised me to sever ties with Dusty's family, completely. That didn't feel fair. Why should the kids suffer, miss out on seeing their grandma and uncle, because of something their father had done? For I think his family felt guilt; we all felt guilt apart from the one person who was guilty. I felt sorry for his mum; how she must have felt. But the police were adamant and, ultimately, I did as they said.

It was another forced choice to keep us all safe. And I had spent years alone, not having my family, or his, or anyone, to help us. So I knew I could cope. Heck, it would be easier without Dusty there destroying everything.

At least we had hope now. At last: we had a future to look forward to.

Chapter Five

As he always did, my ex soon had another card up his sleeve to torment us with. He told the authorities I was a bad mother, and so we had social services breathing down our necks, asking the children even *more* questions to see if his stories were true. 'And does Mummy ever hurt you …?'

To be frank, I didn't much care about the intrusion into my parenting: my house had an open door, always had done for the authorities who deigned to visit, such as when the LEA used to come and inspect my home-schooling, and I was an open book. I had nothing to hide, therefore I had nothing to fear. Social services were in and out; in fact, I became quite friendly with the workers, who told me the children were a credit to me.

Maggie, our first helper, was a kind-hearted lady, older and wise. She knew what the kids were going through and was compassionate and understanding. Jahméne and Corice in particular formed a bond with her quite quickly. Consistency with children and adults is a must, especially at such a sensitive time as this, when they are scared about who they can trust. When a bond is formed it is vital to keep that bond for them to release their inner pain, their worries, their fears. But it wasn't long before we found another flaw in the system, for people in this line of work get replaced frequently. All of a sudden a stranger appears and you have to start all over again, which often leads to many children clamming up and holding in emotions and fears all the way through to adulthood.

Maggie's replacement was Carly, a younger lady. It took a while for the children's bond with her to set. Isaac seemed to warm to her, which helped, as he was still pushing me away, confused and angry. She was a vital source of help and a friend throughout the hardest of times. We were lucky in that she stayed our social worker for many years: a rarity. Even though she isn't our social worker anymore, I'm glad to say that she and her family are still, to this day, a valued part of our lives.

But while the social workers were an invaluable source of support, they couldn't stop my ex playing his games either. For Dusty hadn't forgotten the lessons he'd learned when I'd got away from him the last time. He remembered exactly what he'd done at the refuge in Bath, and how that had ultimately got him what he wanted.

And so, he next demanded that I bring the kids to visit him in prison. I soon learned that what he'd started to study – the educational course that allowed him internet access – was Law. As a consequence, he now began asserting his human rights as a father. He really fought to get me to take the kids to the prison, and we fought really hard back because the kids *really* didn't want to go. They were terrified of him. They were panicking at one point, as legal letter after legal letter came through with the same demand, each putting the living fear into them that they would be forced to see him, saying in scared little voices, 'They're not going to make us go and see him in the prison are they, Mummy?' They looked so frightened. 'No,' I told them. 'No, they can't do that.'

The months passed. Months of interviews and investigations; of reliving the trauma. Months of going up the hospital on a weekly basis as my injuries slowly, slowly healed; as my mouth got put back together, as my hair grew long and thick once more;

as I managed to walk without limping. I still had problems with eating and sleeping, which made my everyday life hard to cope with. I was grasping at low levels of energy just to keep afloat and pretend to the children all day that everything was fine. Then, at night, every night, I would crack up in floods of tears, in desperation for justice and an end to the torment.

A new year dawned at last: 2003. The year I would have my day in court.

The very thought of it made me feel sick.

I was assigned a chaperone to help me through the ordeal ahead. And it would be an ordeal: I would have to stand in the same room as Dusty, without a screen to shield me, and to his face, to those slanted eyes, say exactly what he had done. It would be in contravention to every rule he had ever issued. It would be an open invitation to smite me down. And at the end of it, there was no guarantee that he wouldn't walk out of there a free man, with nothing to stop him wreaking his revenge. I was petrified.

My chaperone's name was Tracy. She was a young woman, maybe in her late twenties, with a sensible square chin and a strong-willed manner. I liked her, even if she couldn't quite convince me, strong-willed manner or not, when she told me to put my faith in the system.

It was Tracy's responsibility to prepare me for and help me during the court case. In those early months of 2003, she went through all the protocol with me and explained what I'd have to do as a lead witness in the case against my ex.

Everything she said struck still more fear into my heart. She took me to visit Bristol Crown Court, so I could see the room where I'd give evidence and understand what I'd have to go through with a judge and jury. I had to watch an actual case and that made things a whole lot worse as I watched a perpetrator 'get off' and his family belittle the victim. I saw how the victim was verbally torn apart by the barristers. Tracy pointed out the witness stand to me, where the poor victim stood shaking, and then she said, 'And your ex will be just over there.' She indicated a wooden box – the dock – only metres from the stand, where this evil man stood with no remorse, laughing and punching the air as he was released. It fed sheer terror into my very being.

'I don't even want him in the room,' I said to Tracy in the courtroom, my eyes on stalks at how close he'd be to me.

'Well, that's the way it is,' she said, apologetically.

I kept thinking over and over, *I can't do this.* Years afterwards, I wrote a full report to complain about attackers being in the same room as a victim giving evidence; to say that when you have a vindictive person that controls your mind, simply his presence in the room, even if you can't see him, even if you can only hear him breathing, is enough to make your fear so alive that you're not able to say things as articulately as you would do if he wasn't there. It can honestly make or break cases: they shouldn't ever have done it like that. Many victims have backed down through being broken this way so the perpetrators have got away with their crimes. Other victims have said exactly the same thing as me to the authorities, and it's changed now, thank God.

But that wasn't the situation in 2003. I would have to 'betray' him in front of his face. It seemed impossibly dangerous. As the trial date drew closer, I grew more and more terrified. I was physically ill with worry. A lot of the time I was being sick and having diarrhoea; I lost over two stone. The closer it got to the date, the more ill I became. I was shaking uncontrollably. I didn't want to be in the same room as him, this man who had torched me, buggered me, defiled me. To know that he was going to stand mere feet away from me, while I had to stand there and say what had happened, in excruciating, embarrassing, shameful detail, was almost too much to bear. I was sick to my stomach. I didn't want to do it.

But I knew I had no other choice. I just kept trying to psych myself up. I said to myself, over and over, *You've got to do this, otherwise he's gonna get off. If you don't do this, he'll walk free.*

Fear is a powerful motivator or destructor – and for me it had to be a motivator, or he would win.

The trial date was set for February. January was too short a month that year – the time raced by, bringing me closer to what I thought of as my doom. I couldn't believe he was going to go down, not after all these years and all the let-downs, so I was trying to prepare myself for what would happen when he was released, as well as for the trauma of giving evidence in front of him. The lawyers went over my statements with me, again and again. I relived the final attack, every minute of it, every strike, every blow, over and over. My physical injuries might be healing – though some never would – but the emotional ones were still as fresh as if he'd burned me the day, the hour, the second before. Every wound in my heart was red raw.

We were only a week away from the trial date when a letter arrived for me from the police. I thought maybe they were writing with a reminder of the court protocol or to encourage me with a final bit of advice, but what the letter had to say made my jaw drop.

'I write to inform you that your attendance [in court] is now not required,' the letter read. It continued: 'The defendant has now pleaded guilty.'

Chapter Six

The breath was knocked out of me.

'How can he do that?' I asked Tracy when we spoke. 'We've been preparing for nearly a year for this trial. How can he change his plea at the last minute?'

It was the law. It gave him the right to change his plea. The police had been telling me for months that there was no way he was getting off, that they were going to slam everything at him, and people were talking about him getting eight life sentences or something ridiculous – sentences that meant he'd never be getting out. I reckon his barrister took one look at the evidence stacked up against him and advised him to plead guilty. And the law allowed him to do that, just like that.

'What about all the police time he's wasted?' I asked. 'What about how much this has cost the government? *What about what he's put us all through – the children's interviews?* Will he be sentenced for all that too?'

But that wasn't how it worked. It made me so mad, when my poor kids had been forced to go through a living hell for a year, that he could get away with changing his plea now. And then Tracy broke the news that, when perpetrators plead guilty, they automatically receive a lesser sentence. He should have had the maximum possible sentence, the longest time behind bars that he could be given for his depravity, but thanks to his legal manoeuvring, he would get a shorter sentence now that he'd changed his plea. It just seemed downright *wrong* to me.

There was only one upside: I wouldn't have to attend the court proceedings. They told me my statements would be taken into account, but because there was a stack of evidence gathered against him I didn't physically have to be in court. I didn't have to be in the same room as him again.

There was no way I was ready for that; no way I would put myself in that position if I didn't have to. So Tracy went to the sentencing hearing in my stead. It took place about a month later, on 3 March 2003: 3/3/03. Three was my lucky number. I only hoped this would ring true that day. I hoped with all my soul that he would be jailed.

Tracy told me later that Dusty stood in the dock as cocky as hell throughout the whole hearing. He might have pleaded guilty, you see, but he was still saying the attack was only a one-off, that he'd gone crazy; that he needed treatment in a mental institution, and not a jail sentence, to help him deal with his 'issues'. *I'm going to go to Broadmoor and walk ...* And after all, what evidence was there that he'd been hurting me for years? There was no way in hell he was going down, in his mind. He thought he had the whole thing sewn up.

The day of the hearing, I stayed at home. I tried not to think about what was going on at court, but I could think of nothing else. The kids were at school so I had nothing to take my mind off it. *Will he be sent to a hospital,* I wondered, *like he told me he would, where he could be 'cured' quickly and set free again on the streets? Or will the judge see through his lies and send him down?* Every atom in my being, every lesson I'd learned, told me he would win.

He always did.

It was the afternoon before I heard a knock on the door. It was Tracy. I let her in and looked at her expectantly, feeling a migraine coming on, the weight of all the pressure crushing me.

'Make me a coffee first,' she said.

I made her a coffee mechanically and placed a warm mug in front of her on the kitchen table.

'Sit down,' she said. 'You're going to need to sit down for this.'

Oh crap, I thought, *if I've got to sit down it's gonna be bad*. I sat gingerly on a kitchen chair, raised my eyes reluctantly to hers. I was trembling. I didn't know how I was going to cope if he was free, where the kids and I would go, what we would do. How could we run after this? My head was in a proper sick spin.

'He's gone to jail, Mandy,' she told me. 'He got six years for rape, and nine years for GBH with intent.'

It was like I'd had the breath sucked out of me and then thrown back in again. I burst out crying. 'Is this real?' I asked her. 'Is he actually going away?'

'Yes,' she said.

'What, for real? You're not gonna let him out? This isn't a fix? You're not just telling me this to shut me up?'

'No, it's real. It's real, Mandy.'

I was shaking and crying. We cried together. We hugged for about half an hour. *Six years for rape, and nine years for GBH with intent*, I thought. I did the calculations. *Fifteen years. Fifteen years! By the time he got out, Darren would be twenty*, I thought. I added up all the kids' ages: Isaac would be twenty-four; Corice, twenty-six; Jahméne, twenty-seven. Dan would be thirty-two. He would be a man. They would *all* be adults. It was more than

I could ever have hoped for. My children were now free to live in peace, to grow up without fear and anger, to follow their dreams unobstructed and unafraid. They'd been given their childhoods back. I clung onto Tracy, squeezing her hard, in wonder that she was there, that it was real, that it wasn't a dream.

'Tell me everything,' I said. 'What happened? What did the judge say? How the hell did the judge see through him?'

It seemed a miracle to me after all the let-downs from the system. But apparently it was a lady judge in charge of the hearing, someone who didn't stand for crap and was strict on justice for perpetrators like my ex. And then Tracy told me something that seemed equally miraculous. She told me that some of the times I'd gone to the hospital or the doctors with an injury over the years – with my bitten, manky hand; with the blow to my head that had started to heal over; with my eye injury – the doctors had paper-filed the incidents. It's standard protocol, apparently, in cases of unexplained injury: it goes on a paper file in case of future investigations. So even though my medical records had mysteriously vanished from the hospital's computer systems, there was still a record. There was hard evidence of his abuse throughout the years. I felt relieved, thankful, that the doctors had done that because I thought all those people had let me down all those times. Now, at least, their record-keeping had helped me out – big time.

My ex didn't know about the paper files either. They proved he was lying, and so the judge came to understand what he was really like. The letters that he'd sent me from prison were also used in the case. He had been claiming to his psychiatrists in prison that the attack on me was a one-off torture; that he had mental problems – he'd been trying to trick them by ticking all the right boxes, acting polite. But those letters proved in black and white and coloured underlines that he was calculated and evil.

Tracy told me that Dusty's jaw hit the floor when he was told by the lady judge that he was going down. He didn't see it coming. But all the evidence was stacked up high against him, and to the judge his callousness was as plain as day.

In her written sentence, she described him as 'devious, evil and calculated'. Because of that, she wrote, she was imposing the maximum possible sentence that she had at her disposal. She'd been a judge for thirty-one years and she said she'd never had a case like it before, where the abuse and torture were so calculated.

When Tracy told me what the judge had said, I almost couldn't believe my ears. I'd seen him twist people – and authorities especially – round his little finger for decades. Now, he was standing exposed, in public, for what he was: a thug, a bully, an evil, heartless man. It felt like a kind of magic in itself; in one statement, the judge had cut through all his cloaks of lies and left him with the naked truth, his deceit unspooling uselessly at his feet. I couldn't wait to tell the kids.

When they came home from school, I gathered them all together in the kitchen. My head went fuzzy as I told them. Like me, they barely dared to believe it. Even as we went out for a meal to celebrate with the DC and our new social worker friends, all of us were convinced that there would be some loophole, some appeal, some last-minute strike that would send him barrelling back into our lives.

But it didn't happen. Oh, he tried various things to get himself off the hook – but not one of them worked. And then I was told he'd flipped in prison and revealed his temper. Showed his true colours. He'd been claiming all along he was not the person I had stated him to be in my police interviews, but then he let his act drop in a moment of anger. After that incident, he got shipped to a prison on the Isle of Wight, one for the most dangerous criminals, where the highest-risk perpetrators are sent. Shortly after he got there I heard he was then placed in solitary confinement 'for his own protection' because the other prisoners had learned what he was really in for – beating and raping an innocent woman, the mother of his kids – and they were not impressed. The using of the blowtorch especially did not go down well with them. I heard they tried to set him alight when they found out what he'd done.

I think what the jail did in segregating him was wrong, actually; I think he should have been put in with the other inmates. Because to my mind he hasn't learned the intense pain he's caused. I don't wish pain on human beings, but he's not a human being in my eyes. He's a monster. He needs to feel what he inflicts so he doesn't do it ever again. If he felt an ounce of the pain he inflicted and still inflicts on me, he would cower and stop for sure … but that's probably the wrong way to think.

Days passed; weeks; months. And the phone stayed silent. No one knocked on the door to say it had all been a big mistake. He stayed locked up. We stayed safe.

There came a summer's day, several months on from the sentencing, when I took the kids to school. I dropped them off with a hug and a wave, and they ran happily into the playground. It was amazing seeing them run, unencumbered by the knowledge of what went on at home; to hear them laugh joyously without a second's hesitation. I smiled to myself as I turned from the school and started to walk back home in the sunshine, listening to the birds singing in the trees and relishing each lungful of fresh air that I breathed. And I felt this wave go over me. It was an overwhelming realisation.

I am free.

I can go home when I want. I'm not being timed. He's not waiting for me. He's not watching. No one is reporting back.

I am free. I AM FREE!

I started crying. Not from sadness, just from that overwhelming sensation of freedom.

I think the only people who will truly understand the depth and breadth of that feeling will be those who have been falsely imprisoned and tortured over a long period of time – so long that you think there will be no end to it. When you have to pretend to act a certain way to stay alive, out of necessity you develop a character that can't express, that isn't you. But to act like that for so long, to not be yourself for so long, well, the day you wake up and you *are* you again, it's … overpowering. Awe-inspiring. To know that you can be you – without fear, without pain, without oppression – is the most immense feeling. There is no feeling like that on earth.

It is freedom itself.

Even acknowledging that now, as I write, I relive that emotion: its power; its ultimate, complete essence of the true meaning of life itself … to breathe freely.

It was strange to feel an emotion that was true and from me alone. It wasn't from anywhere else or prompted by anyone else's actions … it was just me, enjoying the sunshine and the fresh air on a summer's day. Everyone takes breathing for granted, but my breathing had been controlled for eighteen years. Every breath I took on that walk that day felt blessed. Every breath I still take does. I am grateful for the smallest things. For the freedom to feel and experience without control or denial. For the chance to smile and laugh without worry or retribution. For the opportunity to be myself. How blessed we are to be alive.

Daniel came home from school one afternoon around the same time I experienced this epiphany, and he said to me, with clear, shining eyes that I hadn't seen in his beautiful face for years and years, 'Mum, I smiled for the first time today and it was for *real*.'

I grabbed him and hugged him close for the longest time, spinning him round and round in pure joy.

For what he had said was the most profound sentence I had ever heard. I knew exactly what he meant.

We. Were. Free.

PART SIX

BEGINNING AGAIN

How it amused you that you had such power
Over my thoughts every hour
How evil for you to inflict – and enjoy!
How do you feel now …?
I am no longer your battering toy.

Chapter One

In October 2003, with help from our social worker Carly and a friend in a housing association, we moved home. To *our* home. A home untouched by him.

It was in Peasedown St John on the outskirts of Bath: a square, semi-detached, four-bed house that was enormous. It needed loads doing to it, but I got a court settlement payment and I ploughed the money into building our new lives. With Carly's help we had a new kitchen built onto the existing house, and we decorated throughout, together as a family with friends to music. I got all new beds and furniture for the kids, letting them choose what they wanted for their bedrooms. Corice and Daniel were getting rooms of their own, and the younger boys were all sharing.

I was so proud to walk my kids into that house. We were starting from scratch: this is *us*, this is *our* home. The house held no bad memories. Dusty had never, ever been there. He had nothing to do with anything in it. It didn't change what had happened, but the move helped us all mentally with our recovery.

I threw almost everything out. All the clothes he'd forced me to wear went in the trash. Kate and I went shopping and I bought what *I* wanted to wear. It was so liberating. I ripped up loads of old photos; I didn't want to see his face. I took new pictures of the kids having fun, and I started a montage wall of the shots in my bedroom. I made a point of printing off happy photos of the children and putting them up all around the house, and I had one whole wall in my bedroom dedicated to their jolly smiling faces.

Half my bedroom was like an art studio, in fact. I wasted no time in picking up my paintbrushes and *expressing*. I still didn't sleep well at night – old habits die hard – so I would paint and write through the night instead, revelling in the freedom of having no one else in the room with me so I could leave the light on and create all night. I painted portraits of the kids from still photos – there was no way they'd have posed for me, they wouldn't stay still!

They were a bundle of energy, all of them. We went on loads of day trips, getting out and seeing the world and having fun. We'd go to beaches and different towns and events and museums. We'd visit the supermarket and buy loads of sweets and puddings because it was like, 'Yay, we can eat this!' We went out every day because we realised, 'Yay, we can go out!' We were overexcited and over-exuberant, and we revelled every day in our freedom.

The kids started at a new school, closer to our new home. As it always is when children change schools, it was difficult for them – they were bullied for being mixed-race, as well as for being the new kids – but they eventually settled in and made good friends. And I loved being able to invite the children's friends round to play. My kids had never had that experience before; visitors were never allowed in Dusty's day. But I flung open the doors of the house and I invited tens of children at a time. I have five kids of my own, of course, so if each of them brings only three friends back, you've suddenly got twenty kids running round your house – and there were often more. The house was always full of children laughing and playing. I felt so happy with that. It was what I'd wanted before and could never do. Just to see them all so happy made me thrilled.

I'd serve jelly and ice cream and cakes. We did a lot of art. I got a massive twelve-seater table for the kitchen, second-hand, a great big wooden thing, and we'd all sit round it and sculpt with clay or paint and just be messy. I put a huge paddling pool out in the back garden in the summer and the kids would get water guns and play all afternoon out there. It was *fun*. So many of the local kids wanted to play at our house because we were creative and messy, and the noise of laughter and song was always welcome.

Some of my happiest memories are of my kids coming home from school. Darren was bubbly and chatty, and he had about a hundred friends. I can visualise his happy face instantly: rosy cheeks and a big grin. I'd go to pick him up and he'd be charging round in circles. Isaac was like that, too – so much energy. He got into football at Peasedown so he was always kicking a ball about, buzzing around and happy. All my kids, when they got in from school, would try to talk to me at once, wanting to say what their day was like all at the same time. I'd have to say, with a big smile on my face, 'Take it in turns!'

The kids weren't the only ones who made friends. As I was standing in the school playground one windy day, waiting for the kids to come out, the breeze caught my pigtails and whizzed them above my head like rabbits' ears. This tall, slender blonde woman came charging across the playground towards me, laughing, and she told me affectionately that the wind had made me look like Bugs Bunny! I thought that was hilarious, and so we hit it off immediately: kindred spirits. Kath and I have so many things in common; we both love arts and crafts for a start, but the biggest thing is our sense of humour. Alongside Kate, she is the most beautiful woman I know, inside and out. She had three kids at the same school as my lot, so every day we'd meet up a bit earlier, have a chat, and then hang about a bit afterwards too. We went to each other's houses for tea and cake. I'd never been able to do that before, when Dusty was watching the clock, but now my time was my own I could be me again: a bubbly person, jokey and happy and daft. I introduced Kath to Kate and the three of us together would have the best times, laughing and joking. The Three Musketeers had nothing on us. Between them, those women brought me back to life, and I will be forever grateful for their humble, unconditional love.

I made other friends, too. I was a naturally chatty person and friendships seemed to blossom like vibrant flowers. Peggy was our neighbour, a warm-hearted sixty-something who lived in a bungalow across the road from our house. She was a Catholic with ginger-grey curly short hair. A petite, feisty woman, she was a tough cookie with a brilliant sense of humour. She was the first person to come up to me when we moved in and say, 'Hello! Are you new to the area? Aren't your children lovely!' She particularly took a shine to Darren and they formed a bond. He would ask if he could go to hers, which she found strange – 'being an ol' fogey', as she put it.

I also managed to track down the girl I'd met in the refuge in Bath, the one who'd been attacked with the hammer. We'd stayed in contact over the years, but we couldn't be friends because our partners wouldn't allow it. She was still fighting for her freedom. Her bloke would get arrested for attacking her and let off, or be locked up for only short spates of time and then let out – and then he'd come for her, again and again. I spent many hours and days on the phone with her, begging her to hang in there for her freedom. 'It will come one day,' I said.

I met Mike online, too, an amazing illustrator with whom I used to chat about art and poetry. When we met in person, the connection was instant: he's like my soul brother; we're platonically, spiritually connected in some way. Mike opened my eyes up to modern art and we used to go to exhibitions and swap books of reference. He was amazing at night-time, when I couldn't sleep and neither could he; we would chat for hours online, sending our poems back and forth for critique, talking about art and poetry to sideline my thoughts, which always seemed to be drawn to my ex at night, as though the setting of the sun released demons that I could just about manage to keep at bay in the light.

Night-time was a trigger for me, you see. I would remember. I'd have to paint, or write, or talk to Mike or other people online to keep my mind off the memories. Other triggers came unexpectedly – such as walking down a street one day in summer, as the scent of a family barbecue drifted over a neighbour's fence.

Smell that burning flesh …

And I'd be back in the bedroom.

I was paranoid about everything. It was tough, the mental side of keeping it together. If the children went to a friend's house to play and were late back, my first thought was always that their dad had got them: paid his mates in their blacked-out vehicles to snatch them off the street. Then I'd go through and relive the tortures he'd said he'd do. *I'll kill the kids one by one. I am going to gas them all to death …* I'd be thinking that, over and over, so that by the time the kids finally got home, laughing and joking, calling out, 'Sorry I'm late!' in a breezy way, I'd be a nervous wreck. But I knew I couldn't show them my fears so I tried to act as though I wasn't afraid. I don't know that it worked, but I tried my best. I'd have phases where my paranoia and fear were eating me up and controlling me, and I'd have to trick myself into believing I could do this and put those emotions back in their box.

It was a daily struggle, not helped by all the meetings I was still having with the police and the social services. They were in and out of the house; there was never a week when it was quiet and nothing was happening because my ex was still fighting for his rights: his right to appeal; his right to have his sentence reduced; his rights as a father. Early release was his favourite. He played every card he could and, with the new legal training that he'd gained in prison, he now used his human rights to his full advantage – which weirdly overruled our human rights, even though there were six of us victims and only one of him. I couldn't believe he was allowed to study law in prison. Give a perpetrator a rope … and he'll hang his victim.

I felt like he probably knew our life was OK without him and so he wanted to control it and stop it and ruin it. I'd have a good day and then I'd come home and there'd be a letter on the mat saying I had to go to the family court or the children had to be interviewed again about visits to their father, and the day – the week – would be spoilt. The whole thing made me so impassioned I set up a website (www.womeninfear.blogspot. com) and started researching domestic violence in more depth. I wanted to help people who had suffered and been let down as

I had been, to give them an online space in which they could vent, and a place to seek guidance and support. The site was overwhelmed with stories of people who hadn't received justice in the most abhorrent of circumstances.

Justice seemed a long way away even for me. Because even though my ex was locked up, he still made his presence felt in our lives. It was there in the meetings and the legal letters. It was there in my sleepless nights and my paranoid behaviour.

It was there in the constant nightmares and the haunted eyes of my kids.

They'd come home from school every now and again and I could tell something had happened. They might lash out with emotions – crying, or anger – and so I spent a lot of time talking to them and explaining it was OK to feel that way. I'd ask them what had prompted whatever outburst they'd had, and we'd go over it together. They'd often say that something – a smell, a sound, a place, a word – had brought a memory back, and then they'd endure the horror of reliving it all over again. I remember Corice coming home one day after she'd been on a school trip; she came home crying, having a proper fit.

'What is it?' I asked my daughter, blotting her salty tears against my chest as I hugged her.

'We went down that road,' she sobbed.

'Which road?'

'That road that Dad kicked you out the car on!'

She meant when I'd been pregnant with Darren, back when she was five. She was really upset, reliving what her father had done to me in front of her. I always tried to tell myself that the kids didn't see that much – and there was so much they didn't see;

the raping and all the nasty stuff in the bedroom – but because Dusty's abuse had been so constant, and went on for so many years, they still saw enough. I couldn't stop their flashbacks from happening because their dad had done it: it was a real memory, planted deep inside them with jagged edges. I couldn't take it out of their brains; I couldn't repair what he had broken. All I could do was try to make today, tomorrow and the next day a happier memory for them. I hoped against hope that we'd make enough happy memories in the end to override the bad ones.

I tried to keep a lot of their dad's activities in jail from them, but if they were called to interviews, or saw the legal letters before I could hide them, they were straight away back to living in fear. They would panic – 'We need to do this, we need to do that … what if we have to see him again? What if he gets out?' – and I'd have to start their recovery process all over again. It kept happening all the time and I told them, 'We really need to get a grip on this, we can't let him do this to you. Because otherwise he's winning.'

I'd reassure them and remind them: *fifteen years*. We did the calculations together and I kept using that to calm them down. Daniel even wrote the dates in his diary: how many days his dad had left inside. He was marking them off, one by one. That scared me because I didn't want him living like that, under the shadow of his dad's release.

I'd sometimes get calls from the school, or from other parents, worried about things my kids had said or done. Aged about six, Darren drew a picture at school of a man wielding a knife with blood on it and the teacher was really disturbed by that. I had to explain he was drawing a memory, and that the man in the picture was his father.

The children also did what I still do: they spoke openly about their experiences, saying really severe, dark things, without realising the impact it might have on the listener. They might talk about their dad's temper, for example, and how he acted – how his eyes would slant before he'd go for you. They might say what had happened at home one time: their dad punching me, or choking me, or biting me, or kicking me. The teachers would phone me up and say that Isaac, or Corice, or Darren had said this really horribly disturbing thing, and I'd have to say, 'Well, that's what they went through, that's what they saw. I'm sorry they've said it out loud, but I can't repress them and I can't tell them not to speak because we've had enough years of not speaking. Maybe you should try helping them instead of censoring them?'

And so the school got special people in: counsellors who were trained to speak to kids who have been through trauma. And I think my kids did try, on and off, speaking to different therapists, but I don't think it really worked because the counsellors were all quite clinical and there was no consistency to the people they saw.

Dan in particular was struggling. He said of therapy, 'What's the point? I'm getting upset and ill from the sessions and they're not helping me.' So he stopped going. I kept saying to him, 'You need to try different people; keep trying till you find the right person for you,' but he gave up. He couldn't find anybody he could speak to, even though he wanted to explain what was going on in his head. He was scared they would deem him crazy and lock him up. He was afraid to speak of the horrors in his head to a stranger. I couldn't help him as I was part of the nightmare; he needed an outside specialist who would understand and help him adjust.

But I tried my best, all the same. Dan and I spent late evenings talking, for hours and hours. We'd be up until the early hours of the morning most nights, my almost-adult child and me, chatting and drawing and playing Scrabble. It was draining – I would literally give my last legs of energy to uplift him – but I had been saved for a reason, and that reason was to help my kids. It was my purpose in life. *I'm his mum, I need to do this: to keep him alive and well, to see him through*, I thought.

Dan had a little bit of a temper on him and when things built up inside him he would get to boiling point. He used to complain about his head hurting a lot; it was hurting because he was taking on too much, emotionally, without letting anything out. I wanted to encourage him to release his emotions in a positive way. So I used to say to him, 'Use your art to express your inner pain because it releases it.' He used to draw his dreams. We had a similar one, my son and I: we used to dream of flying, in the same way. Walking and then running, lifting our arms up, then reaching up and flying for hours over land and sea, studying people from above. Those dreams felt so real: the ultimate escape. I also suggested he tried some kind of sport because that would physically release his pain, and he got into bodybuilding in a big way.

I used to get him on a high in those late-night conversations. He'd be on a real low and I wouldn't go to bed unless I'd lifted his spirits. Sometimes it would take an hour, two hours, sometimes it would take four or six hours, but I wouldn't stop. I was trying to tell him that there was a whole other world out there from what we knew; a whole world of different things you can be and places you can go. We would get on the internet and I would literally show him. I did that with all the kids – we'd get books and leaflets from the library and I was constantly feeding them the idea that there was an amazing life out there they could have. I spoke to each of them individually, especially as they got older, to find out what interested them – for Jahméne it was music; for Isaac, football – and I'd organise things to help them follow their dreams, entering Jahméne into local singing competitions and getting Isaac on to football trials; he was so talented he even took part in a soccer school at Manchester United, but that was later in our lives.

For the time being, we kept on, keeping our heads above the water.

Praying that nothing was going to pull us beneath the waves.

Chapter Two

'How about this mural then, Mike?' I typed into my computer. Mike and I were planning to create a huge mural together and we were chatting on a public message board about our vision for the piece.

Someone joined our online conversation, some guy called Steve, with a funny line. I smiled to myself at his joke, but I didn't engage with him. I was so anti-men it was unreal; I never wanted another man in my life. After being with my ex all those years I didn't want another bloke coming in and taking over. After what my ex had done to me, I thought there was no way in the world another man would ever want me anyway. I remember thinking to myself, after Dusty had hurt me, down below, *You've got no chance.*

Steve was a chatty guy. He was a bodybuilder, like Dan, and at around the same time he started chatting to me and Mike he and Dan became friends online because of bodybuilding. They'd be swapping tips and recipes for these weird fat-free protein concoctions that Dan had started drinking to boost his weight, and it was banter all the time between them. Steve was very good at banter – he was a really funny guy, and despite myself I found that he was making me laugh with his jokey lines on the message boards: properly laugh – full-on, belly-shaking giggles that would still make me smile days later. I remember thinking, almost in wonder, *I can't remember when I last laughed like that … probably when I was about nine. Before my father died.*

We started regularly chatting to each other online, really casually; Dan was usually part of the conversations, too, and Jahméne would join in from time to time. I just thought he was a cheeky chap. We were friends online for ages before Steve suggested that we meet in person. I was nervous about that and I put him off loads of times, but eventually he persuaded me.

I didn't want him coming to mine because I didn't want him knowing where I lived, just in case. So I said I'd come to his city and suggested we meet in town, in a busy public place. *If he freaks me out*, I thought, *I'll just walk away and go back home again.*

To say I was on my guard when we met would be an understatement. *What am I doing?* I thought, as I boarded the train to meet him. But I still went. I wore, jeans along with a jumper I had knitted myself: a multi-coloured woollen creation in bright pinks and purples. My red hair was long, and I'd plaited and then unplaited it to wear it down, so it was all over the place in kinky waves. I had so much of it that he thought it was a hat when he first saw me.

By the time we met, I knew a lot about him – and vice versa. He knew I was in my late thirties and had five kids, and that my ex had been abusive. I told him right from the start, 'I totally get it if you want to walk away because we're complicated.' I expected him to do that, but he still wanted to meet, this twenty-four-year-old man who had so far shown himself to be polite and caring and funny, and most importantly a friend to my children.

In contrast to my mass of red hair, he was nearly bald. He was taller than me, about five feet eight, and he was properly built because of the bodybuilding, with piercings in his ear and eyebrow. It's hard to describe the feeling I had when we met. It was like … family. It was as if I'd known him all my life. I felt warm and secure just from being with him. His eyes were wide open, brightly coloured like my granny's: grey-blue with flashes of gold; warm and friendly. They were an important feature for me as they say that the eyes are the windows to the soul. But of course I didn't trust my emotions: I thought he was bound to be tricking me. *He wants something else*, I told myself, as my senses remained on full alert. *He can't be who he says he is.* But then I met his parents and his friends, and over the course of several years it kind of gelled for me that he *was* the person he presented to the world. He wasn't just showing me a mask; there wasn't a flip side to Steve; no Mr Hyde lurking in the back of his brain. He was exactly who he said he was: a kind, funny, honest, caring man.

His dad seemed unsure about our friendship at first and didn't want Steve going out with me, which was understandable with my crazy ex lurking in the shadows. But he soon warmed to me as he got to know me; he apologised years later and said he was proud to call me his daughter. He promised, as did Steve, to stick by us through thick and thin.

Eventually I felt comfortable enough to introduce my new friend to the kids; although Jahméne and Dan already knew him from online, they hadn't met in person. He came round one day for the first time when I was having some bunk beds delivered for the boys – the kids had an expensive habit of destroying furniture, another way they released their complicated emotions, so I was forever having to replace stuff – and he helped me put them up.

I remember Jahméne joking, 'Who's that bald man putting the beds together?'

Yet Steve fitted in with the children instantly. He became a role model of sorts, especially for the boys, and he'd do all the lad stuff with them that I couldn't do. He escorted Isaac to football game after football game, cheering him on from the sidelines as Isaac ran about on the muddy pitch. Steve played the game himself so he encouraged him and shared his own knowledge. I remember spending hours standing in a field watching my boy, freezing my butt off or getting soaked with the rain, thinking, *This isn't much fun*, but Steve just loved all that. It was really good for the children to have him around – and it wasn't just the interaction, it was having a man in their lives who was safe, fun and trustworthy.

Daniel, too, seemed on a more even keel with Steve around. The bodybuilding really helped him. Steve would come over maybe once a fortnight in the early days and he and Dan would train together. In time, Dan put on loads of muscle and his arms thickened into powerful limbs. He'd come up to me and say, 'Mum, feel my arm,' and it would be like a rock. Every part of him was pure muscle. When he eventually got bigger than Steve, he used to gloat and joke with him, lecturing him about his poor diet, as Steve would eat pizza and kebabs. Daniel would tell him, 'Your body is a temple: you shouldn't allow anything bad in.' Being sporty, Isaac really looked up to his brother; he idolised Daniel and the two of them grew really close. Dan would teach him all he knew.

I remember an afternoon from that time when I organised a photo shoot with Dan and Steve in the gym and took loads of pictures of them both. Oh, the funny, screwed-up faces they kept pulling to make their muscles pop out! We had a spate where I got Daniel into a fit of giggles by copying them – so much so that he couldn't pull a straight, serious face. Happy memories.

Every now and again, though, Daniel still said things that scared me. Such as that he needed to get the biggest he could get, ready for when his dad came out of prison. He started lifting such hefty weights that he was getting bloodspots in his nose and I had to say to him, 'You're doing too much, those weights are too heavy.'

But he'd reply, 'I've gotta make myself tough, Mum. I need to be able to handle him when he gets let out.'

He started doing some kind of martial art, and he was showing all the moves to Jahméne: a routine they would run through together. Dan would say to his little brother, 'If Dad comes and he does this, then we'll do that.'

I'd watch them and I knew I couldn't stop them because the survival instinct that was driving all this was bred deep into them from all the years of their father's abuse. But I did try to explain, not only that I thought it was unhealthy, but that they shouldn't be planning that way. If they were faced with a scary situation, the chances were they would freeze, stuck in fight-or-flight mode, no matter what they practised beforehand. All the training in the world counts for nothing when you're faced with a psychopath. Above all, though, I didn't want them to have this at the forefront of their minds, to think that they had to do this in order to survive, thinking in constant paranoia how to protect each other if their dad attacked them. I just wanted them to *live*.

The very worst time with Dan, though, was after Steve had stayed over at our house one night, for the first time. My friendship with Steve was deepening, on the cusp of romance, as I slowly,

slowly let my guard down over the years. I'd always been open with the kids, and told them straight that if there was anything they didn't like about Steve or that made them uncomfortable, they should tell me right away. I'm so glad I said that – because if I hadn't made it OK for the kids to talk to me about him, I don't know what might have happened with Dan that horrible day.

I found my son in the kitchen, red-faced and trembling, staring weirdly at the kettle.

'Dan?' I said. 'What's happened? What's wrong?'

I knew my kids inside and out and backwards, and I could tell that something was seriously wrong; that invisible umbilical cord was tugging at my heart with a warning rhythm.

Dan was shaking. He was angry and upset; so confused.

'Is it Steve?' I asked.

He nodded his head, tight-lipped, dangerously close to breaking point.

'What?' I said, worries scattering through my head. 'What is it?'

Dan ran his hands across his skull in desperation. He was seriously messed up. The tension in his muscular body was unbelievable; it was like standing next to a nuclear bomb.

'Tell me …' I pleaded, trying to take his hand, but he pulled away from me. He rarely did that so I was taken aback.

But what came out of his mouth next took my breath clean away.

'Dad said …' he started. He swallowed hard and began again. 'Dad said, if you were ever with another man in the future … that I was to … to boil a kettle of water … and pour it all over you.'

That was what was in his head – what his dad had instructed him to do. His father had warped his mind to carry out his evil.

Poor Dan didn't go through with it but he was so messed up about it. He broke down, his head poisoned by his father's sin. It took me ages to calm him as we talked it through, with tears and hugs, emotions pouring out from all sides. I was scared and angry; I'd had no idea until that point that Dusty had talked to Dan that way about me. But that's what he'd been telling him as a teenager, while I'd been out at work at the post office. That's the kind of filth he'd been filling his son's head with.

It broke my heart.

The other children, too, had dark, dark moments. When Jahméne was about thirteen or fourteen, he locked himself in his room with some pills and said he'd had enough. I don't know what tipped him over the edge; of all the kids, he was probably the most resilient because, like me, he had a kind of inner strength and an inner faith and light that he drew on to get him through the dark days. I guess he had memories that will haunt him forever, and his dad was still regularly trying to get access to him through the courts … but who knows what it was? Only he does.

I was banging on the door, frantic, crying, and there was only an awful silence from within the room, which made me panic even more. In the end, I had to call social services and they kicked the door down to get to him.

Thank God, he was fine, he hadn't taken any of the drugs – but it was still terrifying to go through. I told him, years later, 'You broke my heart that day; I thought I was going to lose you.'

Losing Junior had been beyond my control. I did not want to lose another child. I couldn't bear the intense agony or the suffocating grief. Burying one child … is one child too many.

And still my ex continued to play his games, sending legal letters back and forth and requiring all manner of correspondence to be sent between our solicitors, the police and social services. Maybe in 2005 or thereabouts, as I was helping our neighbour Peggy out – she'd been diagnosed with kidney troubles on top of diabetes, and her liver was failing, so I was going up the hospital with her for her treatment – yet another letter arrived. I'd brought Peggy back to mine that day and we were together when I opened up the plain, large brown envelope that had landed on my mat.

Brightly coloured pictures tumbled out, along with an official-looking letter.

'What's all that?' Peggy asked me.

'I've no idea,' I said. I looked closely at the drawings – cartoon sketches and homemade cards, made by several different children. One colourful message read: 'I hope you get better soon Daddy.' On the official letter were printed five different children's names with birth dates next to them. All the names were unfamiliar – all except one.

It read: Mark.

I couldn't help it: I threw up. Peggy, bless her, even though she was sick, had to look after me and help me. I felt guilty about that. But that letter messed with my head so much. Because it revealed, once and for all, that he'd had *five* other children with this other woman – each spaced neatly with my own five kids. It was a shock. And the message on the drawing made me think, *Do his other kids think he's in hospital rather than prison?* I was worried for them, and worried for their mum, too – did *she* think he was in hospital? Did she know the real him yet? I knew only too well how Dusty could lie and manipulate, and I was very concerned this other family might be in danger.

Then another thought struck me, too. My first reaction had been that my ex must have sent the package to mess with my mind, but then I realised what had happened was actually something far more concerning: it was another careless cock-up from someone in the authorities that could cost lives – posting the wrong envelope to the wrong address. The package wasn't intended for me; it was meant for him or he was returning it to her. Immediately, paranoia and fear shot through me. For if I'd been sent this other woman's name and address and her kids' details by mistake – could she have been sent mine? And would she pass them onto my ex?

I phoned my DC immediately – Bob Eames had moved onto other cases by then, to my great sorrow, so I had someone else in charge who wasn't familiar with our story – and I said, first off, 'Look, I've had this letter through, obviously by mistake, and you need to find out if this woman is safe because somewhere down the line there are lies being told.'

He just said, 'It's none of your business.'

'Well, I'll tell you what *is* my business, then,' I said. 'If I've got *her* letter, has she got one of mine? This address is supposed to be secret so he doesn't know where we are. Can you promise me one of my letters hasn't gone to the wrong place?'

Of course he couldn't. It was an awful time: horrible thoughts whooshing round my head. *Is this other woman on his side or is he controlling her? I don't want anybody else going through what we went through. Are those children safe? Are we safe if he now knows our address?* I was tempted to write her a letter, but the DC told me again, 'It's none of your business – stay out of it,' and I did what I was told.

Our lovely neighbour Peggy died from kidney and liver failure about a week after that debacle. I missed her terribly. I remember on the day of her funeral, I had to go up to the school to see a performance that the kids were doing; Jahméne was in this singing thing, performing a happy song. He sang it, wonderfully, and then he just stopped – in front of about 2,000 people, including all the teachers – and he said, 'I would like to sing a song in dedication to a good family friend who's just died.' And then he started singing 'I Will Always Love You' by Whitney Houston.

You could have heard a pin drop throughout his performance. It was one of the most pure, beautiful renditions I have ever, ever heard. His voice was like an angel's, lifting Peggy all the way up to heaven. And the uproar when he stopped singing! He got a standing ovation and I knew right then, in that moment, that singing was what he was supposed to do. There, stood on the stage, was where he was meant to be.

I helped him pursue his singing through every possible avenue after that. He used to sing with Corice, duetting, the two 'twins' together, but unfortunately my daughter's stage fright was too much so she stopped performing with him, though she still sang her head off at home. To be honest, Jahméne wasn't much better than his sister – he'd be a wreck, fiddling nervously with his jumper onstage as he sang – but I knew it was his calling so I pushed him. He was soon flying through the local competitions, winning everything on his voice alone, but I knew we had to try to sort out his nerves if he was going to get any further, which was what he deserved with his God-given talent.

We used to sit and talk about it. He confessed that he had a recurring nightmare of his dad shooting him onstage. I think that was one of the main reasons he built up his nerves so much, especially as the competitions he was doing started getting more high profile and the audiences he was singing to grew bigger. He used to say to me, 'Mum, if I can't see everybody, how will I know if Dad's there with a gun?' He'd get up on stage to sing and I could see his eyes raking the crowd, trying to clock every face, because he was scared his dad might be there. Even though his dad was in jail, Jahméne had seen him released too many times for comfort. It was a fear that only got worse as the years drew on and Dusty's release date loomed closer on the horizon. I just kept telling Jahméne: '*Fifteen years.*' My son would be a superstar by the time his dad got out.

Dan started doing well in his career, too. He got a job as a lifeguard at a swimming centre and began studying to become a personal fitness trainer. He loved it and he was brilliant at it, too. He studied in depth every part of the body; he excelled at anything he put his mind and time to. When he was nineteen, my 'baby' flew the nest and got a place of his own: a flat in a nearby village. I think he felt our house was too noisy and that he wanted his own space. It seemed like he could never have peace, actual peace, in our house, so even though I was worried about him and wanted him to stay, I hoped, too, that the move would help him find the peace he sought and that it would allow him to get his head round things. He was excited to be going; Steve hired a van and we both lent a hand as he moved his stuff. I got him a few new bits – including a phone so he could stay in touch with his old mum – and he settled in.

But, in the end, I think he was round at ours more often *after* he moved than before. He couldn't stand the silence, he said, so he came back a lot and we resumed our late-night conversations. There was a lot to talk about. Not that long after he moved out, he was trying to cope with a load of stuff that was going on at work; people would upset him and that upset would be channelled into anger and rage. I got a call one night to say I had to collect him from the hospital; he'd punched his hand through a glass panel in a door because he'd been locked out of his building. In his tiredness and temper he'd lashed out and banged the door and his hand just went through the glass.

He stopped at mine for a few days after that incident.

'Look,' I said to him. 'We need to talk. You need to control this anger, Dan.'

He started crying. 'I don't want to be like my dad.'

I spent hours – days – then, trying to explain to him that he was his own character, with his own personality, and that he was *nothing* like his father. But he said he couldn't control his anger, *just like Dad*, and it worried him so much. And while I would never tell him this, because he didn't want to know it, he was visually similar. The way he walked, and with his sun-kissed skin and his deep brown eyes … he did look a bit like him. Sometimes, I'd see Dan in the corner of my eye and do a double-take, *Oh my God, he's out* … and then I'd realise. It was eerie. But similar though their looks may have been, inside they were so, so different. Dusty was fuelled by a rage that gave him super-strength; Dan seemed broken by his.

On 29 November 2005, I would turn forty. Kath was so excited, bless her: she planned a special afternoon tea for me in this posh place in Bath; she got a balloon and a wand with '40 today' written on it; and she bought a white cake with a teddy-bear decoration (but only one candle!). She'd really gone all out. I was so looking forward to the celebrations; we spent weeks beforehand planning what we were going to wear, letting the excitement build. It felt amazing to have such a thoughtful friend to spend such a landmark birthday with, especially in such luxurious surroundings. My thirtieth birthday had been spent in the hell that was Sedgemoor Road. My twentieth had been in the hell of Moseley Road, as I got to grips with being a first-time mum.

But this … this would be different.

I had reckoned without my ex.

Chapter Three

Only a few days before my birthday, a court summons landed on the mat at Peasedown. And the date I would be required? 29 November 2005. You couldn't make it up.

I had to be at court in Bristol at 9 a.m., so all the birthday celebrations were off. It would have been too difficult and expensive to get to Bristol at that time in the morning from Bath, so I asked my friend Mike, who lived in Bristol, if I could stop on his sofa the night before. Graciously he offered to help and his children even let me sleep in their bed. Kath and Kate looked after the kids for me while I was away. Kath gave me the '40' balloon and the magic fairy wand as I left for Bristol and jokingly suggested I attend court with the wand in my hand.

But I couldn't even smile at her jest. I was an absolute wreck. The paperwork didn't say if Dusty would be at court or not so I was terrified that I was going to see him the next day, for the first time since he'd turned around in handcuffs in our old hallway and told Corice, 'This is because of YOU.' I had a physical reaction to my fear, sweating and shaking and throwing up. And then I started bleeding again, too, from internal damage and the keloid scars. The counsellor I go to now says that the central nervous system has a memory, so any trauma that you've suffered has a physical reaction when you relive it or something triggers it. He thinks that's what makes me bleed – which I still do, even today.

Lying in a borrowed bed in the middle of that cold November night, I didn't know what was causing the blood. I just knew that I was back in the bad old days, sticking thick cotton pads into my knickers while my body cried red tears.

I can't tell you the absolute fear it puts in you when you think you'll have to stand face to face with someone who has tortured you. And the fact it was on my fortieth birthday! It was like he'd planned it: he was still pulling the strings, controlling us all. The game was not over.

I dressed all in black, like I was in mourning – which I was. In mourning for the life he was still taking away from me. I was absolutely petrified. Mike came with me to the courthouse, talking to me all the while, trying to keep me safe and well, but all I had in my head was fear Fear FEAR. I was all psyched up for seeing Dusty.

As we entered the room, I could see he wasn't there yet. *They'll be bringing him here in a minute then,* I thought. I sucked in a deep breath, tasting air without him in it one last time before he arrived. I couldn't stop the stream of thoughts running through my head; I was going over and over what he would do when he saw me. How he would act, what face he would pull, what he would do. Would it be the finger across the neck, the silent threat, that he'd done back in the family meetings in Bath? Or would he slide his slick tongue across that same finger, and raise it to the air? *I win again.* I closed my eyes as I heard the door to the courtroom open. I felt so ill, utterly sick to my stomach.

'All rise,' the clerk called.

I opened my eyes again. No Dusty. Just Judge Daniels, who had adjudicated on cases involving me and Dusty before, in our long line of litigation through the courts, looking faintly disappointed to see me there again. He made the pronouncements he needed to – that yet again my kids were to be put through the mill at their father's request – and then he turned to me and he said, 'Go home, Mandy. Go be with your kids on your birthday. You should never have been called up today. I am putting an end to this here and now.' To my mind, he sounded as frustrated with it all as I was.

And that was it. All that stress, all that worry, all those put-off plans – just for a few minutes in a courtroom. Kath and I still had our celebration, maybe the next day or the day after that, but it wasn't the same. It had all been spoilt.

What the judge had requested that day were Cafcass reports; Cafcass stands for Children and Family Court Advisory and Support Service. They're confidential reports so I can't talk about the detail of them here, but basically an independent adjudicator talks to the kids in a series of interviews and finds out how they really feel about their dad. Dusty had applied for a 'parental responsibility' order this time, which meant that, if I was unable to look after the kids, he could make decisions about them. If the order was granted, it would give him valuable information: for example, which school the children went to. It would bring him closer to our new lives; give him names and addresses and details. I felt it said everything that, even though the kids had already told the courts – on at least three separate occasions, in response to previous orders Dusty had filed for access – that they never wanted to see him again and lived in fear of him, Dusty insisted on the full Cafcass process going ahead. He said he thought it was important the court process continue, despite the kids' response, so he could see the report at the end.

So yet again my children had to go through hell.

It made me so mad that he could play the system like he did. I was getting reports from our liaison people that he had stopped flipping out in prison now, and was instead back to velvet-voiced Dusty, saying he was sorry, learning from his mistakes – crossing all the 't's and dotting all the 'i's that he needed to. His risk category in jail was downgraded from high risk to low risk – bypassing medium, which I'm told is unusual. As he applied for early release I got to see some of the reports he was writing, in which he was saying his 'offence' – such a cold, unemotional word for four days of torture – was due to a psychosis brought on by the drink and prescription drugs he'd consumed that day: a one-off, in other words, 'not my fault'. He came across as reasonable and well-mannered in his statements; he was able to switch on his usual charm and pretend that he was fine. It was a double-edged sword for me, because on the one hand what he'd done to me was the work of a madman; yet, on the other hand, what was really chilling was that he wasn't mental, he was *clever* – 'devious, evil and calculated' – which was surely worse. I was so afraid that he would get out early, but his requests kept on being refused. And although DC Bob Eames wasn't in charge of our case anymore, he had my back once again, decent copper that he was. In one pre-release report it said, 'DC Eames reported that the offender was viewed as extremely dangerous … he said he had not seen such a horrendous case of domestic violence in all his years in the police force. DC Eames believed the offender would remain a danger to Mandy upon release.' For the time being – until the next appeal, at least – we were safe.

I tried to relax. Steve organised vacations for me and the kids; we had a holiday in Blackpool and, in 2006, the most amazing time in Greece. I'd never been abroad till I met Steve, never even been on a plane before, and it was just incredible, seeing the clouds around and below you. I was like a kid: I took hundreds of pics of just the clouds and the sun above, glowing.

I think the kids spent ten hours in the swimming pool the first day we arrived, and there was just so much banter between all of us, all week long. Steve and I were a couple by then, even though we still only saw each other at weekends. Happy memories. It was so brilliant to go away together as a family – though to my disappointment Dan had to stay at home on that trip as he had to work – because the kids were growing up fast. Darren was nine that summer, Isaac was thirteen, Jahméne was fifteen and Corice fourteen.

Though I knew it would happen one day, I found it difficult when Corice started dating boys in those heady, rebellious teenage years. I knew I needed to let her have her freedom, but I felt responsible for her safety and it was a hard balance to strike, especially as I could see she just wanted somebody to look after her. It was what I had done at her age. You look for love – and then you're fooled.

Every guy she brought home, I would think, *That's not the right person for you*, but given what I'd gone through with my ex, I also wasn't sure I was the best at judging people. How could I tell who was out to hurt her? How could I keep her safe?

My well-meant concern drove Corice mad, of course. It's the classic thing: no bloke is ever good enough for your daughter. I was just scared that she would end up going down the same path I had.

But as it turned out, I needn't have worried. My Corice won't stand for any nonsense. I'm glad about that, at least. And as the next year or so passed, we all seemed to start new, positive chapters in our lives. It was the best happy ending ever when, in August 2007, after a lovely sunny day and walk through the local woods, Steve proposed to me. I felt higher than high, like the most loved being on the planet. My ex had said over and over that nobody would love me, that nobody would ever want me. He was wrong.

He was wrong about me being useless, too. Over the years at Peasedown I wrote lots of poetry, painted lots of paintings and took thousands of photos – creating a new portfolio of happiness. I was so proud to exhibit my art in Bath's Royal Crescent, and even became a member of the Bath Royal Academy of Artists. Having written hundreds of poems over the years, I then decided to join the Poetry Society. I won many competitions and had lots of poems published in various books and magazines.

In all, our years at Peasedown, though thwarted with troubles, were good. The children were all doing well at school, I was happy and Daniel was happy, too. There was so much laughter in that house. Many hours spent doing fun stuff: family games, parties and get-togethers. We had come so far as a family. At our regular Sunday lunches I could hardly believe my luck as I scanned my eyes around the table, watching all the kids being so blessedly normal, chatting to each other. Darren, coming up to his eleventh birthday, was just Mr Popular at school. He was the most relaxed, joyful boy you can imagine, with an easy smile and an open face and a multitude of happy friends. Isaac was doing his football trials, and he'd started following in the footsteps of Dan, too, doing a bit of training and showing an interest in boxing. It was all a positive way of channelling his boundless energy and any anger he ever felt about his life before. Dan was doing brilliantly: muscle man himself seemed to be letting go of his demons at last, and he was doing well with his studying to become a fitness trainer and live his independent life. Corice was in total teenager mode, with a face full of make-up and an array of admiring boyfriends trailing in her wake; her childhood ambition to be a vet had now switched to modelling, and she was so beautiful that I believed her dream could quite easily come true. Jahméne, meanwhile, was blasting the roof off with his voice, laying down some tracks in a studio, winning singing competitions, and even performing onstage with Pee Wee Ellis, James Brown's saxophone player, who told him, 'See you in America, kid – you're gonna go far ... '

And we still had nine more years before my ex would be released.

Ding dong. The doorbell rang.

'I'll get it, Kath,' I said. A MAPPA meeting – which stands for Multi-Agency Public Protection Arrangements – had been convened at our house one afternoon in spring 2008. I'd had MAPPA meetings before so I wasn't too worried. The team that had requested the meeting had told me that it was to report to us the outcome of an investigation or something; I can't remember the exact words now.

Kath had come over to help me with the refreshments because a lot of people were in attendance – not just our usual social workers and the new DC, but the probation service, heads of department, Bob Eames and loads of other faces, some of which I didn't even recognise. One by one they all traipsed into the house and sat down around the kitchen table, while Kath and I made drinks for them all and I got some food out. I had Steve with me, and his mum and sister had come along for moral support, and Dan was sitting round the table too. He was twenty-two now, no longer a child to be shut out of important meetings about his own future.

All the officials got their paperwork out, and there was general chat about what had been going on with the kids and what was going on with me. They went round the table and all introduced themselves, and maybe that's when my creeping worry began because there were a couple of higher-up people than I'd met before who were present this time. *Uh oh*, I thought, *this is not good*. Every instinct in my body told me: *Something's coming*.

I started thinking about what they possibly might say. *Has he been killed?* I wondered. Stranger things had happened in prison, and I knew from my liaison officers that his evil crimes against me had sickened a lot of his fellow inmates. *Has he killed himself?* My head was spinning and my heart began to pound.

A lady named Alex was sat at the table. I focused my eyes on her. *Where was she from again?* Witness protection, I thought she'd said.

'Look,' she said, 'I'll come straight to it. He's up for release in July. He'll be coming out in July 2008.'

'What?' I said. I was not expecting that. 'What are you talking about? That's only weeks away. Why's he coming out early? All his early-release requests have been denied.'

She didn't answer me – because at that moment Daniel just absolutely lost it. He had a fit, arms and legs going everywhere. He was filled with total anger and fear and disbelief. He screamed, a scream I will never forget, a scream like a trapped, wounded animal, and he was just going mad.

'What are you doing?' he yelled at the people gathered round our table, who were pronouncing our fate like it was nothing, like it couldn't wreck our lives. 'You can't let him out! He's gonna kill us all! Why don't you listen to us? You do this all the time! You're gonna let him out? He's not supposed to get out yet!'

He was storming round the kitchen like a wild thing, muscles bursting out of him in a crazy tangle of limbs and energy, and the police were shouting at him and trying to restrain him. He shrugged them off easily. 'What's the point?' he shouted. 'JUSTICE SUCKS!'

He banged open the back door and stood there looking at the garden. I remember Steve's mum went up to him to try to hug him, but he pushed her off and yelled, 'They don't care about us! They just care about him. They're gonna let him out and he's just gonna come and kill us all.'

I was shocked into silence. Almost without knowing it, I was crying. I felt so very, very, *very* badly let down.

Then the police started shouting at Dan. 'Calm down!' they screamed, like he was a five-year-old having a tantrum. 'Don't have a temper, you need to stop being angry.'

Well, that made *me* shout. I rounded on them as they attacked my boy. 'Don't you *dare* shout at my son!' I yelled, standing up. 'Back off! You've just told him his dad's getting out. You have no *idea* what we've been through!'

And they didn't, half the people in that room. They probably hadn't even read my full statement about what he did to us. They certainly had no clue what it was like to endure eighteen years of abuse and torture and rape and then be told your attacker is going to be out on the streets in just a few weeks' time, free as a bird, ready to start his torture *all over again* … I tried to go to Dan to comfort him, but my own head was spinning too. Tears streamed uselessly down my cheeks. Everything in the room felt raw: raw pain, raw anger, raw fear.

Dan was muttering about getting a Taser to protect himself; they didn't like that. They were telling him to shut up and listen and do as he was told. That made me mad. A few of them did this job day in and day out and they knew that what they had to say in these meetings would cause mayhem, but they were still having a go at him for reacting.

'Why is this happening?' I asked, suddenly calm, as though in the eye of a storm. My emotions were really strange – I'd have bouts of being able to say what I needed to, and then my pain would choke me up and I'd lose it and have to be calmed down. 'Can someone please explain how he's out in a few weeks? We did the maths. Fifteen years, that's what you told me. Six plus nine is fifteen!'

And they explained that his sentences were being served 'concurrently'. So six plus nine becomes nine, and then they only ever serve two-thirds of their sentence, so that's six.

'We've gone from fifteen down to six in one sentence?' I said in icy disbelief. 'You didn't tell me this before. You need to explain this to me because I do not understand your logic. When you go to court and you get a sentence, why do you not serve that sentence?'

They tried to explain the protocol again and I just erupted, 'It's stupid! Why didn't you just say six years in the first place? Then we could have prepared ourselves for … for … for him getting out today …'

I felt woozy with sickness. I sat down heavily, keening with sorrow, this thin wail coming from me, a lost cry for the lost.

Bob tried to console me, as did the social workers. Other people at the table were saying they thought it was wrong, that he shouldn't be let out.

'Well, don't let him out then! He's a danger to society! He *hurts* people. What are you letting him out for?'

'Because we can't keep him locked up forever … '

'But if you let him out and he kills somebody then he's got to go back in anyway. *But someone will be dead.*'

They were immovable: the decision had been made. This was justice. Six years, that's all he would serve. Six pathetic years.

The meeting moved on. 'So, you'll all have to change your names again and go into witness protection and you've got a couple of weeks to move house …' they began.

My head shot up. 'Move? But our home is here. The kids are settled here, the kids are *happy* here.'

'It's for your own safety.'

'I cannot believe you're doing this,' I said. 'Why can't you stick him somewhere else so we can stay here and just live normally?'

But I was told it didn't work like that.

'Where are we supposed to go?' I asked. This house was all we knew now, it was *home*.

'You need to get out; you can't stay here. You need to pick a town, and then you'll have to apply to the council to be rehomed …'

'What about the kids' schools?' I demanded. Corice and Isaac were in the middle of GCSEs; Jahméne was doing a college course. The idea of taking them somewhere new, partway through the school year, where there'd be different curriculums and where

I might not even be able to get them a school place anyway, was just mind-bending. My head was exploding.

'Moving costs money,' I said next. 'I don't have any. You're telling me I've got to do this, but what if I can't?'

'Well, you have to. Find some money,' they said. And then someone pretty much said something like, 'If you stay here and he kills you then it's your fault.'

'He's being released on licence,' another official piped up then, as though this made everything better. A green piece of paper was slid across the table towards me, with neat orderly sentences printed on it, numbered one to eighteen. 'He's being released on a ten-year licence and it's got eighteen restrictions on it. If he breaks a single one, he goes straight back to jail.' They made it sound like a tight plan of defence and protection.

I looked down at the paper. This was when I first found out that he'd been put on the sex offenders' register for what he did to me, which I didn't know before. I read the restrictions. The top one was: 'Not to be left alone with women and children at any point in time.' The next one read: 'No direct or indirect contact with –' and then it named us all. Then I read that he wasn't allowed to go within a perimeter of the zone where we lived.

'Hang on a sec,' I said. 'So we have to move so he doesn't know where we live, right?'

'Right.' They all nodded.

'Well, doesn't telling him where he *can't* go automatically tell him where we are? What's the point in us moving if you're just going to give him the area?'

'Well, we have to tell him where you live so he doesn't go there.'

'But you can't do that!' I said, fear gripping me again. 'If you tell him where we live, he's just gonna go straight there and find us!'

In the end, after we argued about it, they agreed to keep the restriction to Bath. It meant that his restricted areas wouldn't include the new place we would move to, so theoretically he would be allowed there, but I preferred that to them narrowing down our exact location on his licence. That would be like handing us to him on a silver platter. *And*, I thought desperately, the cogs in my brain whirring like they used to, *hopefully the subterfuge will mean he won't even know we've moved cities. We have to keep him guessing.*

The whole discussion had a horribly familiar sensation running through it. After all this time, we were on the run again. I was back to trying to stay one step ahead of my ex.

I could only hope that, this time, I could run fast enough to get away.

It was a raw, raw meeting. I went into a state of shock and panic. I had no idea how I was going to get this done; how I was going to uproot our lives all over again with only a few weeks in which to do it. I had to tell the other children what was happening, but I don't have a clear memory of doing that at all; Kath might even have helped me break the news. All I remember is Jahméne's face being terrified.

After everyone had gone – Steve back to his own house and all the officials back to their own lives – I stayed up late that night, with Jahméne and Daniel, making plans and formulating strategies for our survival. It was strange having them there – when they were kids, I'd done all the planning myself: anything to keep them safe. But now they were here by my side, wanting to know more, demanding answers. It was more difficult for me than I'd anticipated – not because I didn't value their support, but because I still had an overwhelmingly powerful urge to protect them. I knew they already lived in fear; they didn't need any more weight to add to their burden.

They dealt with their fear in different ways. Jahméne was like me: he looked to his faith for strength, and he found something inside himself that bore him up and got him through it. But Dan's fear just seemed to eat him away, from the inside out.

I remember taking their hands at the kitchen table and looking them both in the eye. I said to my sons, 'We can get through this. We've got through worse before; I know we can do it again.'

Afterwards, after the boys had gone to bed, I followed them upstairs, even though I knew I wouldn't sleep. I turned off the lights as I went, and each light I extinguished felt like I was snuffing out one of my children's dreams.

We had lived in the sunshine for the past six years.

But now, as I had always known it would, the darkness had come to claim us.

Chapter Four

It became a life of madness. From that day on, the police were like a shadow, telling us what to do and what not to do. They were in and out of the house and we had no time to sit and reflect on our own view of what had happened. We were constantly being talked at by the police, by the social services, by the witness protection people: a stream of information and instruction barked urgently at us by unsympathetic officials.

The priority had to be to find a new house. We picked a new city, after a family discussion, and applied to its council to be rehomed there. I didn't want to leave our lovely house in Peasedown; I wished I could just pick it up and move it to the new location, but of course that was impossible. We would have to leave everything behind – our home, our lives, our friends. Kath and Kate were in tears about me going; they knew it would be that much harder to support me in a new town far away – and just at the time when I needed help, desperately.

It wasn't leaving the house or my friends that caused me the most heartache, though. I was so upset about leaving the town where Junior was buried. I used to visit him whenever I could, up at the cemetery where I'd laid him to rest. I'd regularly clean the black stone we'd had engraved with his name and leave flowers and toys for him. Everything was always baby blue for my baby boy: blue blooms, blue teddy bears, blue fluffy rabbits. Once we moved, he would be that much further away from me, even more out of reach.

The new council came back to us quickly with an offer: a three-bed flat above some shops in a really rough area. Beggars can't be choosers so, even though it sounded highly unsuitable – our house in Peasedown was a spacious four-bed home, remember, and we were a family of six – I went to have a look at it.

I could smell the dog wee from across the road. The whole flat reeked of it: disgusting. I turned round and said to the person from the council, 'There is no way on this earth I am moving my kids into that. My kids are fearing for their lives right now. They will break. If I put them in that stinking flat, they will break.'

I had to go to the council offices to sort it all out. I couldn't believe that what they'd shown me was a serious offer; surely they must have something else? But they said to me, 'Because you've declined this offer, you now go to the bottom of the list. We don't have to offer you another property.' Yet another hard, cold, emotionless person trying to break me.

'What?' I said. 'What do I do now, then?'

'You're classed as homeless. We have a duty of care to your kids, so we will find beds for you all. We'll have to split the family up and you'll all be put in separate hostels and bedsits.'

'Divide and conquer', isn't that the phrase? How on earth could I keep my kids safe if we weren't together? I narrowed my eyes and said firmly, 'You are *not* splitting up my family.'

But firm words don't build houses. If it wasn't for Steve and his family, we'd have been lost. It was only thanks to their incredible generosity that we were saved. Steve used his savings to rent us a five-bed house, so my kids and I could stay together. Without him, I don't know what we would have done. His selflesness was even more amazing given he didn't live with us full-time.

I began to pack up the house in Bath. I had to do most of it on my own because the kids wouldn't help; they didn't want to move. Tensions were running high because we were all so scared. They kept shouting at me, 'This isn't *fair*!' I agreed with them, but there was nothing I could do about it. Their father being set free meant we all had to be imprisoned.

I felt so ill. I started bleeding again – so badly that I had to go to the hospital and have a tube fitted because it was just constant. Constant stress and pain and blood and fear. I couldn't sleep, couldn't eat; I felt like I could barely breathe. And there was so much to do! *I'm running out of time*, I thought. My heart was like a ticking clock, beating out the last few seconds of freedom that were left to us.

In the lead-up to the move, and beyond, I was also having to sort out all the usual endless rounds of paperwork and bureaucracy – doctors, dentists, schools, colleges, social security, housing benefit, bills – and doing it all in double-quick time because of my ex's imminent release. We had to be out of our home before he got out: the police and witness-protection people were adamant about that. But at each place I contacted, they wanted to put me on a computer system or have a record of our real names. Every single stupid request went *boom boom boom* in my ears until it felt like my head was going to explode. In the end I told the police they had to give me a letter to take to these places to tell them why I couldn't go on the system, but even then it took several rounds of visits and phone calls before I was even halfway sorted.

I don't know how we managed it because I was in a complete state of panic and shock, but moving day came round just weeks after we'd heard the news about my ex. Steve's parents paid for the delivery men. If I'd been on my own and hadn't had their help, I wouldn't have been able to do it. There were no funds available for that kind of thing; we had to run and hide because the system saw fit to release my ex, but the system wouldn't pay to help us do it. It took us two days to get everything out. We had a really small van and it was a long trip backwards and forwards.

I wanted to cry as I shut the front door at Peasedown for the last time; shutting the door on all those happy family memories and fun times. What lay ahead seemed only to be dark days where the unknown could engulf us in its evil at any point.

The new house was nice enough. As it was a five-bed, there were plenty of rooms, and it was a new-build so everything was clean and fresh. But when you're a family on the run, you're not really looking for what normal people look for in a brand-new home. Instead, you're assessing where the panic alarm can go, and asking yourself, how can we make it safer?

We had a panic alarm installed, as well as CCTV inside the house and out. The alarm was another cost because I had to have a phone line for it, and the police weren't about to pay for that. The phone company fleeced me: £200-plus for getting a new line fitted plus various administrative fees over the next few months.

The police did have an opinion on the house, though. They came out straight away and told me all the things we needed to have done to it to ensure our safety – such as inserting steel walls for a panic room in the master bedroom and putting a 12-inch bolt through the framework so my ex wouldn't be able to kick the door in. They were full of all these 'essential' plans for our protection, but then they took one look at the house and said: 'It's not possible.'

We would have to move again! I thought, *Are you kidding me?* The authorities started searching for a property with solid walls for us, but of course they couldn't find anywhere; we'd been down that road before. In the meantime, we just had to sit tight and hope for the best.

Dan was with me when the police said they couldn't help us with the panic room. We just looked at each other. My son's expression said it all: 'The police always say they're going to do x, y and z, and then they turn around and say they can't do any of it to protect us.' Letting us down yet again.

The saddest thing of all was that we weren't even disappointed anymore. It was what we had come to expect.

Dan came with us to the new house. He moved back in with his old mum and his three young brothers and sister. There was no way I would leave him behind, and he needed to be with us for his own safety, too. I worried about him so much. Perhaps for him most of all, the move was a massive loss of independence. But it wasn't just that: it was the thought of his dad being free. Though I tried to stop my brain going there, I just kept thinking of Dan being there as his father had tortured me with the blowtorch. I kept seeing him in my mind's eye, kneeling on the floor in the hallway, by the bedroom door, with his hands on his head: our eyes locked as the flame seared through me. He knew better than any of the kids what his dad could do when he was mad. And Dusty had now had six long years to plan his revenge.

I saw Dan writing in his diary frequently, scoring out the days until his dad's release; crossing off each day of freedom with a thick black stroke of his pen. If he ever had five minutes with me on my own, which was rare at that time as there were so many things to sort out, he kept saying, 'What are we going to do? What's the plan?' He was still thinking of those self-defence routines he used to run through with Jahméne. I had always made extra time for Dan leading up to the move, knowing he was struggling mentally to get a grip. Now, though, I was consumed with so much nonsense I was bogged down with it all.

Like all of us, Dan had to leave everything behind when we moved: his studies and his job. But the one thing he didn't leave back in Bath was his desire to be big, to be muscled … to be ready. He joined a new gym almost straight away and just kept talking about getting bigger and bigger and bigger. I kept trying to tell him not to think like that, not to think of plans and what ifs and strategies – even though I was doing exactly the same thing in my own head – but I don't think a word of it sank in. He was too caught up in his own personal fear.

The police were in and out of this new house, too. Our lives were no longer our own. When we first moved in they gave us a briefing on how to use the alarm and everything if something should happen, and that panicked the kids even more. I'd spent my life trying to un-panic them and reassure them, but the police wanted them to be on edge and alert in case something happened. They wanted them to understand the danger in its full light – as if my kids, who had witnessed first-hand how their dad behaved, weren't already aware of that with every beat of their hearts.

But the worst thing of all – the very worst thing – were the restrictions under which we now had to live. The police kept going over them. We weren't allowed to go to Bath or Bristol.

We weren't allowed to go on the computer or use the internet. We weren't allowed to give out our phone number or address to anybody, even friends and family. We weren't allowed to use our real names. Our steps and movements had to be monitored. It was like we were being punished. Like we were the bad guys.

There seemed to be a hell of a lot we couldn't do.

The frustration of being told you have to live like a prisoner so that a perpetrator can be set free is ridiculously unfair. It is so immense in the way it wears you down mentally. I finally managed to register the kids at new schools – though half their courses had to change as the curriculum was different, so they were starting new subjects in the middle of the school year – and each child once again had to have a new name and a false date of birth. Imagine what that does to a child; to anyone. It messes with your head. You become lost; you lose who 'you' are. We had to live false lives, just to stay alive. Where's the justice in that?

The kids, as you might expect, rebelled. We were now in an age of Facebook and social media, and asking them to stay off that – to refrain from using what was now, in most cases, their only way to communicate with the friends they'd had to leave behind – was akin to killing them. Is life worth living without friends, without what makes life *life*? My kids didn't seem to think so. They had myriad things they weren't allowed to do. I remember one day when the new detective constable who had been assigned to our case came storming into the house. Dan and Isaac were sitting at the kitchen table – Dan was helping Isaac with his homework – and she was properly in their faces, shouting at them because they'd been online. 'What have I told you about going online?' she screamed. 'How can we protect you if you don't do what we say?'

Isaac charged off, swearing, while Dan went off on one: 'Why do we have to live like this because you're letting him out?'

I tried to reason with the policewoman – 'They're kids. This is the way it is now, everything's on the computer' – but it fell on deaf ears. She was just doing her job and I understood the reasons, but I could see her rules were destroying my babies.

The restrictions got to all the kids. Isaac and Dan were the most verbal about it; Jahméne and Corice fell silent. Darren, who had previously been such a bubbly, joyful boy, became completely introverted. Dan classed our new lives as living in a box; living under the police's thumb, with them and the social services coming in and out all the time. 'We're not free,' he said. 'We'll never be free.'

A policeman came out to the house one day, not long after we'd moved in. He had a big file with him, which he put down on the table. And then he told me the exact date my ex would be released: 11 July 2008. It was only days away.

He had come to tell me that my ex was going to be living in a hostel when he was released. He said that my ex would have to sign in at this hostel three or four times a day, and that's how they'd keep track of him. Through my shaking fear, I grilled him on it. Would my ex have time to drive somewhere and do something before signing back in? What would happen if he didn't sign in? The policeman reassured me that they were really good at this hostel and the system worked well. And then he said, with genuine pleasure, as though handing me a gift-wrapped present, 'But Mr Douglas says he has no intention of hurting any of you, so there's no need to worry.'

I smiled grimly. 'Let's just forget you said that because you have no idea what you're talking about or what my ex is like, with his games of Jekyll and Hyde.'

315

The copper told me I wasn't allowed to make contact with my ex, and I wasn't allowed to know where he would be based. But then I noticed that the file he'd placed on the table was open – and had the address of the hostel right there in front of my nose, in neat black type. To this day, I don't know if he did that on purpose. My head started spinning. *Why has he done that? Is it a trick to see if I'll go and do something? Or has he done it accidentally?* The last thought made me feel even sicker than I already did. *If they've cocked up with his address, then what on earth might they have done in front of him with* mine?

If I thought I was in trouble *before* my ex was out, though, it was nothing to the fear I felt once I knew, definitively, that he was loose from prison and roaming the streets: a free man. I bled even more heavily. My meerkat senses came back: I was alert to sounds and smells and anything out of the ordinary. I was on 24/7 alert. There was no way I could sleep – what if that was the moment he chose to strike? My head was full of all the threats he'd ever issued.

'You've got to die. And what I'm going to do is chop your body up into bits …'

'I'm going to kill the kids. I'm going to gas every single one of them to death …'

'You can't run, you can't hide. I will find you.'

He could have been outside, right then, watching, just as he'd done at the refuge.

I was in a complete panic about the kids being safe. Every time I wasn't with them, I felt my fear, *high, high, high* in my throat. I was having panic attacks about it. Which child would he pick? Who would he attack first? Isaac? Jahméne, because he'd always hated

316

him? Corice, because she was the only girl? Lovely little Darren? Or his first-born son …? Everything was happening so fast, complete madness, and I was sooo tired because I hadn't slept for days. I was terrified. I went straight back into that mode of: how can I protect my kids? I remember sitting in my panic-alarmed, CCTV-wired house, crying, and thinking, *I can't do it*. It wasn't like before, when they'd been small. They each had their own lives now, disrupted though they'd been with the move. We were no longer the close-knit, five-headed monster that had traipsed up and down the stairs at the refuge. I couldn't carry all my children in my arms. *There are too many of them*, I thought, *I can't keep up with them all.*

The police issued us with tracker mobiles, with GPS installed, in case one of the children went missing. Each number related back to a specific child so we knew where they were at any one time. I insisted that no child should be allowed out on their own: we had to travel in groups. I'd make sure the kids had someone with them whenever they went out; that at the very least there were always two of them together at any one time. It was yet another restriction, but how else could I protect them? My enforcing rules on them caused arguments too.

The police would tell me: 'If he comes to see you – if he breaches the restrictions – then we'll have him.' They actually told me at one point that they *wanted* him to breach them so they could lock him back up, and I thought, *Oh my God, are they playing a game where they want him to come here? What if it goes wrong? What if he comes here and they get here too late?* I panicked then, thinking, *I can't trust them.*

As I had always done, I tried to rely on my own instincts instead. The kids immediately snapped back into that zone too.

We were alert to everything. We worked out which neighbours owned which cars on the street so we would know if an unfamiliar vehicle drove by. We noticed what colour coats the male neighbours wore. Anything different was a trigger: *that could be him*. We scoped the area to see where the trees were, where the rat runs were. If we went to the shops and he struck, what would our escape route be? Everywhere we went, everything we did, we had to decide: *if he turns up here, what are we gonna do?*

I didn't plan anything with the children, not out loud. All the escape plans were in my head, but I could see their eyes darting this way and that, calculating, just as my own did, and I knew what they were thinking. In contrast, I was trying to pretend to them that everything was OK, that we'd get through it. 'We can do this,' I said cheerily, as I encouraged them to join the library or to go for a family walk. It was July, it was sunny; we should have been enjoying the summer. But how could we? He had stolen our sunshine, our laughter, our future.

Dan finally found a new job that July. He'd had his dream job back in Bath, in fitness, but of course he'd had to leave it when we were forced to move. The new job was at a warehouse, working nights. I was concerned about that, and tried to talk to him about it. 'Swapping days to nights affects your mind, are you sure you can do this?' I could feel how pent-up his emotions already were – he was red-faced all the time and he'd go round fiddling with things, a nervous energy buzzing in his muscled veins. But he said, 'I need the money. I can't stay in this house with you lot forever.'

I didn't blame him. The whole house was tense. We were all getting on each other's nerves, and there were lots of conflicts and arguments. An atmosphere of fear and frustration raged beneath the surface, as we lived by rules that fenced us in, and lived in fear that every day could be our last. It just wasn't fair.

The witness protection people weren't blind to this. Because the kids were reacting so badly to their father being released, they now brought in a special team and told us they could move us to Australia – if we wanted to go.

We had a big family meeting about it. It was a huge move: we would be leaving family, home, everything we knew, heading for the other side of the world – and we would never be able to return. Nonetheless, I was positive about it. I thought, *That's the only sure way we can live in peace.* My ex wouldn't be able to get into Australia with a criminal record. (I say that; with his skills, he probably could, but it was certainly safer than staying in the UK.) We discussed it all and we agreed: it was such a life-changing move that we could only do it if every single member of the family wanted to go.

But Dan and Isaac weren't going for it at all. In fact, they were really angry about the very idea. 'Why should we have to move and never see our friends again?' they said to the authorities. 'Why should we have to run? You should be sorting *him* out.'

I tried to explain to them: 'He won't be able to get into Australia with a criminal record, we will be safe!' But they wouldn't agree to it; and to be honest I understood where they were coming from. Why did we have to keep running? Why did we have to move to different places so their dad could be free to cause disruption wherever he went? Hadn't we been punished enough, without completely losing our identities to start afresh in an alien land?

So Australia was a no. We would have to find some other strategy to survive. From that day on, I think every single one of us agonised over just what that might be.

Only a few days after our family discussion, I was down the council offices yet again, this time to report that Dan had got his new job. Every time our circumstances changed, I had to let them know and jump through all the usual hoops of the false names and the non-computer protocol that drove me insane. Every time I went in it took hours to sort out, and this time was no different. I was so very, very tired, running on empty. I think I'd gone four days without sleep. Everything was spinning round in my head, bringing on a migraine. My fear. My stress. Having to pretend to the kids that everything was fine … knowing it was not. Knowing they were miserable and penned in by the restrictions we lived under. Trying to cheer them up. Trying to make it work.

Trying to keep us all alive, no matter what.

Death was right at the forefront of my mind. I don't know how you're meant to deal with that. My fear levels were at their peak. *He's gonna come and kill us. Any moment now.* And through all this I was dealing with these pompous jobsworths who didn't understand that lives were at stake when they typed our names onto their little screens. It wore me down, inch by inch. I was at the end of my tether with it all, exhausted.

I got back to the house at about five o'clock that afternoon. Dan was sitting at the table with Corice. He had red eyes and he was just staring into space.

'Are you OK?' I asked. For days now he'd been on edge, fidgety. There was nothing calm about him. He seemed confused and angry and scared and tired, and I didn't think the shift work suited him. 'Have you had something to eat? I'm just about to get the dinner on.'

He didn't answer me, so I went off to cook the dinner. A few minutes later, something made me walk back into the living room to see what was going on, and I realised that Dan was going out. I'd seen what he looked like at the table – I'd thought he looked shattered – so I went out to him in the hallway, where he was slinging his black rucksack onto his back.

'Where are you going?' I said.

'I'm going to the gym.'

That desire to build up his muscles even bigger was constantly there by then. He must still have been preparing for God knows what plan.

'You're tired,' I said. 'You should be going to bed.'

He didn't want to talk to me; he was trying to get out the front door. He had his black coat on and his bag on his back. Something was odd about that, and it niggled at me as I watched him open up the front door. *The bag doesn't look like there's anything in it*, I thought. *That's a bit odd. He's taking his bag and it's got nothing in it.*

I tried again. 'Why are you going to the gym? You look tired, you need to rest.'

He pulled away from me, like he knew he had to get away. He wouldn't let me hug him. I tried not to let it bother me; I was upset about so much, and I didn't want to seem overemotional.

I had a weird feeling inside me, though. Maybe it was that invisible umbilical cord again, tugging at my heart. I felt a kind of *knowing*, but there was nothing I could do.

He pulled away from me, and went to walk through the door.

And then he turned back. He said simply, 'See you later.'

With that, he was gone.

Chapter Five

I burst into tears after the door had closed behind him. My migraine and my fear and the stress that had been rampaging inside me for weeks just burst out of me. I felt like I knew something bad was going to happen but I couldn't stop it. Steve shushed me and calmed me. I think he just thought I was losing it because of my ex being released. Of course that was part of it, but this was different. That *knowing* ate away at my insides. It was like I was trapped in a box and banging on the walls to raise the alarm, but everyone just said, 'Calm down, it will be OK,' and no one took any notice of my cries.

The evening passed. I tried to stay calm; I told myself I was just being overemotional. It had been a horrible few weeks. My ex had been out for about ten days at that point and every single hour had taken its toll on me. I started to question my own sanity about how I was reading things. *Maybe it isn't that bad*, I told myself. *Maybe I'm overreacting.*

It got to about ten o'clock and Dan still wasn't home. Whenever any of the kids went out, I couldn't rest until I knew they were safe. I tried Dan's mobile, but he wasn't answering. So I said goodnight to the other children – and I waited up. Darkness slipped through every room in the house, but still there were no footsteps up the front path, no key in the lock. The door stayed shut, the CCTV camera trained silently on it, red eye blinking in the night.

Eventually, I lay down woodenly next to Steve on the bed. My eyes stared unseeing at the ceiling above. I was recapping everything I'd said to Daniel over the past few days. We'd had a row about the tracker mobiles and I played every angry word back again in my mind. I thought over my movements – how I'd been out so much at the council offices, trying to sort everything out; how I'd been trapped in my own fear and panic, worn down by everything that was going on. I hadn't been 100 per cent alert to the moods of the kids at that time. I felt a huge amount of guilt about that. I thought, *I haven't had time for Dan.* I ran through everything, thinking, *Should I have done this?* and *Could I have done that?* I was angry at myself for not stopping him from walking out. I should have stopped him, but I hadn't had the physical strength to battle him, to cling on and make him stay in the house.

I listened intently for any sounds, but there was nothing out of the ordinary. Dan hadn't come home. It got to one o'clock, two o'clock, and still there was no sign of him. Three o'clock, four … I watched each milestone pass on the bedside clock, wide awake and fearful, and still: nothing. My heart was racing, my mind spinning.

At five-past-four in the morning, on Wednesday, 23 July 2008, I felt compelled to go and stand by the bedroom window. I looked out. I have no recollection of what I saw; it was as though I was staring at something way beyond the view that lay before me.

And I felt my son, Daniel Robert Eustace Brian Douglas.

I felt him as he passed.

It was like my soul was being pulled out of me.

There was a sense of parting. A sense of him saying, 'It's OK, Mum.' We had always felt so connected and there was a definite tugging away from me. Our invisible umbilical cord, which had connected us for twenty-two years, was cut clean in two. And then he faded away. Then my son was gone.

The feeling I'd had was that I was meant to be feeling OK about it – but, my God, I wasn't. I was all the emotions: guilt, anger, upset, panic, fear. But never, ever, *ever* OK.

I started crying uncontrollably. I was still stood at the bedroom window, with a sheet of tears streaming down my cheeks. A baptism of sorts. His welcome into a new world – but one I wasn't sure I wanted to be a part of. A world without my son tore at my heart. A pain so deep; so real. I had never felt anything so moving before. The agony of the mere thought that Dan was gone literally stole my breath.

I ran to the bed and shook Steve awake. I told him what I'd felt. He wiped the tears from my face with his thumbs and said, 'Don't be silly, he'll be fine. He'll have gone to his mate's or something.'

But I said, 'I just know. I *know*.'

I ran to Daniel's room. Maybe I'd missed him coming home; maybe this was all just a bad dream. I wanted to see if he'd been in there or had left any indication that he'd been planning to stay at a friend's all along. I just wanted to see a sign.

But there was nothing. Everything was tidy and in its place. The bedspread was smooth and undisturbed. I remember thinking, *God, it's neat*. Not a thing was missing or left askew. It was the tidiest I'd ever seen it.

I ran back out. I paced the house until morning came, then I was straight on the phone to the police. 'Something's wrong,' I told them. 'Daniel didn't come home last night.'

They were completely relaxed about it. They said, 'He's probably gone to see his mates.'

'You need to do something!' I said. 'You need to look for him now!'

Their couldn't-care-less attitude in the face of my urgency annoyed me. I reminded them of my ex and his threats, the risk of my children going missing. But …

'He's an adult,' they said. 'We can't do anything until he's been missing for forty-eight hours.'

That really grated on me, given the situation. Who knew what had happened to him? My ex was never far from my thoughts. Could he be involved in Dan's disappearance? Was Dan the child he'd chosen first?

The police had told me that if any members of my family went missing, my ex would be locked back up straight away to be questioned. Surprise, surprise, it didn't happen – even though we had no idea where Dan was or why he hadn't come home. That just added to my burning anxiety, my panic, my fear, my rage.

Of course, the kids noticed right away their big brother wasn't home.

'Where's Daniel, Mum?'

I couldn't tell them what I'd felt. It could be nothing; it could just be me being overemotional, imagining things, fearing the worst. I hoped against hope that was the case. I wanted so badly to be wrong.

'He's probably just gone to his mates,' I said lightly, parroting the police. 'Why don't we go and check?'

I took them all down to the library with me, and we tried to guess Dan's password so we could access his account and see if he'd emailed anyone about staying overnight. I took the opportunity to email Dan myself to ask him to get in touch. I emailed his friends, too, to see if they'd seen him or heard from him.

But nobody had.

Jahméne and Isaac came to me with an idea: they were convinced that Dan had run away to make a den somewhere, so he could be free of the restrictions of the witness-protection programme. We'd gone on loads of walks together as a family since we'd moved and the kids had often spoken about building treehouses and dens.

So we traipsed round all the local woods, hunting for their brother, looking to see if we could find a den that Dan had built. And, do you know, there was a place, not far from where we lived, which had a little den in it. That made me question myself again. *Maybe he has done that*, I thought. *Maybe they're right*. I was trying to convince myself that I'd been wrong; that he was alive and that we'd find him safe and well. I just wanted to wrap my arms around him and hug him. My son.

I kept thinking over and over my final conversations with him. He always used to ask me about a plan. 'What's the plan, Mum? What are we going to do about Dad?' I thought of the gym membership, the bodybuilding, the training routines, the desire to be big – to be ready.

Dan always wanted to try and sort things out. He was always building up this thing in his head about how to protect us all. He believed that he could do it. I remembered his pent-up tension in his final days at home. The rage, the anger, the fear: his huge muscles used to tremble with it.

And I thought, *Oh. My. God. Maybe he's gone after his dad.*

I felt so much fear for him. His dad was a psychopath. You can't plan to do something to a person like that because it won't go to plan. It's too crazy.

I tried to tell myself that Dan wouldn't know where to go, that he didn't have the address.

But then I remembered the policeman with the open file. I hadn't told Dan the address I'd seen, I hadn't even told him I'd seen it, but if the cops had been that lax with me, there was every chance Dan might have seen it too and stored it away in his head, ready for when he made his move. My panic heightened tenfold.

The hours passed. In time, the days did too. Though I kept my fears from the children, I was pressing the authorities all the time to help us find my son. I was a crazy woman; I don't even know what I said, I was just screaming at people. I went back into Dan's room and searched again, over and over. I discovered that he had left his mobile in a drawer in his cupboard: switched off. No wonder he hadn't answered my hundreds of calls. I remembered the row we'd had about the phones; how he'd felt trapped by the constant surveillance and restrictions – 'We'll never be free,' that was what he'd said. He had left it behind deliberately. He didn't want to be found. Whatever he had gone to do, he didn't want anyone following him.

After he'd been missing for forty-eight hours, the police finally came in and searched his room. They took stuff away with them, but we were still none the wiser about his whereabouts or what he was up to. We searched and searched as a family for our missing member. We went round with photographs on the street, asking if anyone had seen him. We put bulletins out everywhere. But, of course, we couldn't do it nationally because we couldn't draw attention to where we lived, in case my ex caught wind of it and hunted us down. We had to do it pretending we were still living in Bath, and asking people if they'd seen Dan. It was insane.

About two weeks after he'd been missing, the police got the sniffer dogs out in an attempt to try and trace him. Helicopters swooped the land nearby. The police came into the house and got a dog to sniff Dan's pillowcase. The dog caught the scent and went rushing off down the road, pulling his handler on the lead so she had to lean back to stay in control. I was ready: I went behind the group of police officers, following, running to keep up with them as we tore off down the street. I just wanted to see my son again, desperately. *Where's this dog taking them?* I wondered, as I followed close behind.

The police didn't know I was following them. When they realised, two policemen grabbed an arm each and marched me back to the house. They told me I shouldn't be with them. I didn't understand at the time, though I do now: I just wanted to find my son. They understood, however, that we didn't know *what* we were going to find.

Later, they told me the dog had run about a mile from our house. The scent led to a back road, which led to the motorway. The dog had got to a certain point and then stood up and put its front two paws in the air, which meant Daniel had got into a vehicle. We were left with that information, and only that information. We had no idea what had happened. Had he been abducted? Had he hitched a lift? What had happened to my son?

I felt like I was two different people for weeks. Inside, I was in absolute bits, but on the outside I was trying to be positive for the kids and stay normal. Every morning I had to paste on a mask of normality to get us through the day. But, behind the mask, my brain would be whirring and worrying, my pulse racing. Would another child go missing? Would we ever find Daniel? Was my baby even still alive?

Four weeks passed. On Friday, 22 August, Steve and I accompanied Darren to a football club he'd recently joined. Trying to be normal, see? Life had to go on. My boy had finished his game and the three of us were in the car on the way back home; Darren sat in the back and Steve was driving. I was sitting in the front passenger seat, staring mindlessly out of the window, my thoughts full of Dan, when my mobile phone started trilling.

'Hello?' I said.

It was our DC.

'I really need to speak to you right now,' she said. 'Where are you?'

I knew, straight away, that it was news about Dan. I could tell from her tone, and from my own instinctive reaction, that it was bad news. I felt physically sick, like my insides were going to come out, but Darren was sat in the back of the car and hadn't a clue what was going on, so I tried to look calm.

Steve looked over at me. I locked eyes with him and said quietly, 'Something's happened. We need to go somewhere close by.'

Steve's parents lived not far from where we were, so I told the DC we would meet her there. Darren didn't mind the diversion; we were regular visitors at Steve's parents' home and when he got there, he ran straight upstairs to watch a cartoon.

As we came in the back door, Steve's dad was letting the police in through the front. I was trying to psych myself up for the meeting but my stomach was in knots. I was doing my best to keep it together because I wanted to be proved wrong; that what I'd felt on that awful morning four weeks before was nothing, just a ghost of a feeling rustling through me that didn't mean a thing. I was literally trying to trick my mind, saying to myself, over and over, *You're wrong, you're wrong, you're wrong, you're wrong*. I went into the living room and I felt like a crazy woman, just sat on the sofa, waiting for them to come in and say the news. *You're wrong, you're wrong, you're wrong, you're wrong*. Over and over in my head, a mantra to keep us all safe; *You're wrong, you're wrong, you're wrong, you're wrong*.

The DC walked in with another officer, a blonde-haired woman whom I didn't recognise. They both looked at me. There was a beat, a moment hanging in the air: before and after.

And then the DC said: 'We have found a body. We think it's Daniel.'

My pain was like a firecracker curled in a closed-up fist. It exploded, wreaking untold damage, shredding bone and flesh and blood. I shouted out, 'Nooooo!' I banged my hand on the glass table in front of me, angry. I wanted to hit, rage, shout, scream. 'NOOOOOOO!'

And then I remembered that Darren was upstairs and that I had to be quiet. Hold it all in; control. The DC mentioned bits of clothing and so on. Her voice was like a swollen river, carrying me away. I drifted off into a new pain, a new pain of reality.

Every word she said after that was like adding another shard of glass, right inside my heart. I can't remember what she said. It turned out that the blonde woman was with her because she was the officer who had found Daniel's body, so she had come with the DC to explain it in person. But I wasn't really listening to her. They were probably standing there for five minutes, talking about how my son had been found, and I just went off to a place in my head.

It was like when Daniel's father had tortured me, in a way. You have to go somewhere to survive that level of pain. You can't be in the moment and bear it. It is impossible to bear.

Steve was with me. He hugged me, I think, and it just opened up the floodgates. I was crying and crying and crying. I didn't want to believe it, but I knew it to be true. I had known it to be true since 4.05 a.m. on the 23rd of July.

Daniel is dead.

My baby is dead.

And I knew: *This horror world we live in has killed another child of mine.*

There's no greater sorrow
Than the loss of a child.
There's no crueller, deeper pain
Than to lay your born to rest.
There's no cure
No remedy
Or magic potion
That brings them safely back
Into your arms.

Inner grief
Eats at your soul.
With every breath
Your shell cracks as
Tears roll and burn
Like Hell's acid flames
As all strength to fight them off
Is gone
Weakened
By lack of sleep
And food serves no purpose
But twisted cramps.

Futures, dreams stolen …
A new scar is born
As my chest is torn.

I MISS YOU, DAN
Not being here to share with you
The things that could be …
You didn't believe
You couldn't see
Past the hurt and pain
Or even see a future
In your father's game.
You couldn't taste the freedom
You yearned for
For so long
You couldn't see a way out …
Everything was wrong.

Now you have wings, son.
You've earned them: now you're whole.
Fly higher than high with the angels, my boy.
Let the sun shine through your soul.

Chapter Six

After the police had finished telling me about the body – words I didn't want to hear, words I blocked out to stop them from stabbing me over and over – the blonde-haired woman dropped a large brown envelope on the table in front of me.

'I suppose you should have that now,' she said.

'What is it?' I asked.

And then she said: 'Daniel's letter.'

'What letter?' I said. This was the first I knew of any letter.

The officer looked to her colleague in confusion. 'Doesn't she know about the letter?'

'I thought she did,' said our DC.

And that's how I found out that Daniel had left a note behind.

A suicide note.

The police had found it when they'd searched his room, all those weeks before, but had never even mentioned it to me. How had I missed it when I'd combed his room for clues? Where was it hidden?

He writes beautifully, my boy. Wrote beautifully, I should say. I tried to read his words then, but I could barely see through my tears. My broken heart wouldn't let me focus.

I've read them over and over since then.

'My theory is that this life favours suffering over love, hate to happiness,' Dan wrote. 'This world is not meant for me … it hurts me every time I wake. Now my desires are to be set free.'

It was always about freedom. Daniel didn't believe we would ever be free again; he couldn't believe that day would come. As a child, you see, he'd witnessed the constant let-downs first hand. I could still hear his child's voice, as he asked me in confusion, 'Why aren't the police arresting him, Mum? Why aren't they stopping him?' *This life favours suffering over love.* And, as an adult, it was simply more of the same. So Daniel didn't see a way out for freedom. He couldn't see light; only darkness. He thought his father was going to control everything forever.

Sitting there, shell-shocked, on the sofa, I remembered Dan saying to me once that he didn't want his father taking his life. He didn't want his father revelling in that choice. If it came to it, he'd said to me, he'd rather take his own life.

'I have lived long enough to view too much suffering,' he continued in his final letter. 'Too many memories I would rather not have known.'

I saw Dan kneeling on the floor in the hallway, his hands on his head, as the flame came towards me.

'This life served as a prison. I fear that I will only keep living on imprisoned … Now I feel like I just want to find peace.'

He had personal notes for each of us in the family. He wrote about being a 'burden' to me, something he'd often said in our late-night conversations when we'd stayed up for hours talking through the pains in his head. I had always said to him, 'No, you're not, you're my son, I brought you into this world, it's my job to help you, you are in no way a burden.' But those reassurances had never sunk in.

There was one particular line in his note that jumped out at me. It said: 'This is now my time. It is my time to go.'

I was a crumpled mess on the sofa. All the strength seemed to have gone out of me. My bones shrivelled and my spine shrank into nothingness. There was nothing to me, nothing but *pain grief pain grief pain grief pain*. I lived and breathed it. Every heartbeat was a punishment, reminding me that Daniel's heart beat no more. My heartache ripped my insides out. I felt a complete and utter failure. All these years, I had battled to keep my kids safe. Everything I'd done to keep everybody alive … the torture … the rape … the horrors in the house at Sedgemoor Road … I did all that to keep my kids alive. We went through all that, and for what? For *nothing*. There is no justice. There is no hope. There is no sense.

Daniel is dead.

It was the worst pain I had ever felt. Ever. It was so hard to be alive and know that Daniel wasn't. It was a new hell – a new hell I would now have to live with every single day.

I wanted to punish myself for letting down my son, but no torture I could devise would ever be enough.

Daniel is dead.

He had been found at a gasworks in Bath. I found out later he had been to it before, with one of his friends, back when we lived there. You can see all of Bath from the top of it, if you climb up. The world spread out before you. Daniel had climbed up it before – of course he had. It was the kind of thing my little Superman would have loved to do.

My little Superman … every memory choked me afresh.

The police presumed he had fallen from the top. Flying without wings … I remembered saying to the kids at Combe Down: 'No more flying. There's going to come a point when I'm not going to be there to catch you.'

That day had come. And I hated every single second of it.

I knew I had to pull myself together. I wasn't the only one in this family; I had to tell my kids the awful news.

Steve and I got back in the car and drove home. Darren sat in the back, not knowing what was going on. We couldn't speak.

I gathered everybody together in the living room. The police were with us. I didn't know what to say, I didn't know how to say it; I didn't *want* to say it, for I still didn't want to believe it. But eventually, after what felt like an eternity, I said, with all the pain in the world oozing out of every word, 'They have found Daniel's body.'

I didn't have to say anything after that. Isaac ran out of the room and charged up the stairs and started smashing things up. The police ran after him and were shouting at him to stop, so I shouted at them to quit yelling at my son. I'd just told him Dan's body had been found; of course he needed to let out his shock, his pain, his grief. I'd have been more worried if he *didn't* react. Isaac had idolised his brother.

Everybody was crying and hugging each other. Jahméne and Corice looked shocked and paralysed. I felt so lost and guilty and hurt; I felt I'd let everybody down. I was inconsolable: I couldn't stop crying and shaking, I was cold and hot; I was sick. Our family destroyed in an instant. I was the deliverer of this heart-wrenching news. As I soaked in my children's reactions, their tears, their pain, it engulfed me in guilt.

Steve got the doctor out to give me some sleeping pills; I hadn't slept in so long I was a mess. The pills were supposed to knock me out – but they didn't. I'm *glad* they didn't, because Corice and Jahméne and I stayed up all that night talking. We talked about Daniel for the whole night long, all the way through to the next morning.

It was a way of keeping him alive, I suppose. Alive in our thoughts, at least.

We talked about his funny ways: his funny laugh and his funny walk. He always knew how to make us laugh, did Dan. He'd do daft things. We joked about his food: the crazy protein shakes, and the way he used to eat everything in his path in his quest to get big. I talked about when he was small, and I remembered every detail of every part of his life that I'd known. Getting the news I was pregnant in that telephone box in Birmingham. Giving birth to him in November 1985. His big brown eyes and skin the colour of honey. Showing him off to my gran. 'I can hear you, Mummy!' after the operation on his ears.

He was just the best big brother; Daniel shone for us all.

His body was taken by the police. There had to be a coroner's investigation and so on because of the way he'd died. I was asked to verify the body as Daniel's by the bones of his little fingers being curled inwards. His body had decomposed over those hot weeks so there wasn't much to go by. Shreds of his clothes, his trainers. His cause of death was listed as 'unascertained'. They kept him for a month before I could have him transferred to the funeral parlour. The stress and pain of travelling back and forth for paperwork while my head was in a constant, gruelling pain was severe, and I was then told I was to be charged fees for the holding of Daniel and fees for moving him and fees for keeping him at the parlour. It just about broke me; and there were funeral costs piled on top of these. How was all this possible? I was being messed about with the benefits for weeks because of what had happened, reporting changes that stopped our money. I now totally understand what people go through when they lose a family member and how you can get penalised by the system with its cold, hard attitude; no compassion at all.

His body was finally released, which meant we could plan his funeral. It was held on 29 September 2008 at the cemetery in Bath where I'd laid Junior to rest. Maybe they'd be able to look after each other; I felt I'd lost all my powers of protection.

The police wanted it to be a small affair: just immediate family. They were shouting in my ear about safety, because this was a prime place where my ex might make a move, even though it was on the restricted list. Dusty had, of course, been told our son had died. The police said he went quiet when he was told the news, and that was it. They were worried he might turn up at the funeral, even though the specific date had been kept from him and changed to avoid any cock-ups.

But I said it wasn't fair on Dan to restrict his funeral. He had a lot of friends and there were family members who wanted to say their goodbyes. We still had to be careful who we told and who we invited, but in the end I think about a hundred people turned up to pay their respects to my son. It was like a celebrity's funeral in a way, with a police guard and security all around. Watchful eyes, watching us bury my boy.

After someone dies, you can live in a dream and try and trick yourself. *They're just out, they're not dead. Any minute now my son will walk through that door …* But when it came to the day of Dan's funeral, it was like closure. Rude reality intruding on the dream. It was definite: he's gone, he's passed.

It took a long time for everyone to take their place in the church. So many people came. Bob Eames filed in with the rest of them. I can't describe the horrible mix of emotions. A strange pride, to see Daniel so loved, but that pride and love just made our loss even harder to bear. I'd written an eight-page speech about Dan, so everyone could hear what he was like, but when I stood up to read it I lost the power of speech. My knees were shaking, my hands trembling, my heart was ripping me in two. I couldn't speak; my voice was stolen. I had to give my eulogy to the pastor to read instead, but he couldn't read my writing and mispronounced the words, which made me even more upset.

Jahméne sang for his brother. I have no idea how he did it. We also played 'Angel' by Sarah McLachlan. It was now the worst day of my life.

I remember looking out the window as Jahméne's voice soared around the room. The ceremony was held in a chapel where there were large windows all around and the place was filled with light. There was a bright blue sky, with these small white fluffy clouds moving fast across the firmament. I just wanted to get through the service without collapsing or doing something stupid, like screaming. I could feel a scream at the back of my throat, wanting to burst out of me. The service was so, so moving and beautiful – but unbearably tragic.

Towards the end of the ceremony, I had to go up to the coffin and lay a red rose down for Dan. I remember walking over there and my knees going, and thinking, *Get a grip here, I've got to be strong for the children.*

My God, it was the hardest thing I've ever had to do. I was staring at this wooden coffin and it just seemed so unreal that my baby was inside it. I'd put his knitted Danger Mouse that I'd made for him in Woodstock Road on top, together with the ET my uncle had given him as a baby. All his life he'd carried those toys with him, through every move – to Nechells, to the two refuges, to Combe Down, Sedgemoor Road and Peasedown. Now, they would follow him on this final journey, his comfort friends to the end.

Shaking uncontrollably, I placed the red rose down. I didn't collapse; I tried to stay strong for everyone. I spoke to Daniel softly in my mind, saying I understood his fight and need for freedom, his choice, even though I was broken.

I love you unconditionally, eternally. Forever in my heart, Daniel.

No amount of wishes could bring him back to me. He had flown … he was gone.

See you when I get there, xx

Then it was time for the closing of the curtains for the cremation. It was time for goodbye. The curtains were red and they slowly shut out the coffin from view. At that moment fire-hot pain seared right through me. Ashes to ashes in a puff of smoke. Daniel was finally free … his spirit free to fly.

The final thing Dan had written in his note was a message for us all: 'See you when you get there.' It's a lyric from a Coolio song. We picked all the music for the funeral, and the kids wanted that to be the last song played. So we did that. It starts with a violin playing, before the beat kicks in. And that was how we said goodbye. With a hope that we will see each other again. Somewhere, somehow, someday.

After the funeral we went to watch Isaac and Darren at boxing. They had taken this up when Dan had gone missing. It was surreal, beyond words, watching Isaac in the ring releasing his pain and anger. I actually started to question my own sanity. Had this day really just happened?

We held the wake at a pub, a few days later – and I had a breakdown there. I'd held so much in that it all just came out. Jahméne was singing, Stevie Wonder songs and all sorts, and I don't know now if one of the songs set me off, but I started bawling my eyes out and I couldn't stop. I was shaking, and I remember Steve's mum gripping me and telling me to snap out of it, because I was in such a state. I pulled through and I stopped. I told myself sternly, *You're not allowed to do this. For the kids' sake, you need to be tough. You can't break down.*

Back at home that night, the guilt and hurt and grief I'd been feeling for so long started turning into anger. I was angry at the police: if they'd done their jobs properly in the beginning, none of this would have happened. I was angry at the system: for letting us down; for letting him out. I was angry at myself: I hadn't been able to stop any of this.

But, most of all, I was angry at my ex.

I hadn't felt an anger like it ever before in my life. I was completely consumed. It seemed to eat me up, stiffening my spine where my sorrow had wilted it and pumping blood through my veins with a newly hot hurt. I started pacing up and down the house, muttering to myself. I thought of the tension we were living under still. How all the children were broken and sad. How any one of them, at any moment, might make the same choice Dan had. How any one of them, at any moment, could be stolen from me by their dad. And I thought, *I can't have any more children die.*

I still remembered, with crystal clarity, the address of the hostel where they were keeping him. Keeping him *safe*. My pacing sped up. An idea started forming in my brain. My anger fed it, and made it grow and burn and build.

And then, with anger simmering in every drop of blood in my body, I turned to Steve and I said, 'I'm going to hunt him down and kill him. I know where he is. I can go and hunt him down; I can pay somebody to do this.

'I'm going to end it, once and for all.'

Chapter Seven

Steve grabbed hold of me and wrapped me up in his arms. 'It's OK to be angry,' he said, as I raged and schemed, 'but you don't really want to do that. You're just venting. Let it out, Mandy, let it out.'

I was talking like a crazy woman for about two days, absolutely fuming. Steve let me talk and talk. But he was right: I was apoplectic about the downright *injustice* of it all, but I wasn't a killer. I'm not the kind of person who would ever wilfully hurt another. In the end, I realised my ex had done enough damage without making me scar my own soul as well. I found it almost impossible to bear the thought of him walking the streets while Dan was dead and gone, though. How was that ever fair?

A month after we buried Dan, the council told me they'd found us a house with solid walls for us to move to. We had to move again, to keep us safe from my ex. It was a three-bedroom house on the other side of town. It was disgusting. No one had lived there for years, so a load of stuff had been dumped out back. The garden was so overgrown that the trees looked like they were going to smash through the back windows of the house; and the inside was no better. The walls were peeling and lumpy, showing about ten layers of wallpaper underneath. There was dog wee and hairs up the walls and on the floor; urine stink everywhere. The smell alone was just nastiness.

I wanted to turn it down. But, looking out for our interests, our no-nonsense DC told it how it was: 'If you don't accept this, you're going to be homeless because you're running out of money.' The rent for the five-bed place was crippling, and Steve and I didn't have the funds to stay there anymore. So I was forced into accepting it, but I thought, *I can't move my kids into it like this: it will kill them.*

I was so worried about all of them. How they hadn't lost their way, given everything they'd been through, I had no idea. The family felt fractured without Dan, and I felt like I'd lost my power of protecting them. I was supposed to be a rock, but I couldn't keep up that role anymore. In the wake of Dan's death, I had turned into another person. I felt like I'd failed in everything I'd fought for up to that point, like it had been snatched away from me. Now I felt I wasn't good enough to be their mum, that I wasn't doing the job properly. Looking around the house to which I was now planning to move them – once again – I didn't think any person on the planet would disagree. It was madness we were being faced with.

We had two weeks to move: two weeks to make it habitable for my kids; to pack and rearrange our lives yet again. Steve's parents and sister helped me paint and strip the walls when they could, but most of the time I was going there on my own during the day while the kids were at school. It was two bus rides away from our current home, and I'd do fourteen-hour shifts there, working my butt off, scrubbing and cleaning because it was so disgusting. It wasn't fit for an animal to live in, let alone human beings. I was grief-stricken, and bleeding and ill, and I had to scrub and clean and strip and paint, almost robotically, but exhausted mentally and physically fit to crack.

I was there on 10 November: Daniel's birthday. There was no electricity in the house, so it was freezing cold. I spent the day scraping filthy woodchip wallpaper off the walls for hours and hours. When the sun set, just after 4 p.m., I picked up a torch and kept going in the dark. I remember sitting down on the kitchen worktop at the end of the day, waiting for an electrician, completely exhausted. Then I sat in the dark, waiting for Steve to come and pick me up in the car. I didn't want to be there on that day doing that. I wanted to be with the kids, because I knew they'd be hurting like I was hurting. I wanted to be with *all* my kids.

The police installed a panic room in my bedroom. They put a spyhole and deadlocks on the super-thick door. The steel plates and bolts made the walls stick out unnaturally all the way round the room. When I was in there, the shape of it reminded me instantly that it was a safe room – and why I needed one. That made it hard to relax and, to be honest, I wasn't convinced about the whole concept of a safe room anyway. Trying to think like my ex, I said to the police, 'What if he sets fire to the bottom of the house and I'm in the room upstairs? He'll do that to flush me out. What do I do then?' They just said, 'We hadn't really thought of that. But if you ring us from your tracker mobile, we will be with you in minutes!' *Yeah*, I thought, *I've heard that one before.*

Moving day was a killer. My friend Kath came over with her family to help out. It was a real physical slog, moving furniture and so on, and I was in absolute agony inside and out from my internal bleeding and the physical exertion. It was really stressful, hard labour. I was on the final van trip, and I remember thinking, *I've done it.* It had been two horrible weeks of cleaning and scrubbing and painting, but we were in. The relief was overwhelming and as I walked up the path to the front door, I collapsed, my legs going every which way and my head smacking hard on the ground. Perhaps I just didn't want to move into a new home without my first-born son. It all felt wrong: I was just going through the motions, doing as I was told.

We still had whole communities of people traipsing in and out the house. Grief counsellors. Social services. Psychologists. MARACs – Multi-Agency Risk Assessment Conferences. The police. Witness protection. Every single day for months. It was constant. Questions; interrogations; the police shouting at the kids for going on Facebook. They were just doing their job, but it left a bad feeling. The kids were miserable; they'd had to change schools again – and subjects and friends – as we now lived on the other side of the city. The witness-protection restrictions were a daily pressure on us all.

I was also battling the bureaucrats about all the paperwork to do with Dan's death because his gym and his bank and his opticians refused to cancel his direct debits and close his accounts because they said they couldn't do it without his permission; even though I told them he wasn't alive, I had to prove it. But because his cause of death had been ruled 'unascertained', it took about a year to get the death certificate and so they simply kept on charging a dead man for services he would never use. It was a massive headache: salt in the wound of my still-raw grief. I also had to sort out all the paperwork for our new address, the new schools and colleges and doctors; I had to pay the phone company yet another cancellation fee for moving and then another reconnection fee for yet another line for the panic alarm to be fitted. The hassle of just that part alone can break people: lack of money, lack of choice; forced into situations you'd rather not be in, on top of trying to stay one step ahead of the crazy ex.

As the months passed, our DC changed. Over the next two years, we would have about three different coppers heading up our case. And each time we were handed over to a new person, the 'handover notes' got shorter and shorter. It was like Chinese whispers. We had a massive file about our case – my statement after the final attack had been fifty-seven pages in itself, and there were all the letters my ex had sent me from the prison with his sick threats, and all the paperwork from the court cases over the years – but by the time it filtered down to our new contact, they pretty much knew nothing. I had to keep telling them the facts and they'd say, 'Oh, I didn't know that.' It annoyed me. I'd try to get across the point, 'We are under witness protection, you're supposed to know about the tracking devices and the panic alarm, the ten-year licence and the eighteen restrictions, and the fact that my ex is a "devious, evil and calculated" monster.' But they knew nothing.

It was a new DC who handled the issue when my ex put in a request to read the coroner's report into Dan's death, maybe a year after he had died. I went into panic mode. I didn't know what was in the report; I was worried it might have information that would lead to us. I didn't want my ex to find out anything because I knew from experience: if you give him even a little bit he works his way up and then before you know it he'll know where we are. I had to be in that alert mode, even though I was still swamped with the grief that I had not yet had a chance to release. So I ordered a copy of the report from our new DC, so I could read it all before it went out to my ex. I said, too, that in my opinion he shouldn't even be given the report. He was the *cause* of my child's death: why did he even have a right to read it? But that was the law, I was told. I couldn't stop him.

The DC printed off a copy as I'd requested and gave it to me in a car park. I had no idea what coroners write in such reports, and the DC gave me no warning as to what was in it. I thought maybe it was going to list dates; when the body had been released and where to, and things like that.

But it wasn't dates. And what I read has scarred me eternally. I am a creative person, I'm an artist: when I read things, I picture them viscerally, in technicolour – and that's what I did with that report as it went into graphic detail about how Dan's body was found. I had visuals in my head as I read that report that I can never erase. I wish to God I'd never read it, but I had to, every word, in case it gave anything away that could put us in danger.

In the flying dream my son and I had shared when he was alive, it was always such a peaceful experience: walking and then running, lifting our arms up then reaching up and flying for hours over land and sea, studying people from above. The ultimate escape. It wasn't like that in Daniel's last moments of life. No soaring freedom. Instead, I read word for word in all its gruesome detail how my baby had been broken apart as he plunged towards the earth. He had literally been torn apart by this world, in every single way.

I threw up as I read, vomiting in the car park with the DC beside me. He didn't even ask if I was all right. I said to him, 'What is going on with you people? Why didn't you warn me?' And he said to me, deadpan, 'You asked to see it.'

There wasn't a single personal detail about our new lives in it. No address, no hint of the city in which we now lived. No reason for me to have read it at all.

So off the report went to my ex. And I thought, *If anything is going to change this man into a human being, it should be the death of his first-born son. This should be it. Hopefully, after this unjust tragedy, he will leave us alone.*

But I was about to learn that he hadn't forgotten us at all.

Chapter Eight

It was August 2009. I was making a pilgrimage to the cemetery where we'd laid Junior and Dan to rest. It was now fifteen years since I'd buried Junior; a year on from when the police had found Dan. I didn't get to go to the cemetery very often now we lived in a different town, but I went as often as I could, and whenever I did I felt completely alone and safe. Our new home wasn't on my ex's list of restricted areas, but the cemetery was, so it was my place to sit and talk openly and outwardly to my boys, just to release and feel some semblance of peace.

My grief still felt incredibly raw. It was raw because it was wrong. If somebody old dies, it hurts, but they have lived their life and you can deal with it because death is part of life. But when somebody dies tragically young, like my two boys had done, you never get over it. You want to make it right, you want to fix it, but you can't, so it's ongoing: a daily struggle to get by. No justice, no peace: just grief and pain.

I walked up the path to where the plot was. As I got closer, I thought, *There's something on the stone*. Something was painted on the stone, and beside it was a laminated sheet of paper, with handwritten lyrics to a song. I came close enough to read them – and the bottom dropped out of my world.

It was one of the many songs *he* had tortured me to. It triggered me massively, a whoosh of memory and pain and hurt shooting like ice through my veins. I went into a blind panic. *He has been here. Is he still here now? It's his writing, his words: a message to me.*

The grave is surrounded by bushes so I was spinning round, looking, thinking, *Is he hiding in the bushes?* I feared for my life, there and then, and my heart pounded with its horribly familiar refrain – *live die live die live die.* I grabbed the sheet and ran back up the path, back to the supposed security of the main entrance. But this place was on my ex's list of restrictions. This whole place was supposed to be safe, yet he had been here. It was then I knew: nowhere was safe, no matter where I ran. How had this happened?

I phoned the police straight away, in a panic. 'He's been here! He's left a message!' I felt such shock and horror I could barely get the words out. All the while his grin was embedded in my brain: *One to me, Mandy – I win again.*

'Oh,' said the officer. 'I don't know how that's happened. We'll ring you back.'

I got on the bus and started heading back home, my heart in my throat. The kids were back at the house – were they safe? Panicking, I rang round to see if they were all OK. If he'd been here and moved on, where had he gone? My fear was right up in my face, clouding everything before me.

I cast my eyes down at the sheet in my shaking hand, trying not to read the words that would trigger my memories. It was a bit manky, I realised; it had been at the grave for a while. But because it was laminated, it had lasted well. He wanted me to see this. He wanted to be sure I'd know he'd been.

And that's what this was all about, I knew instinctively. The song was one thing, because he'd deliberately chosen it, but it wasn't really about the words or the memories they provoked. It was a simple message: *I'm out there. I'm still here. I'm coming to get you, one of these days* ... And the fact the cemetery was on the restricted list was to say: *I can go wherever I please. No one can stop me doing what I want. I am invincible.*

It was just like the bad old days, all over again.

I think the police took about a week to get back to me with an explanation – a week I spent in petrified fear. Any minute, I expected my ex to knock on the door and come swanning back in, with murder in his eyes and untold pain in his fists.

'There's been a cock-up ...' the police began.

This never ends, I thought. *The cock-ups never stop. They are letting me down, all the time. The torture game is not over.*

'He could have been there when I was there,' I said to them, interrupting their half-arsed attempt to explain. 'He could have killed me – your ineptitude could have killed me – and then what would you say? "Sorry, it was a bit of a cock-up"?' I was fuming.

'The thing is,' they said, 'he got locked up for something else but he's out again now ...'

'*What*?!' This was the first I knew of it. 'Was it for violence?'

I wanted to know because I thought, *If it is for violence, he has definitely not changed his ways and we all need to be even more on guard.*

'It's nothing to do with you, you're not allowed to know,' they said.

'Go on, then,' I said. 'Tell me what's happening. When are you locking him back up because of him breaking his restrictions?'

'Well, that's the thing,' they said. 'When he got locked up and they let him out, they forgot to put his restrictions on. They forgot to put him on any kind of licence at all.'

I went mad. All this time the police had been telling me he was in this hostel, signing in, safe as houses, and now I learned they'd been lying to me.

'We didn't want to upset you ...' they said.

'If you lie to me,' I said, 'it's false hope I'm living under. False security. That's dangerous. I'd rather know the truth, however harsh it is, so that I can strategise to protect everybody. How did he get to the cemetery? Does he have a car?'

But I wasn't even allowed to know if he had a car. I only wanted to know so that, if I saw it parked down our road, we'd know it was him and have a head-start to get away but, apparently, it was against his human rights for us to know. Apparently his human rights outweighed ours, every time.

I could not believe it. I was so angry: when he was let out, he was let out as a normal citizen. No restrictions, no licence – nothing! Of course he saw that as his chance to leave me a message. Of course he wanted to tell me: *I'm still here, I can still get you*.

Let's give him the benefit of the doubt here: let's say he saw it as his chance to pay his respects to Daniel. If he'd visited the grave out of remorse or to say sorry then, in some ways, fair enough. But to go there, to a place he knew I thought was safe, and leave words that hurt me ... that was just to tell me he'd been there. He didn't visit for the right reasons: he did it because he is evil. He hadn't changed – no way, not one bit.

There was the paint on the stone, too. I had to scrub that off, inch by inch, with my bare hands, to restore the grave to how it should be. Once again, he'd spoilt what had been a sanctuary for me. Now nowhere was safe. He was like a deadly disease that followed me everywhere, tainted everything.

I assumed, once the police realised their mistake, that the eighteen restrictions would be immediately put back on. But that wasn't the case. Oh no. I had to fight for that. They were telling me, 'Oh, there's nothing we can do about it.'

'Are you being serious?' I said. 'If a judge sets in place a thing like that, how come you're now saying there's nothing you can do about it?'

I had to go through so many channels of people to fight to get it put back on. 'You can't do this,' I said, 'it just makes him a free man before he should be; you've got to put the restrictions back on. Do you not know how evil this man is?'

Finally, after many months, and only at my request, they sent me through some paperwork to reassure me that my ex was back under licence. When I opened up the letter, I thought they'd sent me the wrong paperwork, but they hadn't.

There were the restrictions, set out in black and white. There they were, neatly numbered one to eight. That's not a typo, by the way: they were numbered one to *eight*.

Ten restrictions had been dropped from the licence, for no apparent reason.

That is our justice system for you.

It was like they were taking the mick but, believe me, it's exactly what happened. It was as if they'd stuck their fingers in my eyes when they told me they cocked up and shoved them in again when they told me they couldn't do anything about the licence, and then given a final good old twist by reducing the restrictions to boot. It made me sick to my stomach. The torture and the injustice never ends.

It was a dreadful time. The entire family was miserable as hell. Every day we missed Daniel. And every day we had to endure the witness-protection restrictions that saw us living under false names, looking over our shoulders, banned from doing things we loved, while my ex was allowed more and more freedom. Dan had been right. We were not free. We would never be free.

I think it was Steve who started to chisel away at the prison we had found ourselves living in. Like an expert escape artist, he began to find a way to lead us to the light. I still wore Steve's engagement ring on my finger, but we'd done nothing in the intervening two years to plan our wedding. Too much had happened for us even to think about it. And since Dan had been gone, there was nothing good in our lives. It had been one thing after the other: the funeral, moving house, the coroner's report, my ex's message to ensure we lived in fear. We were all depressed from grief and fear. We couldn't adjust or fit in, relax or live like normal people.

'Why don't we get married?' Steve said to me one day, in the autumn of 2009. 'Let's set a date. How about it, Mandy?'

I thought about it. I think the wedding had always scared me in a way – just think of the official paperwork; it would be yet another way for my ex to get to us. But I saw what Steve was trying to say, and I saw the love in his eyes too. Just as he'd always promised, he had stuck by us through thick and thin. If we held the wedding, it would be a celebration. It would be security for the whole family. It would be saying we were loved and needed and wanted as a group. It meant we were OK, not that bad; that there was somebody out there who thought we were worth something, who thought we were worth saving. I knew I had to give my children some form of light and inspiration to lift them up; I feared that, without it, we would all sink down and I'd have even more deaths on my hands.

We called a family meeting; an informal one – we're not big on ceremony. It was a Sunday and, like most families, we always tried to have our Sunday dinner together. We all sat round the table and ate a meal I'd cooked, and then we got talking.

'We need to do something positive,' I said to all my kids. 'We've got to move on with our futures. We need to have a change of plan here.'

I think one of our old DCs was there too, and I said to her frankly, 'I can't do this anymore. We can't keep the kids locked up in a prison so that he can just do whatever he wants. He's doing what he wants anyway. If we carry on this life, the way we live now, I'm going to bury more children. They can't live like that.'

'You know what you're doing if you do that …' she warned.

'I've got to let them be themselves … and *live*,' I said.

I told the kids the happy news that we were going to have our wedding. I said, 'Let this be our fresh start. Live for your dreams, kids, live for your dreams. Whatever it is you want to do … let's do it.'

It didn't mean the fear was gone or that we could be mindless to the threat. We live with fear every day. But I knew we had to learn to live with it differently. We had reached the point where living with fear at the forefront of our minds meant we were not living at all. We were existing for pain alone … and that is no life. It wasn't the life I wanted for my kids.

We all seemed happier after we'd reached that decision. Deciding to make a conscious effort not to live in the shadow of fear – it's then that you feel the warmth of the sun on your skin. The kids could pursue their dreams with real ambition. They could be normal. They could use Facebook and stand up for who they were. They could be them again: Jahméne, Corice, Isaac and Darren. Using the names we had chosen for them, no longer hiding away.

Steve and I got married on 8 May 2010. Corice, Kath and Kath's two daughters were my bridesmaids. They looked beautiful in their lilac dresses. I wore a gown of pink silk, with my red hair in ringlets and a shimmering tiara on my head. My now-eldest son Jahméne gave me away; that job had been stolen from my father, then my favourite uncle (who had died the preceding Christmas) and then Dan. Isaac and Darren were the ushers.

I was so nervous on the day – not because I had any doubts about Steve, but because I had a recurring nightmare that my ex was going to shoot me in the church – like the *Kill Bill* scene. It never ends, see? But the day was a flawless celebration. Every single person there was so happy. And it wasn't happy like back in the day, when you had to smile for a picture for my ex, it was genuine, having-a-good-time happy.

As Steve took my hand at the altar and I became his wife, I felt like I was *loved* and *wanted*. It was such a massive, overwhelming feeling. My ex had drummed into me that nobody would ever want me, and tried scarring me enough to make it true, mentally and physically, but as we took our vows it was like we banished the spectre of his hate with a magical spell of our very own ... LOVE.

The wedding lifted us all up. And, as a family, we thought, *What can we do next that's happy?*

I don't think any of us are ever going to be normal, but we try. We try to be happy. I've realised that's all you can do. Love and be loved. Be good, be nice, be happy.

And so I try, every second of every minute of every day. I try to be happy.

Epilogue

'I am not what happened to me.
I am what I choose to become.'
Carl Jung

In the spring of 2012, having just flown back from holiday, I headed straight for the O2 in London. Jahméne had a singing audition to attend, and he needed support.

He was going to try his hand at *The X Factor*.

It had been just over two years since we had decided we were choosing *life* over *fear*. And I knew what I wanted to do with my life: I wanted to help people. How I saw it was: if there are lives at stake, if there are innocent victims in need of help, then surely we have a responsibility to protect them and put things right. There's an anonymous quotation I love: 'The purpose of life is to discover your gifts and the meaning of life is to give them away.' That inspired me. I believed strongly that helping people was my reason for being alive when I shouldn't be. I had come so close to death so many times, and been given so many chances, that I now believed I had been saved for a reason. And that reason was to save lives myself.

I had started campaigning for victims' rights since we made our choice to live. I threw myself into the system to try to change things. Having used nearly all the services over the years myself, I had hands-on knowledge of what worked and what didn't, and I began advising people and working with victims. I had already helped a lot of people with the website I'd set up back in Peasedown, but now I took it further. Paulo Coelho said, 'The universe stands aside for those people who know where they are going' – and I found there was nothing standing in my way. I spoke to everyone I could about domestic violence and I had a lot of meetings with social services and the police to explain the pros and cons of all they did to help – or hinder – victims. I believed the system desperately needed people like me on the inside, pointing out where they were going wrong and what could be done to avoid mistakes, and so I stepped up to try to make a difference.

My work spanned out from there and I had recently begun to counsel victims at SARCs (Sexual Assault Referral Centres), as well as online. I was advising on a lot of raw cases – how the women could get out of their abusive relationships and where to go for help. I knew only too well that I was alive because I'd had somewhere to run to when I was close to being killed, back in Christmas 1994. Because I'd once been helped by being given advice and shelter, I now tried to help others.

My experiences with the rape victims taught me that massive lessons still needed to be learned in how the police treat victims. I tried to explain that to the authorities in the formal meetings I had with them. The official approach was way too clinical; a lot of women simply couldn't hack that way of being interrogated after a violent sexual assault, no matter that the police's intention was to help them. I have sat in SARCs and a female official interrogates, writing everything down on her clipboard and asking probing questions, but without having any compassionate response to what is being said. *That needs to change*, I thought. I wanted to be the one to make that change.

It wasn't easy work. Hearing other people's stories reminded me of my own. It took me a long, long time to control my triggers, and I'm still not fully the master of them, even now. When I first started sharing my story, with a counsellor or with others to help them through their own pain, I was a nervous wreck. I used to have panic attacks a lot. I couldn't write a paragraph or say Dusty's name without being physically sick, with vomit or diarrhoea or stomach cramps for days. But over the years I was taught to concentrate on the here and now, bringing myself to the present, so my triggers didn't take me back to those dark places. I was taught to focus on my breathing to remind myself: *I'm here and this is now*. I never thought I'd be able to do it but, with time, I got a lot better at it. And now I was trying to help other people do it with their own trauma, too.

I didn't just do the counselling and the website and the meetings. I also got involved with Women's Aid and helped them with raising money and raising awareness. I would go into stores with information boards and to hand out leaflets. Anything to get the word out there: *These women need help. They're suffering in silence. Please do not turn your back*. And, of course, I was still a mum, trying to support my kids, to celebrate them and encourage them to live the best lives they could and to follow their dreams.

And that was what Jahméne was doing on that sunny spring day. We were both beyond nervous as we joined the queue for the *X Factor* auditions and the line crept forward, inch by inch.

It took hours, and as we got closer and closer to the stage it got harder and harder for me to breathe.

It wasn't just nerves for Jahméne that had given me palpitations and stolen my breath away. It was a fear of my ex, too. We would never have dreamed of doing this kind of thing before. It was so high profile, so public – he would know exactly where we were and what we were doing. But it was such a huge opportunity for Jahméne that we had to go for it. If it worked out, it would be worth the risk so he could live his happy dream of being a famous singer.

Jahméne was his usual nervous self. He kept going to the toilet every five minutes and he kept telling me, 'I can't do this, I won't be able to sing,' right the way up until he took to the stage. His hands were shaking as he held the mic. They kept interviewing him and all the traits he'd had to battle with for all the years we'd fought to stay alive were clearly there.

'People that know me know that I'm the biggest worrier, I get so nervous,' he said. 'I don't mingle very well.' His breathing, like mine, was shallow and short. 'But everyone has their thing, and my thing is singing. I've always dreamed about being a singer.'

My emotions were right up through the roof as he walked out onto the stage in the big arena. He looked shy and anxious, uncomfortable in his smart grey suit. He had the same nervous laugh that I did, the one that used to get me hit. He stuttered over his words as he introduced himself to the four judges: Louis Walsh, Gary Barlow, Tulisa Contostavlos and Nicole Scherzinger. And then he opened his mouth and started singing – 'At Last' by Etta James. And I thought, *Well, that's it. That's all they need to hear.* This was his time to shine.

There was a stunned silence in the arena, and then people started to clap at the high notes as Jahméne debuted this masterclass of vocal acrobatics. His voice was pure and strong and beautiful. It raised the hairs on my arms – on every arm in the arena. Tulisa said afterwards that he had 'the shock factor': 'When you stepped on that stage you were a timid little soul and you couldn't actually express yourself. But do you know when you started expressing yourself? The moment you started singing.'

It was what he had always done; what we had always done, as a family, singing our heads off when my ex was away. Let it out, express your feelings: live, laugh, love. I watched him sing on that stage, and saw the audience's and the judges' reaction, and I couldn't help the tears that sprang to my eyes. For years and years I had said to myself, *He is going to be this star, I just know it, I can see it*, and that moment onstage was the moment it came true.

He got a standing ovation at the end, rapturous comments and four heartfelt yeses from the judges. Steve and I were in bits backstage, hugging each other and crying. It was so overwhelming. And then Jahméne came out and said, 'Was that all right? Did I do all right?' And I just said, 'It was brilliant! You did it, you did it!' Such celebrations.

As he moved through the competition, each week we became more and more proud as a family. I think Jahméne's singing has brought more celebrations into our family than anything else. Every week we would all get together to go to the show and watch him shine onstage, his love of singing and for us clear in his eyes.

We didn't tell anyone about our family background. I think I lost a stone in weight from worrying about what his father might do when he saw him on national TV. Had Jahméne's old nightmare been a vision of the future? Might his father come to a show and shoot him dead? Jahméne was the same as me, sick with worry. I wondered if I should print off a picture of his dad to give to the security men at the doors to say, 'Don't let anybody come in if they look like this,' but I thought that would just make us all more paranoid and ramp up Jahméne's fear if he found out I'd done it, so I trusted my old meerkat instincts instead. Jahméne would be onstage singing and I'd be on high alert, scanning the crowd to see if his father had got in, looking to see if anyone was reaching inside their jacket to pull out a pistol, straining to see a cold hard gun.

It was about halfway through the series, I think, that the papers dug up our family history. They kept sending journalists out then, trying to interview us about it. I refused to speak to them, but this reporter said to me, 'If you don't speak to us we're just going to put what we know already.' I thought, *What can they know already?* Nothing should have been on the system; it should have been locked down and watertight.

But I had underestimated the British press. I was shocked at what they dug up, what the press can gain access to. Because they hadn't spoken with us, too, they got loads of stuff wrong, like Daniel's age and how he had died. Some of the stuff they printed they plain made up. But the worst thing of all was that they splashed it all across the national papers in big bold print, and they called my ex something horrible in a huge headline. I could just imagine how Dusty would react to that … fuming with rage and revenge.

I asked for an interview then. I wanted to tell them: 'Do you realise what you've done by doing that? Are you trying to get us killed?' They obviously didn't know anything about domestic violence. So together with Women's Aid we build up a protection system.

The newspaper apologised and promised to do another story, a nicer one. Jahméne and I talked about Women's Aid on the show and in the press – and donations went through the roof. That's when I realised: we could flip this exposure and just go all out to push the message – and it's not stopped since.

Everyone wanted the story. I went on TV, on *Newsnight*, and on the radio; I gave interviews. It was so surreal. We'd gone from hiding all our lives, being different people with fake names, not being ourselves, to suddenly being out there in the public eye for everyone to see who we were, and what had happened to us. It was massive. And it was hard, too, because everyone wanted to know *everything*. But, in some ways, I'd had enough of shying away from it all. I wanted to stand up and be counted. We were going back on what the police had harassed us with verbally, and we were standing up for our rights.

The press, being the press, wouldn't let the story lie. What's that saying? 'There are two sides to every story.' Can you guess what happened next? Of course you can.

They went after my ex.

I heard, later, that they tracked him down and hounded him. I was told, later, that was when he went on the run. The police haven't told me anything, so as far as I know, that's where he still is today: on the run. Out there, somewhere. Unlicensed. Uncontrolled.

I hope the public shaming has caused him to think about what he's done. I worry that it might just have pushed him over the edge – to end his game by killing us all. But that thought has to be tucked away so we can live our dreams.

Jahméne came second in the competition. It was an amazing achievement. His first album went to number one and he's currently working on album number two. I literally could not be prouder of him – and that goes for all my kids. Corice is a carer in an old people's home now and the residents all say 'she is a little ray of sunshine'. The idea of modelling got set to one side – she is so beautiful, though, she could easily be on the front cover of *Vogue* (one of my dreams of her) – but I think this suits her better anyway. From a little girl, she was a caring child, whether looking after rabbits or her brothers – or even me. She's settled down with a lovely boyfriend now, too, and I hope she won't mind me saying that I think this one might be *the* one. I get a warm whooshy feeling when I see them together; when I see how much he loves her. It's all a mum could want for her daughter: good health, to love and be loved.

Isaac is still doing his boxing and training, as avidly as Dan once did. He still goes to the gym frequently to pump up. He recently landed his dream job at a building society and I was so excited for him. He had to do so many interviews, because they're really picky, but he nailed it finally. Each of my kids has to have a goal and a thing to strive for and that was his. I wanted to hug him and kiss him and jump up and down when he told me the good news, but of course I just had to say, 'Oh, well *done*,' and play it down. No eccentric crazy mum here! I was really happy for him, though. He is the Isaac Newton of the family, with the brains and ambition to go far in life. He loves his cars and bikes. He has a huge heart and I know one day he will make some girl out there blissfully happy. He will succeed above and beyond what we think is possible and I can't put into words how proud I am of him.

As for my youngest, my baby boy Darren, he is at college studying engineering. He doesn't know exactly what he wants to do yet, but he is only eighteen. He has years ahead of him yet to make that choice. Whatever he decides, he will have my full support. His smile warms my heart and his laughter rings round the house. Hearing Isaac and Darren sing together, as they do at times, reminds me that we can be sort of normal, sometimes.

I think daily of my first-born son. Of my Daniel. The pain never gets easier; my grief is still raw. We still have his favourite chocolate cake every year on his birthday, and remember. He had written, in his note, 'I can let you know how I get on if you can understand the messages I send to you.' And so I search all the time for a message from him. It could come from anywhere: the weather, or a passing bird, or a swirl in the sand. He and I had been so connected and spiritually linked on earth that I was convinced when he passed he would get some kind of sign to me. I waited and waited – and I am still waiting. It's been seven years now and I've not had a message from him personally. And that makes me think, *Maybe he thinks it's all my fault.*

Corice tells me that's not true. She went to a medium in 2014, using a false name and giving false information, and Daniel came through for her. I was sceptical, but the medium properly got Daniel down: the way he looked, walked, his character, some of the things he'd done; things that only Dan and I knew. Corice played me the tape of the session and we both had our jaws on the floor and tears flowed.

Daniel said to get a message to me to stop tormenting myself because what he did was a decision he made for his freedom. Corice was really crying at that, and she said, 'See, Mum? See?' Daniel said through the medium that he was really happy – and that he'd found love. I don't know whether to believe it, but I hope it's true.

Some people say there can't be a God because he wouldn't let evil things like what happened to me and my children happen in the first place. But I don't think that's true. God can't stop evil people doing what they do, but He can encourage the people that believe in Him to be stronger to cope with it. It's something you can cling onto, to tell you that there is something better. My ex, despite his best attempts, could not break my faith, which in turn meant he could not break me. Faith and hope together can move mountains to achieve the impossible.

A change has got to come in our society. I've got this oomph and angst in my stomach to make that happen and, as I'm getting older, it's getting more and more powerful. The anger and gripes I have over injustice weigh heavy on my mind. I feel like I'm running out of time – I'm fifty this year. There is an urgency to my campaigning now because when you put things off, tomorrow never comes. Now I have acquired a voice, I will not shut up. I will shout my message from the rooftops. The bare bones, heart and skin of me breathe every day for justice.

Domestic violence needs to be taken seriously. It's a life-threatening issue. People are dying all the time in our country: two women a week are killed by their partners. One in four women will experience abuse. They are being raped, tortured and murdered – and then forgotten about by the system.

And domestic violence isn't just a woman with a black eye – although that is bad enough in itself – it's a hundred things and more. Because it doesn't just affect the woman at the heart of the abuse. As you have seen from my story, my ex's violence didn't just affect me: it affected my children, and their teachers, and their school friends, and our neighbours; and it will affect my children's children too. It spirals out from the moment a man hits a woman to affect the whole of society – and no one can honestly say it doesn't. It affects every person walking down the street.

Yet services that are vital to the life of a survivor are being cut up and down the country. Refuges are closing. Who is in charge of these decisions? Do we mean nothing? Are we just stats to these people – the faceless 'one in four'? Every victim gets numbered as a code, as a statistic; my code was '808'. I wasn't 'Mandy' to the system; my children weren't 'Daniel, Jahméne, Corice, Isaac, Darren and Junior'. We were '808'. I always come back with the line: 'If it was your daughter, your wife, your sister that this was happening to – would you still cut the services, or would you make a change?'

As I write this my heart is racing with anger at all the stupid mistakes that are constantly being made, which are *costing people's lives*. Sort it out; make the change *today*. Because, for sure, tomorrows aren't promised for some of us.

I have come to the stark conclusion that I was tortured for a reason: to make a change in the world; to expose all the sectors involved; to reveal the mistakes that have cost lives unnecessarily. My main goal is to make changes in the justice system that will make a difference. Sentencing should make sense. Life should mean life – not early release or out 'on licence'. It needs to deter criminals, not encourage them. The system lets monsters do what they want. When they get caught, it's a short sentence, a slap on the wrist and 'don't do it again', and then they're set free, while their victims continue to exist in a living hell. It's gone beyond stupid. Make sentencing fit the crime. Make sentencing make sense!

I feel like I have been banging my head on a wall for years. There are not many people who will stand up and say the truth, because you do get bullied and threatened – or, worse, people turn away. They don't want to hear it. There are times I've been to conferences where I've been told to shut up because what I have to say is too raw. But this is what the subject is ... RAW and ugly. People used to edit my speeches to take out the harsh reality of what I've been through. I was told to be careful what I said. No more. I write my own speeches now. And I have gone from talking nicely to screaming for justice. It is time for voices to be heard. It is time for *my* voice to be heard. United, our voices can make a difference, make that change.

And that is why I am writing this book. I am not writing it for pity or even understanding. It is part of my purpose. I hope it makes a difference – a huge difference. A change has got to come. For I am not the only one to suffer in the way I have. And I have a message for anyone reading this book who is experiencing domestic violence: SPEAK OUT – REACH OUT – GET OUT. 'Domestic violence' applies to any form of control from your partner, verbal or physical. Please don't read this book and think, *My fella's not* that *bad*. Don't ever think your story is too small or weak or that it's not as bad as mine, and therefore you don't need help. Living with someone like this never gets better – in fact, it's guaranteed to get worse. If you are living with a control freak

– *get out*. Now. Today. Your life is precious and your freedom is worth fighting for. Nobody should steal your dreams. Nobody should take your happiness away. Stand up for what you believe in and stand up for your rights. Miracles do happen: I am a living witness to that.

It has not been easy to write this book. It's been beyond hard, beyond stressful, dredging up pain, grief and tortures I want to forget. I have had numerous breakdowns. I have even questioned if I was doing the right thing by writing it, questioning purpose, reasons for being, the big WHY? But if I can save just one beautiful life by doing this, then every moment suffered in my life will be worth it. If I can save hundreds by changing the system … then it's God's work, done.

I can never forget what happened to me. I am reminded of it daily. I will have to live on painkillers for the rest of my life. My hearing is rubbish because of having my eardrums smashed and being hit round the head so many times. Even now sometimes I question whether I really did go through everything I did – because I have reality and I have my nightmares, which are just as real, and sometimes I think, *Did that really happen? Did he really attack me with a blowtorch? Did he really try to bite my nose right off my face?*

But then I'll look at my body, or examine my features in the mirror, and I'll think, *Yep, there's the scar for that one. It was real. It did happen.*

The worst scar of all is the one in my mind, though. What he did to me affects me in so many unseen ways, daily.

I can't listen to certain songs because they're the ones he used to torture me to, crooning away as he cut and sliced and *hurt*. When I hear those songs now, it makes me go cold. My husband likes songs from the past, and I sometimes say, 'Oh, I don't like that song,' and he'll say, 'Why not? It's a brilliant song!' And I don't say anything, but then Steve says, 'Oh, your ex.' And I just say, 'Yeah.' There are about twenty songs I can't listen to. He has ruined them for me forever.

The same goes for smells and sounds, people and places, clothes and furniture, and more.

There is no time of year that does not have bad memories. There are so many triggers, all around me, that I have to fight against them every moment of the day. They cause a feeling of being crushed so it's hard to breathe. My mouth goes dry and my heart goes fast, and I want to cry and scream and panic. I try to remind myself: *I am here and now. This is the present. The past is in the past.*

But, of course, part of the problem is that it is not. Because he is out there now, a free man, even as I am writing this account of all he has done. Telling you all how it really was; telling how he 'got' me for a bet, a stupid bet – but then never, ever let me go. People have told me I shouldn't write this book because it might make him angry and set him off, but I've already given him enough fuel for his particular fire in sending him down in the first place. This is just my chance to tell the world what he did and all that's happened – before it's too late.

I was once told that his licence – not that it is worth the paper it is written on – would expire in autumn 2014. And I do wonder if, after all these years, that's what he's been waiting for. Because he wrote that in one of his letters from prison: *It doesn't matter how long it takes. I'm just gonna take my time. I'll get you when I'm ready. You won't expect it. It will be a time when you* least *expect it.*

He could be waiting for me now, outside this room. I could leave this room tonight – I have to get two buses home – and he could snatch me at any point along the way. He could be waiting for me anywhere. I'm a walking time bomb now his licence has expired. *You've got to die. And what I'm going to do is chop your body up into bits …* It may seem an idle threat to some, but to me it's a genuine possibility. Because I know the way his mind works. It's a game to him. A torture game.

And my ex wants to win.

The police don't tell me anything; I no longer bother to ask. As I was writing this book, in May 2015, a police officer came out to my house and said lightly, 'Don't panic, but have you still got your alarm fitted in?'

'What? Why?' I asked.

'I'll get somebody to ring you,' she said, but they never have. I don't even know who's in charge of our case anymore. Every time I go up the police station, it's someone different. We're supposed to be updated regularly, but we're not.

So, as we did in our family meeting where we chose not to live in fear, I have a choice to make about how I deal with that. Do I keep hounding the police and pressing them for information – information which at times in the past has been proved to be a lie anyway – or do I try to switch off from it and be free … to live?

I have come to the conclusion that we should just live. I hope if something bad was likely to happen, they would let us know, if they had advance warning. But I don't know. He could turn up tomorrow and wipe us all out. And that's the worst part: the not knowing.

I try to stay on top of it. Although Jahméne's success and my campaigning have raised our profile, we are still in a protection programme. We are still kept off the system, and our address and personal details are kept under wraps. I still have a safe room, in which I am meant to sleep; but I don't – can't – sleep because he haunts me in my dreams. My 24/7 alertness is something I cannot cure or stop. It's my cross to bear.

The children ask me why I bother with all the subterfuge. They say to me, 'Don't you think he doesn't know where we live?' And I think he probably does. They have said to me, 'He's just waiting for a time.' So they have it in the back of their minds, too. It's not done and dusted; not for any of us.

I know I'm supposed to forgive him. I know that's what so many people preach. But I feel if you forgive a person like that, it makes it so that you're condoning what they've done, and I don't condone any of it. My counsellor says it's not about that. He says it's about letting go and to let go you need to forgive. But my nightmares are too real. My scars are too numerous. I have buried too many children.

I can't do it. I just can't do it.

And so I continue my fight for justice and freedom. I don't want to be just another person who went through it, and either got killed or simply dismissed. I want to be somebody who says, 'No, this isn't happening anymore. Let's stop it. Let's make a change.'

Back in the day, I used to think I had been saved for the children, to get my family through it, but I know it's bigger than that now. The burning inside me to stand up and be counted is greater than that. Each deep, painful wound has made me stronger. I have lost two sons, but I fight on for their freedom, for my freedom, and for the freedom of all those out there who are suffering under perpetrators. A change is going to come.

So let me paint a picture for you. Imagine it as I swirl my colours in my palette and sketch out a vision on the most enormous canvas you have ever seen. For I am riding into battle, with my red hair plaited and tied up for the fight ahead. I am small, but I am mighty. And I have a message for all the perpetrators out there, who think they can get away with what they've done. I am coming for you. I will fight this system tooth and nail to see that justice is done. I will not back down. I will not be silent.

YOU can't run.

LET SENTENCE REFLECT REPENTANCE

You lured me down to hell's hot pit
And there I stayed for eighteen years
You preached the devil, mocked my god
You brought me to a thousand tears.
You believed everything you did was right
As you tore my soul apart each night,
My pain became a source of your needs
It powered you to watch me bleed.
Your hate, your evil, your vulgar tongue
An eternal game. Destruction done.
Inflictions, wounding, terroristic gore,
You abused me, used me, till you could no more.
Your aim was to daily, mentally, break me
Yet not forsake me: no death to set me free.
You dangled me, hung me, burnt me to the core,
You beat me, raped me, kept coming back for more.
You wouldn't leave me,
Wouldn't let me … escape your nightmare world,
Your laughter at my suffering in agony as I curled,
A scuttled shiver racing down the centre of my spine,
Continuous bombardment of words would all unwind,
Slicing like shards of glass in the corners of my mind
Shadows and reflections of a horrifying kind,
A past that haunts the present, a future I can't find.
Sleep a gift to those who can, I beg to see me through
Yet no amount of tiredness will allow me to.

Inflictions run through veins of pain
Affecting generations, driven insane
In their eyes and on their minds embedded, impossible to erase
Nightmares, infernal, internal, senses triggered in a blaze
This damnation, this affliction of which there is no cure
Survive, strive … reason for being alive.
I must endure.
I must implore.

'I am that I am': not by choice, but by force
Now it's my time: I am on freedom's course,
I have reason to shout, I have full cause to complain,
No amount of screaming will bring my babies back again,
Nothing can remove the emotional damage that's been done,
The visual recollections from the senses … I can't run.
They are engraved and controlling my central nervous system,
A multitude of messed-up perpetrations: counselling lists them.

So this book I have written to expose a myriad of mistakes
That did not have to happen if the system wasn't fake.
If truth and justice had've ruled and reigned unto this day
I wouldn't have this story, I wouldn't have to say, that
I pray my words rattle the heads of those who know and understand
How fear lives and breathes under the surface; it demands
A control that shakes your very bones to sand.
This tainted, warped perception engraved into my soul
The reasons for my being, my God will mend me whole.

It's clear for me to see now: I've dug up and revealed
The devil's work for you to read; and the fact I am not healed,
I am the subject of discussion, many minds I wish to feed.
Revenge for me could be no sweeter
Than justice birthed from need, not greed.
No repercussions, so let the victims speak,
Listen to their inner pain, give strength to the broken and weak.

What I seek is a global discussion, where in the past
we have been failed,
Let sentence reflect repentance, a fitting time to be jailed,
All pasts, present and future seek systems of justice, of truth,
For those we have lost to this growing disease.
Let's educate with awareness our subsequent youth,
Take a vow, speak out now, for all the voices that have cried
Tomorrows are not promised – so remember those who've died.

Make our world a safer place, where peace and love would reign,
Let our united voice shake the earth,
Let our words fall from heaven like rain
Soaking and disseminating the hearts and souls and brains
Of those who have the power to make the all-important change.

Note from the author

My aim is to change sentencing because as I see it, 'Sentence does not reflect Repentance,' and the laws attached to domestic violence do not make any sense to the victims having to live under these laws. Domestic violence is not seen or dealt with in all its seriousness, depths and entirety. The ripples of destruction it causes affect not just one person, it spider-webs out across generations, affecting children to the point where it destroys their hopes of a safe future.

The mental side of D.V. is also never really covered, to explain its depths and mind control. My son Daniel would speak of his head nearly exploding with pain. Not sleeping – because you're always on your guard in your own home – affects all natural bodily functions. It's not something that goes away or ends. It grows and infects the mind. Fear destroys the widest smile, the brightest day. It eats you from inside out. When justice systems allow such things to be rife in our world, it breeds its own form of control. It spreads through people; it destroys everything in its path. A silent deadly disease.

Having a voice breaks the silence. Speaking out gives hope to those who feel alone and lost in their pain. United voices make for change. Whatever your reason for buying my book, you know in your heart that these crimes should not continue. Please step up for change. Voice your concerns, your pain, your loss, your anger and your frustration. Together we can make our world a safer place. A place we can be proud of, a place we can call home, a place built on love's foundations. Our children and their children's children deserve a better life.

By writing my story I do not wish to put the police in a bad light. I understand that they only follow guidelines and rules set to them. Let this NOT be a reflection of their hard work. I am aware of the pressures enforced due to cutbacks, laws and rules. If a family's safety is compromised because of a lack of service, then surely it's the government's job to address this issue of human worth?

As human beings we need to show compassion for those suffering. Help the weak get strong. What we need is love to guide us, empower good over evil.

For all those who have lost a family member to D.V.

For all those affected by and still living with D.V.

It's time to make that change today – because tomorrows are not promised.

Recognitions

I dedicate this book to Daniel, my first born. Everything about you from your soul to your heart overflowed with love. You live on in this family now and always. Your death shall not be in vain. Fly free with the angels now, my boy, sing loud and proud and I will see you soon, SON xxx

My children … Jahméne, Corice, Isaac and Darren. You are the reason, the light and love in my world. Your strength is to be commended. Your spirits are blessed with greatness. Know that I will love you all eternally. I wish for you all happiness, good health and real love. For within your laughter and smiles lives a beauty only a mother knows. Blessings are in my babies' eyes. There is no stronger bond of love on earth.

My husband Steve – for your never-ending support and love through thick and thin. For your years of dedicated time and unconditional love. Know your worth, know that you are loved. A blessing to me.

Mother, Suzanne, Julie, David and Jaqueline, we are connected in blood and spirit. I share your pains and love throughout our parted lives.

My father in heaven taken way too soon, alongside my dear sweet Granny, Junior, Uncle David and Paul (Dad). Hear my prayers … for you are not forgotten.

Marlene, Rachel, Peter and Isabel: my new-found family. Thank you for your support, your time, laughter and love. Praying we have many years ahead of us to enjoy together. Happy holidays. Happy memories.

Marlene and Bev from Wales. You have been there, opened your doors to me and my children when we needed you the most. Your worth is etched upon my heart eternally.

My best friends, Kath and Kate, you have kept me going through so many years. We have grown up together and been through so much. Our laughter and jokes as the Three Musketeers continually lift me. You show me true love and true friendship does exist.

Carly and David – for getting me through the horrid years, for bringing smiles, laughter and normality into our crazy world of pain.

Bob Eames – for your dedication, support and understanding of my children's needs. For fighting our corner for freedom.

Margaret and David – for being there always, for showing me love never fails, for your healing hugs and time.

Michelle and Billy, for laughter and hugs and a lifetime of friendship.

Sally, for showing me us crazy artists need to stick together, for your love and friendship.

Mike Stuart, for your endless hours of brain-picking and friendship, your amazing art and poetry.

Rhona and Bhari – for your spiritual healing and friendship and keeping God close.

Sikeena – for understanding. My soul sister.

Tina Turner: for making me believe in myself. For giving me the strength to leave, for being a beacon for so many women across the world.

Whitney Houston: for her powers to lift the spirits up and sing to the world, for being 'The Voice' in our home for so many years.

Geoff Thompson: for your words of guidance and light; for your inspiration to an enlightened path. Your Romans 12:20 ... pure brilliance.

Bill: I owe you so much. You are my rock when I am weak, my guide, my strength. You are the only person in the whole world who truly knows me inside out. Thank you for the endless hours you have worked with me over the years.

My family and friends far and wide who have walked this path with me, you know who you are. Thank you.

Women's Aid, Refuge, Victim Support and all the other organisations helping victims worldwide. I thank you for your ongoing hard work, for picking up so many broken souls and guiding them to freedom.

Raj Holness, for her ongoing fight for justice. For my 'Grace House Award'.

Marie Hanson of S.T.O.R.M., and her team, for their continued dedication to raising awareness and hands-on helping of victims, and for awarding me 'The Women of Power Award 2014'.

Katie Piper, for being such a beautiful soul and an inspiration to so many.

Duncan Bannatyne, for being a Real Man, for listening and understanding and supporting us at Women's Aid.

Rosa Matheson, 'Respect Not Violence' campaigner, for her dedicated work globally; she makes changes happen.

The Women's Aid team at Bristol, Theresa in particular: you are movers and shakers, creators and change-makers. Through hard work and pure dedication, you achieve beyond the impossible. Without you, I would be voiceless.

Thank you to my publishers, Ebury Press, for making this book possible and for enabling me to get this message out globally.

Thank you to Kate and Sara for their untold hours of patience and understanding.

LINKS

www.mandythomas.com

https://twitter.com/goldylonglocks

http://www.mandythomas.blogspot.co.uk

http://www.paintingsilove.com/artist/mandythomas

http://fineartamerica.com/profiles/mandy-thomas.html

http://www.womensaid.org.uk

http://www.everyclick.com/helpwomensaid

http://www.refuge.org.uk

https://www.victimsupport.org.uk

http://www.rapecrisis.org.uk

http://www.womeninfear.blogspot.co.uk

http://www.btsuk.org/aboutus.html

http://stormempowerment.com

http://www.katiepiperfoundation.org.uk

To the good times
Love Always, Unconditionally,
Mandy
XXX

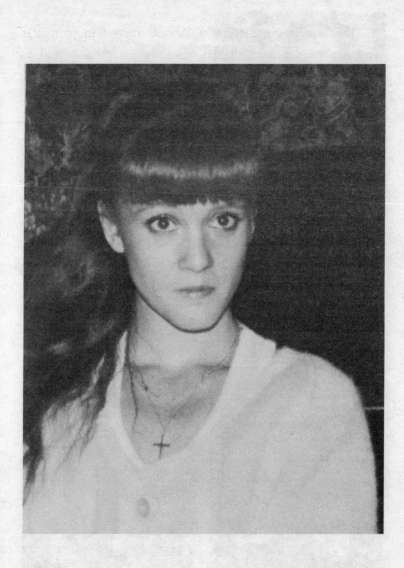

This is me around twenty-four years old. It was taken at Nechells, Birmingham.

My granny and baby Daniel.

Daniel and Jahméne: Dan kept giggling during this photo.

Jahméne, Corice and Isaac smiling for their school photo.

Daniel's school photo. He was around sixteen years old.

My babies: Corice, Jahméne, Isaac and Darren in 2002.

The last picture taken together, 2008.

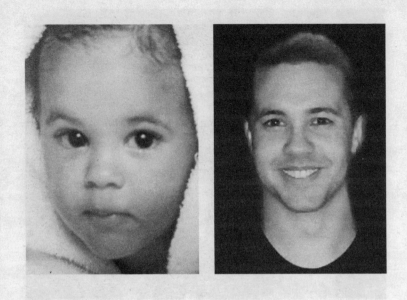

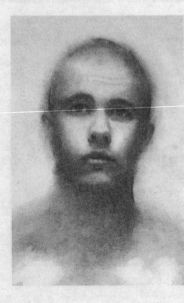

Daniel

Me in my studio. *Sacrificium* (below left) and *Baby Chimp* (below right).

Me and Jahméne at an awards night at Grace House, Birmingham. My 'Woman of Power Award' from Marie Hanson and the team at S.T.O.R.M. London.

Family holiday: Jahméne, Isaac, Corice and Darren.